Transforming Technologies to Manage Our Information

The Future of Personal Information Management, Part 2

Synthesis Lectures on Information Concepts, Retrieval, and Services

Editor
Gary Marchionini, *University of North Carolina, Chapel Hill*

Synthesis Lectures on Information Concepts, Retrieval, and Services is edited by Gary Marchionini of the University of North Carolina. The series will publish 50- to 100-page publications on topics pertaining to information science and applications of technology to information discovery, production, distribution, and management. The scope will largely follow the purview of premier information and computer science conferences, such as ASIST, ACM SIGIR, ACM/IEEE JCDL, and ACM CIKM. Potential topics include, but not are limited to: data models, indexing theory and algorithms, classification, information architecture, information economics, privacy and identity, scholarly communication, bibliometrics and webometrics, personal information management, human information behavior, digital libraries, archives and preservation, cultural informatics, information retrieval evaluation, data fusion, relevance feedback, recommendation systems, question answering, natural language processing for retrieval, text summarization, multimedia retrieval, multilingual retrieval, and exploratory search.

The Future of Personal Information Management, Part II: Transforming Technologies to Manage Our Information
William Jones
September 2013

Information Retrieval Models: Foundations and Relationships
Thomas Roelleke
July 2013

Key Issues Regarding Digital Libraries: Evaluation and Integration
Rao Shen, Marcos Andre Goncalves, Edward A. Fox
February 2013

Visual Information Retrieval using Java and LIRE
Mathias Lux, Oge Marques
January 2013

On the Efficient Determination of Most Near Neighbors: Horseshoes, Hand Grenades, Web Search and Other Situations When Close is Close Enough
Mark S. Manasse
November 2012

The Answer Machine
Susan E. Feldman
September 2012

Theoretical Foundations for Digital Libraries: The 5S (Societies, Scenarios, Spaces, Structures, Streams) Approach
Edward A. Fox, Marcos André Gonçalves , Rao Shen
July 2012

The Future of Personal Information Management, Part I: Our Information, Always and Forever
William Jones
March 2012

Search User Interface Design
Max L. Wilson
November 2011

Information Retrieval Evaluation
Donna Harman
May 2011

Knowledge Management (KM) Processes in Organizations: Theoretical Foundations and Practice
Claire R. McInerney, Michael E. D. Koenig
January 2011

Search-Based Applications: At the Confluence of Search and Database Technologies
Gregory Grefenstette, Laura Wilber
2010

Information Concepts: From Books to Cyberspace Identities
Gary Marchionini
2010

Transforming Technologies to Manage Our Information: The Future of Personal Information Management:
William Jones

ISBN: 978-3-031-01201-3   print
ISBN: 978-3-031-02329-3   ebook

DOI 10.1007/978-3-031-02329-3

A Publication in the Morgan & Claypool Publishers series
SYNTHESIS LECTURES ON INFORMATION CONCEPTS, RETRIEVAL, AND SERVICES
Lecture #28
Series Editor: Gary Marchionini, University of North Carolina, Chapel Hill

Series ISSN 1947-945X Print   1947-9468 Electronic

Transforming Technologies to Manage Our Information

The Future of Personal Information Management, Part 2

William Jones
University of Washington

*SYNTHESIS LECTURES ON INFORMATION CONCEPTS, RETRIEVAL,
AND SERVICES #28*

ABSTRACT

With its theme, "Our Information, Always and Forever," Part I of this book covers the basics of personal information management (PIM) including six essential activities of PIM and six (different) ways in which information can be personal to us. Part I then goes on to explore key issues that arise in the "great migration" of our information onto the Web and into a myriad of mobile devices.

Part 2 provides a more focused look at technologies for managing information that promise to profoundly alter our practices of PIM and, through these practices, the way we lead our lives.

Part 2 is in five chapters:

- Chapter 5. *Technologies of Input and Output.* Technologies in support of gesture, touch, voice, and even eye movements combine to support a more natural user interface (NUI). Technologies of output include glasses and "watch" watches. Output will also increasingly be animated with options to "zoom".

- Chapter 6. *Technologies to Save Our Information.* We can opt for "life logs" to record our experiences with increasing fidelity. What will we use these logs for? And what isn't recorded that should be?

- Chapter 7. *Technologies to Search Our Information.* The potential for personalized search is enormous and mostly yet to be realized. Persistent searches, situated in our information landscape, will allow us to maintain a diversity of projects and areas of interest without a need to continually switch from one to another to handle incoming information.

- Chapter 8. *Technologies to Structure Our Information.* Structure is key if we are to keep, find, and make effective use of our information. But how best to structure? And how best to share structured information—between the applications we use, with other people, and also with ourselves over time? What lessons can we draw from the failures and successes in web-based efforts to share structure?

- Chapter 9. *PIM Transformed and Transforming: Stories from the Past, Present & Future.* Part 2 concludes with comparison between Licklider's world of information in 1957 and our own world of information today. And then we consider what the world of information is likely to look like in 2057. Licklider estimated that he spent 85% of his "thinking time" in activities that were clerical and mechanical and might (someday) be delegated to the computer. What percentage of our own time is spent with the clerical and mechanical? What about in 2057?

KEYWORDS

PIM, personal information management, information overload, HCI, human-computer interaction, cognitive science, keeping found things found

Part 2 is dedicated to my sister, Pamela Jones, most especially for her love of learning and her passion for teaching.

Contents

Preface

This is Part 2 of *The Future of Personal Information Management: Transforming Technologies to Manage Our Information*.

In Part 1, we covered:

- *Introduction to PIM* as an area of research and as our daily challenge (Chapter 1).

- *Fundamentals of PIM*, which discussed the six distinct senses in which information can be considered "personal" and the six basic activities of PIM (Chapter 2).

- *Our information always at hand* took up problems and possibilities we face when our information is "always at hand" on mobile devices and a general ubiquity of computing (Chapter 3).

- *Our information, forever on the Web* considered the problems and possibilities of our information living "forever on the Web"—outliving us and standing in reflection of and legacy for our lives (Chapter 4).

Part 3, called *Building a better world with our information*, will look at:

- *Group information management and the social fabric in PIM.* How do we preserve and promote our PIM practices as we interact with others at home, at work, at play, and in wider, even global, communities? (Chapter 10).

- *Designing for PIM* in the development of tools, techniques, and training programs. What principles guide us? (Chapter 11).

- *To each of us, our own* broaches the larger question of how we assemble and apply what we've learned to build a better world with our information and through own custom practices of PIM (Chapter 12).

In the present volume, Part 2, we face a more basic, "show stopper" question: Is personal information management really necessary? Will it be so in the future? Rather than *Transforming Technologies to Manage Our Information*, a more catchy theme might be "Technologies to Eliminate PIM." Can technologies do this?

A quick response is to note that, with information so integral to the lives we lead, we will always need to manage it at a personal level even as we seek to manage our lives.

Fine. But can't we do so in ways that don't require a separate treatment of PIM? Can't we just get on with the lives we wish to lead? If so, then isn't PIM, effectively, eliminated as a separate area of concern?

Consider, for example, the taking of a photograph as an action of information management. We see a beautiful sunset. We are part of a special event such as a surprise birthday party for a friend or loved one. Even as we enjoy the moment an inner voice calls to us. "Stop! Don't forget to take a picture!" We must then step out of and away from the event in order to create and save an information item, the photograph.

Why do we do this? We do this to "capture" the event or, more accurately, to create a photograph as a way to trigger and share with others our good memories for the event later on. Certainly some of us enjoy taking photographs. Some of us may enjoy playing the role of the photographer at an event. But for many of us, the taking of photographs is tedium and a distraction whether we are taking the photograph or posing while someone else takes the photo. Taking the photograph takes us *away* from living in the moment and *into* information management.

Enter the SenseCam.[1] And soon (if not now as you read this) a commercial variant that is small and less obtrusive.[2] Chapter 3 (Part 1) considers the implication of being about to take a picture—or make a full-motion video—using a camera unobtrusively embedded in a necklace, necktie, eyeglass frame,[3] or belt buckle.[4] In a party area, cameras might be scattered about, embedded within decorations, and placed strategically for coverage. In many homes and offices, the cameras are there already as part of the security system.

A camera worn in this way would be calibrated to take a photo of (approximately) what its owner is looking at. Information so captured might be sent and stored initially on a palmtop device stowed in pocket or purse and then relayed to the Web. The device might be set to snap a picture automatically every few seconds. Or the device might be triggered to take a picture on command—whenever its owner says "say cheese." The pictures may not be perfect but then neither are the pictures we hurriedly take with our smartphones today. If continuous photo logs are almost here already, continuous full-motion video may not be too far into the future.

---

[1] See Gemmell, Williams, Wood, Bell, & Lueder, 2004.

[2] See http://memoto.com/.

[3] See, for example, Google Glass (http://en.wikipedia.org/wiki/Google_Glass; http://www.google.com/glass/start/) and Microsoft's efforts to support an "augmented reality" via glasses (http://www.slate.com/blogs/future_tense/2012/11/28/microsoft_augmented_reality_glasses_patent_rival_to_apple_google_glass.html)

[4] Try searching, for example, a question like "how small can a camera be?" or "spy camera" to find links such as these: http://www.protectiondepot.com/Spy-Mini-Covert-Cameras.html; http://www.youtube.com/watch?v=do6m2pKWIZ0; http://en.wikipedia.org/wiki/Lipstick_camera. http://en.wikipedia.org/wiki/Hidden_camera.

Some may recoil at the thought of devices continuously recording our lives. But this is happening already. Walk into any convenience store and we're likely to be on camera.[5] Likewise, we and our cars are on camera when we drive through many intersections or, perhaps, when we trigger a "speed" or "red-light" camera.[6] Attend a public event and we may be captured in hundreds or even thousands of photos and videos taken by surveillance cameras and by other people. If this bothers you, then wear a disguise. The days of public anonymity are over.

On the brighter side, we can now return to our enjoyment of the sunset or the party—already in progress. We're back to the living of our lives and away from a moment-killing management of information. Our enjoyment of the sunset or the party is, blessedly, PIM-free.

Or is it? To be sure, we've mostly sidestepped the burdens of one basic PIM activity—that of *keeping*. But decisions relating to *meta-level activities*[7] of PIM remain. We make these by default even if we do nothing at all. What is our policy, for example, with respect to privacy (and the more general management of information flow)? Do we inform our guests that the room is "bugged" for sight (as well as sound)? Does a red light blink whenever the camera we wear takes a picture?

And how, later, do we maintain and organize (another meta-level activity) the pictures and video clips captured? Many of us already experience gnawing pangs of anxiety at the thought that those digital photos we so easily take may not be really "taken" after all and may easily be taken from us as a web service goes out of business or local storage is corrupted. Even if these photographs aren't actually lost from physical storage, where are they really? Will we be able to find them again later? Even if we know where to look, will we ever remember to look?[8]

These questions, in turn, bring a rejoinder from the technology advocate. Pictures and videos might be uploaded and shared so that they are robustly stored in many places and, for better or worse, are nearly impervious to the dangers of physical loss. As described in Chapter 3 (Part 1), photos and videos might be interwoven into our item-event logs ("i.e., logs")[9] which provide context and a rich source of indexable content to enable us to locate this information later on. Photos and videos are further indexed through technologies for face and scene recognition. Further, the photos and videos we share can be indexed and organized by the commentary of others (see Chap-

---

[5] Surveillance cameras played a key role, for example, in case of the Boston marathon bombing prompting discussion afterward concerning the tradeoffs of security vs. privacy. See, for example, http://www.slate.com/articles/ technology/technology/2013/04/boston_bomber_photos_the_marathon_bombing_shows_that_we_need_ more_security.html; http://www.cnn.com/2013/04/26/tech/innovation/security-cameras-boston-bombings; http://www.huffingtonpost.com/geoffrey-r-stone/the-boston-bombing-the-ri_b_3223871.html or try a search such as "surveillance cameras Boston bombing."

[6] http://en.wikipedia.org/wiki/Red_light_camera.

[7] For a more complete description of meta-level activities of PIM see Chapter 2 of Part 1 (William Jones, 2012).

[8] See for example Steve Whittaker, Bergman, & Clough, 2010.

[9] Recall that an item event log is simply a sequence of events each of which, minimally, is stamped with time, location attributes, a URI addressing the item (e.g., web page, local file/folder, email, etc.) and an action taken toward this item (e.g., Open, Close, Create, Delete, Move, Rename, etc.).

ter 10 of Part 3). Let our photos and videos be a part of a never-ending story told, re-told, and continuously enriched by us and an interconnected web of colleagues, family, and friends.

Will technology eliminate PIM? Assuming a world where actions that manage personal information are perfectly in line with and a byproduct of actions of "life management" we might say "yes." We could elaborate to say that there is information management, but there is little point to its separate treatment—information management 'happens' as an integral part of living.

On the other hand, given that information is a second-hand reflection of life, there are stronger reasons to say "no." Information management and, at a *personal* level, PIM must remain separate categories of concern.

We can more easily respond "yes!" to another question: "Will technology transform PIM?" Absolutely. Even if the basic PIM activities are always with us in some form, the actual actions we perform may bear little resemblance to the PIM actions we perform today. If we already notice that we're using the hanging file folders of a paper filing cabinet much less than we once did, can we imagine a similar trajectory for our use of, for example, the "Save As" dialog as a means of keeping and organizing electronic documents?

Technologies may not eliminate PIM but they will certainly transform it. So the question is "how?" How will technologies transform the way we work with information in our practices of PIM? What about PIM will change or become unnecessary? What will stay the same? And how can we prepare? How can we influence the trajectory of technologies to better suit our needs? How can we transform the technologies that are transforming us?

SAVING, SEARCHING, AND STRUCTURING OUR INFORMATION: THE EXAMPLE OF EMAIL

We can group PIM technologies into three broad areas: Technologies that help us to **save** (capture, store) our information, **search** our information, and **structure** our information. The first two areas, technologies to save and technologies to search, generate tools in support of the many event-driven actions of keeping and finding we do in a typical day. The third technology area, structuring, aligns more closely with meta-level activities of PIM, that is, maintaining and organizing, managing privacy and the flow of information, measuring and evaluating and, most of all, making sense of (using and making decisions based upon) our information. However, as we shall explore later, each technology area—technologies to save, search, and structure—impacts each of the six activities of PIM and each of the six senses of personal information.

Technologies of saving, searching, and structuring. We need all three. The example of email illustrates.

In the early days of email (back in the 1960s and '70s), digital storage was dear and the initial focus for email was communication. Little thought was given to saving email messages, either sent or received. Once the message was communicated, we were done. But as storage got cheaper, the value of saving email messages became increasingly apparent.[10] We can check sent email messages to see if we've received a proper response or as proof that we've responded. We save incoming emails for a closer reading later on, possibly days or even weeks after their initial receipt as our attention finally turns to a related project.[11] Even better, this useful log, this memory, is a cost-free by-product of actions we must take in any case: the actions to communicate and coordinate with others.

But as we saved our emails and they continued to increase in number, we needed ways to return to a desired email or grouping of emails. It was no longer feasible to scroll through the entire sent mail folder or the entire inbox.[12]

Search? Until fairly recently search was not supported by an index and could take long minutes to complete. And it frequently failed. For even a reasonably sized email collection, there can be no interactive, exploratory search without the requisite speed-up of an index.

In the absence of fast, index-supported search, people developed sometimes elaborate schemes for the use of folders and tags.[13]

But now that fast, indexed-assisted searching is commonplace, many of us appear to be abandoning our schemes for the manual organization of email. Why bother to organize email into folders for sender and subject if these same groupings can be realized, in seconds, through a simple search by sender or subject?[14] Many of us have taken to leaving our emails in an ever-growing inbox, a practice encouraged by online email services giving large amounts of storage. Do search technologies obviate structure? Not at all. The need for structure remains but is transformed. Email messages have structure already. An email has a subject, a sender, intended recipients, and a record of the time it was sent and received. A search that could not be restricted by this structured information would be far less useful.

Will email go away?[15] Possibly. More likely, email stays but is much less central to our practices of PIM. Email may be pushed aside by other modes of digital communication such as texting, instant messaging, and tweeting. Or, even more so, in favor of persistent "places" of sharing supported by services such as Facebook and Dropbox.

If so, with each alternative to email, we will still be looking to technologies to save, search, and structure in support of managing our information.

---

[10] See Lovejoy & Grudin, 2003 for a historical perspective drawing parallels between the history of email and the more recent history of instant messaging.

[11] I have emails going back for 10 years or more. I used emails sent and received some four years ago to resolve a difference of memories between me and an acquaintance from college.

[12] For studies on the use of email in PIM (with entry points into others), see Bälter, 1997; Bellotti, Ducheneaut, Howard, Smith, & Grinter, 2005; Bellotti & Smith, 2000; Berghel, 1997; Dabbish & Kraut, 2006; Ducheneaut & Bellotti, 2001; Gwizdka, 2002; Mackay, 1988; Whittaker, Bellotti, & Gwizdka, 2007; S. Whittaker & Sidner, 1996.

[13] See Whittaker & Sidner, 1996.

[14] See Whittaker, Matthews, Cerruti, Badenes, & Tang, 2011.

[15] See Chapter 10, "Email Disappears?" in W. Jones, 2007.

Technologies to save, search, and structure. Each will get its own chapter. As we consider each technology in its turn, we pose the same questions. What technologies will the next 10 years bring? What impact will they have on how we manage our personal information? How might even small quantitative changes over time, such as the decreasing cost of storage or the increasing speed of search, produce qualitative changes in the way we manage our information and our lives?

But first, what else? What other technologies are likely to have a major impact on our practices of PIM?

In Part 1 of this book we considered two general areas of impact: 1) Palmtop devices and, more generally, an increasing presence of computing resources. 2) The Web with its world-wide, universal reach as a place we go not only to "read" (and learn about things) but also to "write" (share, influence, convince, impress) and, increasingly, to "execute"—that is, to get things done both in virtual and real worlds.

Input/output, or I/O, is another large area where developments in technology have the potential to have enormous impacts on the way we work with computing devices and, through these, with our information. This is the topic for Chapter 5, the first chapter in Part 2, before we dive more deeply into an exploration of technologies to save, search, and structure.

CAVEATS AND DISCLAIMERS

References to scholarly articles of direct relevance to personal information management (PIM) are grouped together into a bibliography at the end of Part 2.

Web references and references for non-PIM background reading are often included directly in footnotes. I include no references to information you can easily find on the Web. Instead of references, I sometimes include suggested search terms.

I am an unabashed citer of Wikipedia (http://www.wikipedia.org/) articles when these are reasonably clear and objectively written. The interested reader should use these articles not as a final destination but as a springboard (through references cited) for further study of a given topic. You the reader may discover—especially if you are expert on the topic of a Wikipedia article (whether or not cited here)—that the article is inaccurate or incomplete. If so, you should change it.

As with Part 1, Part 2 is not a step-by-step "how to." It aims to help you in your efforts to figure things out for yourself.

Even though Part 2 focuses on technologies of PIM, Part 2 is not a review of the latest and greatest in PIM tools and technologies. Such an effort is out of date even as it is being written. Likewise, Part 2 is no crystal ball. Instead, Part 2 makes reasonable extrapolations from present trends into the future. Also considered is a "present perfect" of basic truths concerning our ways of processing information.

WHO SHOULD READ PART 2?

As with Part 1, Part 2 is intended for the following audiences:

Faculty who are teaching PIM-related courses can use Part 2 for a review of technologies of i/o and technologies to save, search, and structure information—with special focus on the impacts these technologies are having and are likely to have on PIM.

People in PIM research can use Part 2 as an update of PIM-related technologies.

People in related/contributing fields—including human-computer interaction (HCI), information retrieval (IR), library and information science (LIS), artificial intelligence (AI), database management, cognitive psychology, and cognitive science—might find that Part 2 addresses questions similar to those they have concerning the impacts of the technologies reviewed.

People in business can use Part 2 to know "what they should know" about the technologies reviewed especially as these relate to employee productivity and the criteria for the selection of tools spawned by the technologies.

Interested laypeople can use Part 2 to know more about the exciting potential for technologies to impact the ways they manage their information and the ways they lead their lives.

Acknowledgments

I thank the following people for their careful review of Part 2 and their good suggestions toward its improvement: Maria Staaf, Gary Marchionini, Heiko Haller, Max Van Kleek, Lars Johansson, and Peter Kemmerle. Part 2 is much better for their efforts.

I thank Yaron Galitzky for the many useful references he provided to work on gesture recognition and, more generally, on *natural user interface*.

I thank Gary Marchionini for his excellent leadership as editor of the "Synthesis Lectures on Information Concepts, Retrieval, and Services" lecture series in which Parts 1 and 2 of *The Future of Personal Information Management* book appear. (And soon, Part 3).

I thank Diane Cerra for her assistance in getting this book to press.

I thank both Gary and Diane for their support and patience even as I repeatedly missed my (mostly self-imposed) deadlines.

CHAPTER 5

Technologies of Input and Output

We don't—can't—interact with our information directly but only through the tools that we use. The tools influence not just the ways we interact with information but also our ability to apprehend it. Though we may not usually think of it so, paper is a tool (and the ability to produce paper is a technology). So too are leak-proof pens, paperclips, staplers, and filing cabinets with hanging folders. They're all tools for managing paper-based information.

Even if some of us can contemplate a gradual obsolescence of the paper-based book in favor of a digital delivery of information via tablets, pads, and palmtops, we should all acknowledge the profound impact that the bound book, as a tool, has had on our ability to work with information.[16] Contrast the use of the book with an earlier use of scrolls and it's easy to believe that quantitative changes—e.g., it's faster to leaf through the pages of a bound book than to roll and unroll a scroll—might add up to qualitative differences in our ability to work with and understand our information.

We interact with our digital information via a computer in one device or another. Computer-based tools—devices, gadgets, desktop and web-based applications, etc.—are having a profound impact on our interactions with digital information. The technologies behind these tools can be grouped in two general areas according to whether these support the output of information from the computer or the input of information to the computer.

5.1 TECHNOLOGIES OF OUTPUT

How do we get our information from a computer? Some of us can recall mainframe computing days when the results of a "run" were communicated via paper printout to a designated bin in the anteroom of the computer area. The teletype was a big improvement. Now we have display screens of ever better resolution for laptop and palmtop use. We can elect to get our textual information spoken to us (e.g., as we walk or drive) via voice synthesis.[17]

---

[16] See a short write-up on the history of the book: http://en.wikipedia.org/wiki/Book. For a humorous take on initial "user interface" challenges posed by the book when first introduced, see http://www.youtube.com/watch?v=pQHX-SjgQvQ.

[17] http://en.wikipedia.org/wiki/Speech_synthesis.

We may soon be looking at our information through glasses we wear either as a tiny separate display embedded within eyeglasses or as "augmenting" overlay to the sights and sounds of the physical world.[18]

If we'd rather not wear glasses, we might accessorize in other ways such as through a "watch-watch" as discussed in Chapter 3 (Part 1). The "watch-watch" was originally discussed in 2007[19] as a way to connect a palmtop in pocket or purse with an item many of us habitually wear in any case—a wristwatch. The watch then provides a display surface for much that is timely beyond the time of day. Who is calling us right now? What meetings do we have today? What's the traffic like on the 520 bridge? How are our stocks doing?[20]

Given these new devices, some have enthused that "the end of the smartphone era is coming."[21] Others are more skeptical. Google glasses, for example, have been likened to Apple's ill-fated Newton; that is, they may be years ahead of the supporting technology needed to make them mainstream.[22]

More likely is a future of several devices including a palmtop device with a long battery life kept in pocket or purse as a kind of data hub connecting the other accessories we wear to the Internet.

Also on the output side of our interactions with computing devices are animations and an ability to "zoom" into and out of our information. Zooming and other animations provide a powerful way to apprehend a large volume of information.[23]

If "today is the world" (courtesy of Google Earth, Bing Maps, etc.) then perhaps tomorrow is our own personal space of information (PSI). Suppose, for example, that a Steinberg-like map of our personal world were used to organize and provide access to all our information. We might zoom into a particular area—a project we are working on now, a special party we are planning—

---

[18] http://en.wikipedia.org/wiki/Google_Glass; http://www.google.com/glass/start/. http://www.slate.com/blogs/future_tense/2012/11/28/microsoft_augmented_reality_glasses_patent_rival_to_apple_google_glass.html; see also Krevelen & Poelman, 2010 and http://www.businessinsider.com/this-is-what-apples-curved-glass-iwatch-might-look-like-2013-2.

[19] Jones, 2007.

[20] There was speculation not long ago that Apple had plans to realize a watch with such a configuration. Via Bluetooth (4.0), the iPod Nano as a wristwatch would serve as display for information pulled in from a nearby iPhone. See http://www.cultofmac.com/189414/will-apple-save-the-wristwatch/, and http://www.digitaltrends.com/apple/baseless-speculation-the-new-ipod-nano-will-be-a-wristwatch-for-the-iphone-5/. However, no more recent word on when or whether this will happen. Meanwhile, at least one other company is working on a wristwatch as display for an iPhone or Android (http://getpebble.com/).

[21] Carlson, 2012, see also http://www.businessinsider.com/the-end-of-the-smartphone-era-is-coming-2012-11#ixzz2LNdIR2AP.

[22] Chen, 2013 (http://qz.com/61145/google-glass-will-be-the-next-apple-newton/). See also, http://www.tgdaily.com/opinion-features/69806-google-glass-vs-apples-iwatch-when-will-screenphones-become-obsolete#b-ZzBDWW2Tr5XCcPE.99; and http://techpinions.com/apple-iwatch-vs-google-glasses-and-the-next-ui-battle/14497.

[23] See The Economist, 2012b and also http://en.wikipedia.org/wiki/Zooming_user_interface.

only to zoom out and back in again to another area—plans for ski trip over the weekend or for a summer vacation.

Figure 5.1: What if we could access our informational worlds via a customized, "zoomable," 3-dimenensional version of Steinberg's New Yorker-centric map of the world?[24] From Steinberg: illustration for the cover of *The New Yorker*, 1976. Copyright © 2013 Condé Nast. Used with permission.

5.2   TECHNOLOGIES OF INPUT

In the mainframe days of computing, we may have given our information to the computer via keypunch cards[25] that may themselves have been punched via keypunch.[26] The keyboard, whether attached to a keypunch, teletype, terminal, or personal computer was our primary means of input for decades. Then came the mouse—mostly as complement to, not a replacement of, the keyboard. The promise of "keyboard-free" voice recognition seemed for decades to be a mirage on the horizon. But voice recognition continues to improve and may be good enough for use even in noisy environments—good enough at least for simple messages (e.g., "on my way home").

Voice recognition (and handwriting recognition) are not the only means of input. The gaming industry has implemented gesture recognition (and a form of face recognition) "in the large" for

---

[24] Taken from http://theruralsite.blogspot.com/2011/12/winter-colds-new-yorker-state-of-mind.html.
[25] http://en.wikipedia.org/wiki/Punched_card.
[26] A special kind of typewriter (see for example, http://en.wikipedia.org/wiki/Keypunch#IBM_029_Card_Punch).

big gestures.[27] Gesture recognition is already being used as an aid in stroke rehabilitation,[28] where it enables self-paced training by the patient as a complement to the sessions with a trained professional.

Now we are beginning to see technologies to support "in the small" gesturing and other touch-free ways of interacting with our digital information.[29] Through eye-tracking technology[30] we might communicate our changing focus with a glance. We might select with a wink.[31]

I met a salesperson recently who spends up to two days out of three on the road. His office is his car for much of his day. Seconds matter. If he can't respond quickly to a request for a quote, the business may go elsewhere. His palmtop is his lifeline. Even as he drives from one meeting to the next, he "hears" text messages and email via voice synthesis. His response is converted from speech to a text or email message.

This is task switching to be sure.[32] Even if hands and eyes remain on the road, attention is divided between tasks: 1. Driving (often in unfamiliar circumstances). 2. Responding to a client with a quote. 3. Possibly also ancillary tasks to look up information in order to give the quote. Potentially dangerous? Certainly. He might agree. But this is his reality. He considers, rightly or wrongly, that the risk is worth the savings in time.

Technologies of input and output are incorporated into efforts to support a more natural user interface (NUI).[33] NUI promises—some might say threatens—to further separate us (some would say "liberate," others "alienate") from the immediate physical world in order to interact, typically via Internet connection, with digital information and people at long distances.

We have already grown accustomed to people talking into thin air as they walk along. Sometimes they really are crazy. But more often, they are talking to someone via headset. In a near future we may encounter people not only talking into thin air but also gesticulating and apparently seeing things that aren't there.

When we're the ones looking, talking, and gesticulating, we may realize whole new levels of freedom and power in our interactions with information. For much of my day, I still carry a laptop

---

[27] http://en.wikipedia.org/wiki/Gesture_recognition, http://en.wikipedia.org/wiki/PlayStation_Move, http://en.wikipedia.org/wiki/Kinec. And of course, touchscreens support gestures on a small scale (select this, delete that, make this view bigger/smaller, etc.).

[28] http://www.onwindows.com/Articles/Kinect-aids-patient-stroke-rehabilitation/7506/Default.aspx.

[29] Leap Freehand 3D Computer Interaction Without Gloves, http://research.microsoft.com/apps/video/default.aspx?id=173838&l=i; (Knight, 2012), What Comes After the Touch Screen? See also http://www.economist.com/node/21548486.

[30] M. Bell et al., 2009; The Economist, 2012a. For eye-tracking, http://www.tobii.com/.

[31] There are also "cyborg" technologies already being realized for a greater synthesis of the digital and the biological. and already here in research prototypes for people with special needs (people unable to see or hear; people with artificial limbs) are computing interfaces in support of control of an artificial limb or synthetic vision. http://en.wikipedia.org/wiki/Cyborg.

[32] See Chapter 3 (Part 1), William Jones, 2012.

[33] Bowman, McMahan, & Ragan, 2012, see also http://en.wikipedia.org/wiki/Natural_user_interface#Examples_of_interfaces_commonly_referred_to_as_NUI, http://whatis.techtarget.com/definition/natural-user-interface-NUI.

around with me. I once felt liberated by this arrangement—how nice to be able take my work with me from place to place rather than having to return to a desktop computer in my office! But more recently, I feel the burden—my backpack with my laptop inside is my constant companion and the thing I'm always worried I'll forget. How liberating instead to carry my work with me via wearable accessories!

Still, even as these NUI technologies become mainstream, they don't eliminate the need for PIM. On the contrary, technologies of input/output force with even greater urgency the need to manage. How, for example, to protect privacy in an age when we are openly, continuously interacting with our information, leaving a record that others might inspect?

If technologies of NUI don't eliminate PIM, they will certainly transform our ways of doing it. Technologies of NUI and ubiquitous computing will complete a revolution already underway, thanks to our palmtop devices and a greatly improved connectivity of these devices to the Web. To the good, we'll be able to work on our information anywhere via exchanges that are faster, easier, and more "natural" than those we have currently (and with no need to carry backpack or briefcase). To the not-so-good, as we realize these new abilities we are even more separated from our actual physical environment with consequences that range from the comical and crazy (in appearance) to the dangerous and deadly.

Technologies of NUI and their impacts on our practices of PIM are explored further in the context of the remaining chapters in Part 2.

CHAPTER 6

Technologies to Save Our Information

There is a story of a young man—a promising playwright—who decided to part with all of his worldly possessions and to walk across America as a "pilgrim for peace."[34] He divested of the digital as well as the physical: He gave away his computer after first wiping the hard drive clean of all data, including all the plays he had written over an eight-year period.

What to do later, when he decided to abandon his pilgrimage and reconstruct the pieces of his former life? How to recover eight years' worth of plays?

The answer: Email.

I don't know how exactly he got back copies of his plays. The plays in one version or another had been sent to other people—friends, colleagues, prospective producers, etc. He may very well have sent drafts to himself as insurance against the failure of local storage. Perhaps recovery was as easy as the reactivation of his Gmail or Hotmail account and an inspection of sent mail. Or, perhaps he had to ask the indulgence of the people to whom versions of the plays were sent ("Er… remember that play draft I sent you?…").

That his digital trail was not so easily erased was a good thing. This is a story with a happy ending. We can be sure that such stories end less happily in other instances: digital trails may persist like a bad memory notwithstanding all our efforts to delete them.

6.1   THE POSSIBILITY OF "TOTAL CAPTURE"

The story tells us that digital capture—automated and passive—is here already. Capture is a by-product of our activities. How can we use this information to advantage toward the "goals and roles" in our lives? How can we avoid being "framed" by digital information (e.g., pictures, videos, emails, and tweets) which may, taken out of context, portray us falsely?

We might strive toward a "total capture" of all our daily experiences. Imagine, for example, a camera worn as jewelry or apparel to record everything we see and hear during the day. The recording is our alibi, our record, our memory that stays even as our internal memory fades with the passage of time.

---

[34] The story comes to me via a local KUOW radio broadcast of the Jan. 4, 2013 episode of "This American Life" (http://www.thisamericanlife.org/radio-archives/episode/483/self-improvement-kick).

Dreams of saving it all (aka "lifelogging" or "total capture") can be traced back to Vannevar Bush and his sketch of a Memex system.[35] Memex was described in terms of conventional cameras and microfiche. More recently, we have systems of digital capture and preservation. The Lifestreams effort explored the potential to organize all personal digital information along a timeline.[36] MyLife-Bits explored the feasibility of storing all of a person's digital information, including digitized copies of paper information, into a single database, organized for rapid searching and the dynamic construction of collections (groupings) of information on demand.[37]

Mann conceived of "wearable computing" as a way of capturing the interactions people have with their surroundings. Eyetap devices might record continuous video.[38] SenseCam, a device that periodically and automatically records still images, has been extensively tested by volunteers, who wear a rather largish pendant around the neck.[39] More recently, there is even a start-up proposing to commercialize the SenseCam approach.[40]

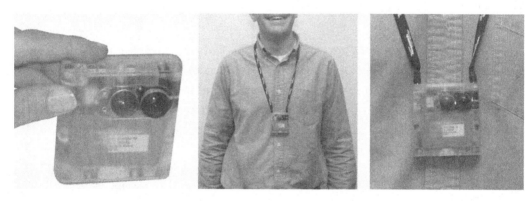

Figure 6.1: Images of the SenseCam v2.3 prototype. Used with permission from Hodges et al., 2006.

Gordon Bell estimated in 2001[41] that a lifetime video (DVD quality) record of a person's experiences might be recorded in a petabyte (a million gigabytes) of data and that associated costs of storage might, two decades hence (i.e., 2021), be as little as $100 per year.

---

[35] Bush, 1945.

[36] Fertig, Freeman, & Gelernter, 1996a; Freeman & Gelernter, 1996.

[37] Gemmell, Bell, & Lueder, 2006; Gemmell, Bell, Lueder, Drucker, & Wong, 2002; Gemmell, Lueder, & Bell, 2003.

[38] Mann, Sehgal, & Fung, 2004.

[39] Byrne et al., 2008; Hodges et al., 2006; Siân E. Lindley, Harper, Randall, Glancy, & Smyth, 2009; Sellen et al., 2007.

[40] Ref http://memoto.com/.

[41] G. Bell, 2001.

Bell's projections may even have been conservative. Advances in the technology of storage promise more storage lasting over longer periods of time, for less money and less energy.[42] From 1986 through 2007, the world's per capita capacity for information storage has doubled roughly every 40 months.[43]

With the use of social media we can anticipate an ability to reconstruct a digital record of events from multiple perspectives. We are already beginning to see, for example, web queries that can retrieve "pictures and clips" within a given range of time and location.[44] Furthermore, recordings might be interleaved with an item event or, i.e., log.[45] The log provides a searchable index into the video stream; the video, in turn, provides an indication for our immediate environment at the time we were sending an email, tweeting, texting, surfing the Web, etc.

Recordings and the log might be further enhanced through the use of *telematics*[46] to record data concerning the automobiles we drive. We might also track the ebb and flow of energy use in our homes and correlate with our activities.

We're never done. For everything recorded, there is always something left unrecorded. What about smells? Tastes? Feelings? What about a back-mounted camera to record, literally, what's happening behind our backs? And if we take care of these, there is still always a larger context, the ground to our figure, that goes unrecorded.

If "total capture" is impossible by strict definition, lifelogging by relaxed definition is already here. We have fragmented logs in the form of time-stamped emails, text messages, tweets, "Instagrams," etc. We can imagine a future in which our lifelogs are an integration of these and other sources of time-stamped event information. Events might point to pictures and video clips. Events might include measures of heartbeat, blood pressure, glucose levels, and so on. Logging can happen not only during our waking hours but also as we sleep.[47]

So, given a lifelog in some form or another, what good is it? How would we use it?

---

[42] Read, for example, about recent developments in Phase Change Memory (PCM) and Resistive Switching Random Access Memory (RRAM); see (Wong et al., 2011) Farther out is the potential of DNA storage (Goldman et al., 2013). An article in the *Economist* describes the many potential advantages of PCM over flash memory including speed, capacity for much greater miniaturization, with much greater density of storage, and also characteristics of dynamic random-access memory with the potential to serve as "storage-class memory" (*Economist*, from the print edition: Technology Quarterly).Q3, 2012.

[43] Hilbert & López, 2011.

[44] See, for example, "Geofeedia helps journalists locate real-time photos, tweets where news breaks," "Simple Tool Lets You Dig Up Instagram Photos by Time and Location" and "neartime: find flickr photos taken nearby in time and space" each returned with a Google search for "search for photos by time & location."

[45] W. Jones, 2007; William Jones, 2012, Chapter 3 (Part 1).

[46] http://en.wikipedia.org/wiki/Telematics.

[47] http://www.usatoday.com/story/news/nation/2013/03/24/sleep-tracking-devices/2007085/.

6.2   PERSONAL POTENTIALS OF A LIFELOG.

Sellen and Whittaker[48] describe "the five Rs" of benefits that might accrue "if we could digitally capture everything we do and see." With capture we might better:

- **recollect** so that we could recall, for example, the name of the person we talked to at a party last night or the instructions we received from our supervisor during a drop-in meeting.

- **reminisce** (as a special case of recollecting) in order to re-live past experiences (especially the good ones).

- **retrieve** specific items of digital information such as an email, document, or web page.

- **reflect** upon past events including our interactions with other people. Could we have been more understanding? Less argumentative? In correlating our activities with physical measures, we might reflect upon situations that tend to make our heart rate or blood pressure go up (or down). At what times of the day are we at our best for completing tough tasks or making difficult decisions? Does the second cup of coffee make us more or less productive? Are we getting good sleep at night? Does it matter what we ate for dinner? When?

- **remember** our intentions. Did we remember to pick up the milk?

A recall benefit was observed in one study involving the use of a SenseCam for a 12-month period by a patient with amnesia. "The results of this initial evaluation are extremely promising; periodic review of images of events recorded by SenseCam results in significant recall of those events by the patient, which was previously impossible."[49]

A benefit for reminiscing is reported in the description of another study by Lindley and colleagues where members of a household each wore a SenseCam during the same week. Household members then shared their SenseCam images with each other. "The time-lapse nature of the image stream led participants to romanticize the mundane and find sentimentality in unexpected places, and was particularly effective at portraying personality and play."[50]

Lindley and colleagues also report a benefit for another "R" in a study involving the use of SenseCams by members of four separate households. Images viewed some 18 months after their capture appeared to be especially effective in support of reflection: "The findings reveal how images captured by different family members led to new insights around normally unremarkable routines, and provided new perspectives on how children experienced the world, while the 18-month interval

---

[48] Sellen & Whittaker, 2010, p. 70.
[49] Hodges et al., 2006, p. 177, see also Kalnikaite & Whittaker, 2012.
[50] Siân E. Lindley et al., 2009. See also, Harper et al., 2007.

prompted some reinterpretation of the past and made participants aware of incremental changes in their everyday lives."[51]

More generally, as we combine recordings of "the same" event via devices worn by different participants, an objectification of multiple viewpoints—possibly quite divergent—becomes possible.[52] Mann speaks of sous-veillance (from the French for "to watch from below") as a counterpoint to a more "God's eye" surveillance provided by cameras placed in fixed locations that often "watch from above."[53]

6.3   CAVEATS AND DISCLAIMERS

Notwithstanding these potential benefits of digital capture and an approach of "saving everything,"[54] an accounting of actual benefits is more nuanced. Sellen and Whittaker go on to review[55] studies that suggest the following:

- Digital information such as pictures and SenseCam images can help us recall a particular event. "Oh, that's right. Mike was there and told that interesting story about the election."

- Images that are passively and automatically captured may be more effective in supporting our recall of an event than, for example, pictures we consciously take with a camera.[56]

- At the same time, our ability to recall declines with the passage of time with or without the "prosthetic" of SenseCam images. Apparently, as our memories fade with the passage of time, the effectiveness of images in evoking these memories also declines.

In another article, Sellen and colleagues note "… in the case of remembered events, we failed to find an interaction with the length of the test interval. In other words, there was no evidence that SenseCam images provided any greater (or lesser) benefit over time, …with SenseCam images, we can remember more, but the power of these cues to spark remembering also deteriorates over time."[57]

In relation to recall (and reminiscing) a distinction is made between the function of external memory as a record of "what must have happened" as opposed to a cue for internal memories. In

[51] Síin E. Lindley, Glancy, Harper, Randall, & Smyth, 2011. See also, Isaacs et al., 2013.
[52] We are reminded of the story and film, Rashomon wherein different characters provide distinctly different versions of the same incident. See http://en.wikipedia.org/wiki/Rashomon.
[53] Mann, 2004.
[54] See also Chapter 7, W. Jones & Teevan, 2007.
[55] Hodges et al., 2006; Sellen et al., 2007.
[56] Why would pictures automatically taken be better than pictures actively taken in the support of recall? One explanation may be that, if we are taking a picture, our attention is already focused on the event, thus strengthening our memories for the event whether or not we view the picture later. On the other hand, pictures taken automatically may remind of events we were less fully attentive to at the time of their occurrence.
[57] …"page 88, "Sellen et al., 2007.

the complete absence of a recalled internal memory of an event, we can often piece together an understanding of what "must have" happened. A picture of a younger us in a graduation gown with the main building for our high school in the background "must have been" taken at our high school commencement. (And, yes, we'd forgotten how pimply-faced and thin we looked back then.)

The time intervals studied so far have been relatively short—up to four months. What is the value of information like pictures, video, sound, text, email, and tweets over much longer periods of time? Will that external information do more, over time, to compensate for the decay of internal memory? And, on a darker side, is it possible that doctored records might lead us to construct a false memory for an event that never happened?[58] These are good questions for which we do not yet have an answer.

As another practical limitation of total capture, we can note that, even as the capacity to capture and store continues to increase, the time we have to retrieve and review is fixed. Studies suggest that information recorded digitally is rarely accessed again[59] or as in the case of digital photographs, only a tiny portion is ever accessed again.[60]

Time considerations support another observation on the practical limits of lifelogs: People often settle for imperfect, internal memories quickly in preference to a more time-consuming retrieval of external information, which might represent a particular event more completely.[61]

"Total capture" might also lure us into a false sense of security. We don't pay attention in a lecture or meeting thinking "I can always look at the recording later" but we may have trouble doing so and, by not being actively engaged during the event, we miss an opportunity to interact and ask questions to better understand the material. Lansdale[62] expressed this as a dilemma—"the more we automate the process of storage and take responsibility away from the user, the less he is going to remember, and therefore the less he is going to be able to retrieve." And then, since lessons build the new on the previous, so too do the negative effects of inattentiveness.

The importance of active, meaningful engagement as a means to understand and form durable memories for the material (e.g., of a meeting or lecture) is well-established from basic research in cognitive psychology.[63] Studies of note-taking[64] indicate that we're more likely to remember the

---

[58] Loftus, 1993.

[59] Petrelli & Whittaker, 2010.

[60] Steve Whittaker et al., 2010.

[61] Gray & Fu, 2001, Kalnikaité & Whittaker, 2007.

[62] Lansdale, 1988, p. 65.

[63] Original "levels of processing" work by Craik and Lockhart, 1972. http://en.wikipedia.org/wiki/Levels-of-processing_effect, demonstrated superior memory for words processed more "deeply" for meaning rather than for superficial features such as appearance and sound. A related "generation effect" (Slamecka & Graf, 1978) points more generally to a benefit for paraphrases generated by recipients in their own words. A technique follows that many of us, when giving instructions to others (especially to our own children) have learned apply: Ask the recipient to repeat the instructions in his/her own words.

[64] For an extensive review of note-taking studies, see Williams & Eggert, 2002.

more important points from a lecture if we take notes, even if we never consult the notes again.[65] As we take notes, we paraphrase, expressing the content again in our own words. In so doing we process the information we are receiving more "deeply," forming new associations to the material within our internal memories.

With respect to activities of keeping, a contrast can be made between activities that promote a richer engagement with the information and activities that distract from the information being presented. Simple note-taking focused on understanding and recording the main ideas may improve the quality of our engagement with the information. On the other hand, a more mechanical attempt to record the lecturer word-for-word may distract us from engaging the information more deeply. In a best of both worlds, the "gist notes" we take might be interleaved in time with a recording of the presentation. Notes then serve as a kind of index into a selective review of the recording.[66]

Our attention, like our time, remains a precious resource in short supply even as ease, economics, and capacity for information capture and storage continue to improve.

It is generally a good thing that we no longer need to agonize over what to keep and what to delete—why bother when storage is so cheap?[67] However, although we may not need to delete, we are well advised to remove old items from our *attentional surfaces*.[68]

One important surface that gets our attention, our email inbox, does this for us. As new emails arrive, old emails are pushed down and out of sight. This also happens in our digital calendars. If we view a week at a glance, then our view of the current week displaces the view of the previous week.

For other surfaces, such as a frequently used folder or a to-do list, moving older items out of the way (e.g., into a subfolder) requires our conscious time and attention. Future applications might more routinely include a "shelf-life" logic so that items are archived or sorted to the bottom if we haven't worked with these items in some time.[69]

6.4 THE PIM TRANSFORMED, THE PIM THAT REMAINS

As we consider technologies for saving our information, remember that a given item of information might be personal—might be "ours"—in any or several of the senses determined by its relationship to us. The senses in which information can be personal were illustrated in Figure 1 of Chapter 2 (Part 1, "The Basics of PIM") and this diagram is repeated again here (Figure 6.2).

[65] See also, Kalnikaite & Whittaker, 2008; Williams & Worth, 2002.

[66] See, for example, Kalnikaite & Whittaker, 2012.

[67] Bergman et al., 2009, note a "deletion paradox" that when storage space is dear and needs to be managed we may find ourselves spending time on the wrong kind of information—information that is old and slated for deletion but that we agonize over nonetheless "to be sure." W. Jones, 2007, describes a related "old magazine effect" that, when attending to an item for deletion (such as an old magazine), we're likely to notice all sorts of potential uses (e.g., interesting articles we'd like to read some day).

[68] W. Jones, 2007.

[69] But perhaps we should hold our collective breath. Malone had a similar proposal back in 1983 (Malone, 1983).

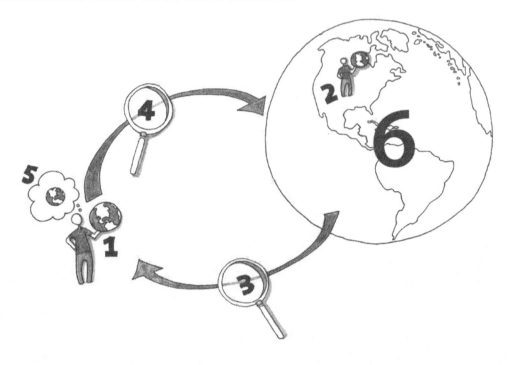

Figure 6.2: Six senses of personal information combine to make a personal space of information (PSI), Based on an illustration by Elizabeth Boling.

Information can be personal in relation to you or me because it is: **P1.** Owned by us (and at least partially under our control). **P2.** About us. **P3.** Directed toward us by others. **P4.** Sent or shared by us. **P5.** Experienced by us. **P6.** Relevant to us.

We note again that these senses are not mutually exclusive. Far from it. An item of personal information is frequently personal in several of these senses. In aggregate the six senses combined exclude very little, especially when P6 is added. These senses are useful for the complementary perspectives they provide on our information. The six senses will be used as a yardstick by which to assess each of the technologies we review in this book.

For any piece of information or for any tool that would manage this information, it is illuminating to cycle through each sense of the personal and ask, "In what way(s) is this personal?"

We began this chapter with notions of "total capture." By an information processing approach to intelligent behavior[70] all of our experiences of the world are informational, that is, products of our processing the worldly data that impinges upon our senses. This includes information

---

[70] An information processing approach to human psychology was pioneered by Broadbent, 1958. See also, http://en.wikipedia.org/wiki/Broadbent's_filter_model_of_attention.

packaged into items such as email messages, paper documents, and web pages. But more generally, *anything* we experience is information and potentially subject to capture and storage in some form.

This is the **P5** sense of information: what we experience. We can attempt to "capture," with varying degrees of fidelity, the information of the original experience. This produces new information in some format that represents the original experience. The new information might, for example, be a video clip stored in an MPEG format, a verbal description written in plain text, a digital photograph stored as a JPEG or TIFF file, or even a pen drawing on paper.[71]

To the extent that we have control over this representation, the information becomes **P1**, that is, "owned" by us. As soon we share the information, it becomes **P4**. To the people we share it with—our Facebook friends, for example—the information is **P3** (information directed to them). As it gets shared, the photo, clip, or text message representing an experience we had becomes from our perspective an important subset of **P2**—information about us but under the control of someone else.

We can also consider the impact that technologies for capturing and saving will have upon our six activities of PIM. Recall again from Chapter 2 of Part 1 that the six activities of PIM are keeping, finding (re-finding), maintaining and organizing, managing privacy and the flow of information, measuring and evaluating (of our practices of PIM) and making sense of and using information.

The discussion about finding (and re-finding) information will wait until the next chapter, which deals with search. Keeping activities may be altered by saving technologies but perhaps not as much as we might initially have thought. Yes, the recording we make during a lecture might free us from scribbling down a word for word transcription. But if we elect instead to catch up on email or complete some form-filling busywork, we should be doing so because the lecture is information we know already or know we don't need. Unless some other task needs immediate attention, we should **not** attend to these tasks merely so that we can later attend to the recording of the meeting. Where, after all, is the savings in this?

We may, in fact, take notes even though a faithful video recording will be available for the meeting. Notes might be time-stamped and then synched with the recording so that the notes serve as an index of the recording and provide useful entry points into the stream.

Or we may take notes not as a thing to be used later but rather as a means of more fully comprehending the lecture. Paraphrasing the lecturer's ideas helps focus our attention. We're recording to internal "wet" memory. As we paraphrase through notes, we're more likely to be aware of gaps in our understanding and points of disagreement. The notes may be illegible. We may never consult them again. Even so, they have served their purpose.

---

[71] Don Norman describes his experience during a journey to the Yellow Mountain (Huang Shan) in China. Many tourists simply took pictures with their cameras. However, a group of artists chose sketching and painting as a means of recording their experiences (http://www.jnd.org/dn.mss/chapter_1_i_go_to_a.html).

What about other kinds of keeping such as taking a picture or video? In the introduction to this chapter, I suggested that we might happily forgo picture-taking if the process could somehow be delegated to our friends, a professional photographer, or a device like the SenseCam. But here, too, some of us might consider the taking of a picture of, say, a beautiful sunset not as a distraction from the current experience but a way of more fully attending to the scene.

As for our keeping activities, so too for meta-level activities of PIM: Saving technologies do not save us from the need to manage:

➢ **Maintenance and organization.** Saving technologies mean there is even more of our information (especially **P1**) to maintain and organize. Digital photographs are a case in point. Their capture is easy. We can store gigabytes of photos on our palmtop devices. Photos can be uploaded automatically to a laptop computer or to the Web. But then what? Is this information safely backed up to guard against crashing hard drives or the theft of our devices? Is this information organized for use later on? Or consider our methods of document versioning. Many of us still save versions of a document in separate files even if only a few words are different between versions. Wasteful in storage but who cares? Storage is cheap. But we may care a lot later if, lacking a system for organizing versions, we accidentally edit and distribute the wrong version.

➢ **Managing privacy and the flow of information.** With technologies of web-based information saving and sharing, the senses of our personal information can be likened to blotches of paint in a watercolor. Information experienced by us (**P5**) runs into information we own (**P1**) and then into information we project (**P4**) via sharing on the Web. Cheap and easy storage means that others also keep huge amounts of information about us (**P2**). Our connections to the Internet greatly increase the opportunity for others to send information our way (**P3**).

Technologies that enable us (and everyone else) to save information make it even more imperative to manage not only privacy but also "publicy"—how do we appear to others.[72] We may have reason, for example, to maintain a lifelog not as something we'll necessarily ever have time to consult, but as a "for the record" alibi. As our lives and ourselves are increasingly mediated by the Web, we also need to address issues of search engine optimization (SEO)[73] in our projections of ourselves onto the Web. And we need to

---

[72] Marchionini coins the term "proflection" to describe the interplay between projections of a person's information into cyberspace and the reflections that others (people and machines) create to those projections (Gary Marchionini, 2008).

[73] On the topic of "personal SEO" see, for example, http://socialwebthing.com/2010/03/10-tips-to-boost-your-personal-seo/, http://blog.kissmetrics.com/personal-branding-seo/, and http://www.slideshare.net/bencotton/presentation-to-london-met-on-personal-seo, and http://www.slideshare.net/RossHudgens/how-to-get-hired-in-seo?from_search=6.

understand and be able to trust the privacy controls provided through web services for sharing and syncing.[74]

➢ **Measuring and evaluating.** Given an ability to record our interactions not only with digital information but also with the physical world, opportunities for measuring and evaluating greatly increase. We measure to evaluate our practice of PIM and our lives more generally. The "quantified self" movement loosely groups various efforts to understand ourselves better and to make life improvements based upon logged data.[75] Are we making the best use of our time, energy, and money? Are we eating well (but not too well)? Are we getting enough exercise? Enough sleep? Saving technologies will provide us with increasing options to measure and, through measurements, to evaluate. To the good, we may learn and so make changes toward a better life in which we are better people. To the bad, we risk becoming inwardly focused and obsessed with our measurements so that there is little time left to live. "Know thyself" is a Delphic maxim. But so too is "nothing in excess."[76]

➢ **Making sense of and using our information.** Saving technologies will make it much easier for us to save (pile, group) information for review later on. This might be information for a trip we're planning, a decision we need to make, or a project we need to complete at work. When we find the time to review this information, we face a more general problem of evaluation. What is the information telling us? How to make sense of it all? And do we need more? Do we have enough to make a decision? In organizational contexts, we hear discussion of data mining and "big data."[77] How to make sense of very large sets of data? Where are the hidden "gems" of understanding and actionable implication? As in so many other areas, as information resources move from the organizational to the personal, so too do issues of information management. Recently then,

---

[74] For example, a search on "privacy in facebook photos" in June of 2013 produced several interesting articles including, http://allfacebook.com/people-arent-stealing-your-facebook-photos-a-lesson-in-privacy_b117857. A search using the template "How secure is …" applied first to Facebook and then Dropbox in each case produced the standard reassuring articles form the websites for these services but then other articles from independents such as: http://www.pcworld.com/article/249727/how_secure_is_my_facebook_information_.html, https://nolancaudill.com/2013/04/14/how-secure-is-dropbox/.

[75] Search "self-tracking," "the quantified self," and "personal informatics" to locate websites such as http://quantifiedself.com/guide/ and http://personalinformatics.org/ and short articles such as Hollindale, 2013; Singer, 2011, or the Wikipedia article on "Quantified Self" (http://en.wikipedia.org/wiki/Quantified_Self). For more scholarly articles use search expressions within Google Scholar or the ACM Digital Library (http://dl.acm.org/).

[76] http://en.wikipedia.org/wiki/Oracle_of_Delphi#Oracle.

[77] See http://en.wikipedia.org/wiki/Data_mining and http://en.wikipedia.org/wiki/Big_data.

the phrase "small data" (or "little data") has been coined.[78] The expression nicely riffs on the "big data" theme to provide a PIM emphasis. Whether the "little data" movement produces more than a new perspective remains to be seen.

Our information… sort of. And then there is information about us that is "ours" and protected but not fully under our control. In this category are monthly statements from our bank, credit card, and brokerage accounts. We used to get these as paper documents via surface mail. We now increasingly opt for paper-free, on-demand transmission. Statements can be downloaded as PDFs, but do we always remember to look?

Often more useful are the dynamically generated listings of account activity that we get through interactions with a database. Working through a financial institution's database, we can receive a customized listing of transactions that we can then elect to download (e.g., as comma-separated values or "CSV") for import into a spreadsheet. The data in this form is generally more useful than that in PDFs. We can, for example, do subtotals to find out where the money goes.

But a problem arises. Institutions may keep data for only a limited period in databases to which customers have ready access. Institutions may even keep PDFs of monthly account statements in a readily accessible location for only a few years. And what happens if you switch banks or your credit card number is compromised and needs to be changed?

We can make copies of all our monthly PDF statements. We can update our spreadsheets periodically with database listings. But will we? We have to remember to do this. Copies of our electronic statements do not stack up in the manner of paper copies delivered via surface mail. Usually, this is a good thing. But what if we really need this information some day? Making copies and doing updates takes time. More likely, we won't. As time goes on the information is available only in less useable form, such as PDFs, and may eventually only be accessed via special request.

It may be time, therefore, to think about another more practical kind of "total capture." Forget about a total capture of all that we see and hear. What about total capture of all that we spend and earn via a special kind of "crawl?"[79]

An increasing reliance on digital information brings up other new issues of maintenance. How long does a given medium of digital storage last? And what happens if "the lights go out" for

---

[78] See, for example, http://blogs.hbr.org/cs/2013/05/little_data_makes_big_data_mor.html and http://www.guardian.co.uk/news/datablog/2013/apr/25/forget-big-data-small-data-revolution. There are also advocates for "slow data" (see for example, http://www.perceptualedge.com/blog/?p=1460, http://brandsavant.com/the-slow-data-movement/).

[79] There are an increasing number of web services that promise to provide integrative views of your different banking, spending, and investment accounts. Mint (https://www.mint.com/) is arguably the most well-known of these services. But several alternate services are also available (see for example, http://www.moneyunder30.com/mint-alternatives-comparing-adaptu-personal-capital-and-manilla, http://www.xconomy.com/national/2013/02/22/i-switched-from-mint-com-to-pageonce-maybe-you-should-too/, and http://www.dailyfinance.com/2010/08/11/look-out-mint-moneystrands-worthy-money-management-competition/).

a prolonged period of time or, cataclysmically, forever?[80] If our lights and electricity are really out, we obviously have bigger problems to contend with, but those of us who survive these problems might be very happy for non-digital backups to our digital information.[81]

With lights and electricity still on we must deal with the reality that media for digital storage are not forever; each has a limited lifetime. For information kept on the Web in readily accessible form, we can continue to copy the information from place to place and into newer formats so that it stays "fresh." But information kept readily accessible on the Web consumes enormous amounts of energy.[82] Why spend all that energy when the likelihood we'll ever need the information again is extremely small? One interesting alternative for archival is storage based upon artificially constructed DNA where the bases of DNA—adenosine (A), thymine (T), cytosine (C), and guanine (G)—are used to encode information.[83] Encoding is currently costly but, once encoded, the information might persist for thousands of years.

In summary, with one technology area—for saving our information—considered, the need for PIM is still firmly intact. But what if we could summon the information we need when and where we need it? Would we still need PIM? We're on to a consideration of search.

---

[80] The made-for-television series "Revolution," for example, portrayed a world after the lights (and electricity) have gone out (http://en.wikipedia.org/wiki/Revolution_(TV_series)).

[81] For non-electrical options in the high-capacity storage of information, you might also track developments in Microsoft's "immortal computing" initiative (http://www.technovelgy.com/ct/Science-Fiction-News.asp?NewsNum=924).

[82] By Google's own estimate, for example, "2010 footprint was 1,449,825 tonnes of CO_2" using as much electricity annually as 220,000 people (http://www.google.com/green/bigpicture/references.html). "Google accounts for roughly 0.013 percent of the world's energy use" (http://techland.time.com/2011/09/09/6-things-youd-never-guess-about-googles-energy-use/#ixzz2YNVH1i4i). See also http://www.nytimes.com/2011/09/09/technology/google-details-and-defends-its-use-of-electricity.html or http://www.dailymail.co.uk/news/article-2035382/Google-discloses-energy-consumption--power-Salt-Lake-City.html or try searching on "power consumption by google" (as your search completes you will have consumed the approximately the electricity needed to run a 60W light bulb for 17 seconds).

[83] See http://en.wikipedia.org/wiki/DNA_digital_data_storage. "DNA-based storage may be cost-effective for archives of several megabytes with a 600–5,000-yr horizon" (Goldman et al., 2013, p2). See also popular coverage, http://online.wsj.com/article/SB10001424127887324539304578259883507543150.html, http://www.bbc.com/future/story/20130724-saving-civilisation-in-one-room, http://www.economist.com/news/science-and-technology/21570671-archives-could-last-thousands-years-when-stored-dna-instead-magnetic, http://www.computerworld.com/s/article/9236176/DNA_may_soon_be_used_for_storage.

CHAPTER 7

Technologies to Search Our Information

A search that succeeds can seem like magic. The words of our query function literally as "key words" that unlock the information we need. If it works, we get the right information, at the right time and place, in the right format, and in the right amount to address our current need. That's one of the originally stated ideals of PIM.[84]

Search can be characterized as a two-step of recall and recognition:[85] First, *recall* (and articulate) something about the desired information (e.g., author, title, content words) to specify the query; second, scan among the results returned to *recognize* and select the desired information.

We can do better. Web searches sometimes return just the snippet of information we're looking for, at, or near the top of the results listing, with no need for us to scan and click (Figure 7.1).

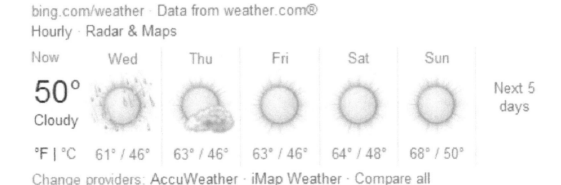

Figure 7.1: A search in Bing on "Seattle weather" brings back a results listing with a 5-day weather forecast included directly at the top of the listing.[86]

---

[84] W. Jones & Maier, 2003.

[85] Lansdale, 1988, Jones 2007, Chapter 2 (Part 1), broadens the process for re-finding to include an initial step of remembering (to look) and a subsequent step of repetition to expand and fine-tune results).

[86] Retrieved on March 27, 2013 (not bad for Seattle for this time of year ☺).

Some searches return snippets called "search clips"[87] with fields we can specify, such as the date range of a stock price (Figure 7.2) or dates of a vacation (Figure 7.3). As we do so, we search more deeply into structured, special-purpose databases (e.g., for stock prices or airfares). Snippets work now only for the most popular search queries, but we can well imagine coverage extending into the "long tail" of a frequency-ordered distribution of search queries.

We can do even better. In the spirit of "read, write, execute" discussed in Chapter 4 (Part 1), we might actually do something via the results page of a search: Make a reservation for dinner or purchase a movie ticket or order a delivery of groceries. With credit cards already on file, transactions can be as easy as entering or saying[88] a search phrase followed by a few clicks (or gestures, or utterances) to confirm.

Figure 7.2: The top-ranked snippet of information returned by Google in response to "Boeing stock." Buttons at the bottom can be clicked to show (in place) stock prices over varying periods of time (5 days, 1 month, 6 months…).[89]

---

[87] "Search Clips" is one of the patents I was awarded while working at Microsoft in the '90s (http://patft.uspto.gov/netacgi/nph-Parser?Sect1=PTO1&Sect2=HITOFF&d=PALL&p=1&u=%2Fnetahtml%2FPTO%2Fsrchnum.htm&r=1&f=G&l=50&s1=6256623.PN.&OS=PN/6256623&RS=PN/6256623.)

[88] Capra, III & Pérez-Quiñones, 2005.

[89] Retrieved March 27, 2013.

Flights to **Honolulu, HI**

bing.com/travel

From	To
	Honolulu, HI (HNL) - Hor

Leave		Return		
04/19/2013	▦	04/21/2013	▦	**Find flights**

Figure 7.3: A top-ranked "search clip" of information returned by Bing in response to "Expedia airfares to Hawaii." Fields can specify departure airport (though this should be defaulted) and travel dates.[90]

If we can do this on the Web for public information and services, then why can't we also do this for our own information and when interacting with our applications, either desktop or web-based? Why can't we ask, for example, "What are the names and spellings of Bjorn and Ami's children?" and get back a direct answer?

Or consider the help we sometimes search for within an application in order to find out how to format a document or to change the settings of our email application or even to access advanced search features of our desktop search application. We often go through several steps: Specify the query; scan the results listing; open one, perhaps several, help topics. And when we finally find the right topic it often involves a long sequence of instructions to carry out. Why can't our computer "just do it!"?

The visible search box or its audio counterpart then comes to support a kind of universal command line interface. Our wish is our search genie's command.

Ironies abound. The original command line interface was fussy and unforgiving. We looked to "WIMP" interfaces[91] for help in communicating with the computer. New search interfaces, by contrast, apply sophisticated methods (e.g., of text, language, link, and statistical analyses) to give us an interface that is potentially both flexible and forgiving but also fast and efficient in the manner of a conventional command line.

Of course a search-enabled command interface is no longer limited to typed-in text. We might speak our request instead. Or we might point to or take a picture of a person or thing as a kind of query ("Who is that person at the table over there?" "Can I get a better price on this item at another store nearby?").

---

[90] Retrieved March 27, 2013.
[91] See http://en.wikipedia.org/wiki/WIMP_(computing).

And we may be selecting this or that result via gaze and eye movement. We may broaden or narrow our search through gestures that interface with a zoomable display.

Whether or not search will ever totally eliminate the need for PIM,[92] it has already transformed it. We've noted the emails that many of us are now more inclined to leave in our inbox rather than filing or tagging. We use fast, index-supported search to get back to emails we need.

In general, we're less inclined to remember the "what" of information we encounter than the "how" and "where" needed to get back to our information later (e.g., which website? Via which search service? Using which keywords in the query?).[93] Our decision to do so can be seen as rational.[94] Why memorize the phone book if it is always easily accessed? Similarly, if time is short, we may choose to remember only the gist of the content on a website, knowing that we can easily return to this page later. There's no need to gorge ourselves or hoard when information is plentiful and its access assured.

Search is about much more than just the search box or simply searching and getting good results (as important as this is). Modern search brings to bear a wide array of sophisticated technologies to the access and analysis of information. The potential benefits of search in PIM are enormous.

7.1   WHY DON'T WE USE SEARCH MORE OFTEN? (AND HOW WE MAY ANYWAY)

Given the magic of search (when it works), why don't we use it even more?

Teevan et al.[95] describe a "teleporting" form of search where we jump directly from a well-formed query to just the information we need: We describe our information needs and—presto—we get back a listing of results or even the actual information we need (e.g., a sports score). Even better, we might jump to an option to actually "do" something, such as make dinner reservations.

However, Teevan and colleagues go on to observe that people more commonly practice what they refer to as "orienteering… Instead of jumping directly to their information target using keywords, our participants navigated to their target with small, local steps using their contextual knowledge as a guide, even when they knew exactly what they were looking for in advance."

Similarly, Barreau and Nardi[96] contrasted keyword search or "logical finding" as a means of returning to files with "location-based finding" where "the user takes a guess at the directory/folder or diskette where she thinks a file might be located, goes to that location, and then browses the list of files or array of icons in the location till she finds the file she's looking for. The process is iterated as needed."

---

[92] Cutrell, Dumais, & Teevan, 2006.
[93] Sparrow, Liu, & Wegner, 2011.
[94] J. R. Anderson, 1990.
[95] J. Teevan, Alvarado, Ackerman, & Karger, 2004. The quote about orienteering is on page 415.
[96] Barreau & Nardi, 1995, p. 40.

Marchionini[97] notes the general importance of *browsing* in information seeking. Indeed, searching and browsing are commonly contrasted with one another as distinct ways of retrieving information.[98] However, the word "browsing" is burdened with one meaning that doesn't work for our purposes: "To scan, to casually look through in order to find items of interest, especially without knowledge of what to look for beforehand."[99] The situations described above involved very purposeful searches. People often knew exactly what they are looking for. They simply chose to take smaller steps along the way to their destination.

Here we will use the term "navigate"[100] to represent a class of methods for the access or re-access to information that are used when the user has a definite destination in mind but chooses to take smaller steps to get there. In navigation people make more use of the informational "lay of the land" such as folders and intervening web pages.

But why give up the "magic" of being teleported to desired information for the slower "ground transportation" of navigation?

Teevan et al. describe the advantages of orienteering and, we can say more generally, of navigation to include:

1. *Cognitive ease.* When steps are smaller there is less to articulate, less to hold in our minds at the same time, less syntax to worry about, and a better chance of getting closer (if only incrementally) to the desired information.

2. *A sense of location.* We may know "where to go" even if this is not easily expressed in a search query. For example, we may know that a link can be found near the top right of another web page that will bring us closer to the information.

3. *Understanding the answer.* Orienteering/navigation preserves a surrounding context for the information that helps us to assess whether we have the "right" information. For example, navigating to a desired file in the context of its folder can help us to determine that we have the most recent version of a file (i.e., based on a sort by "last modified").

Often we're not just looking for a single email, file, or web page but rather a grouping of items. Even if we are mostly after one item, we get valuable additional information from noting its place within a larger structure like a folder and in noting the item's relationship to other items.[101] When making a decision about which hotel to book for the conference, we want to see all our top-choice

---

[97] G. Marchionini, 1995.

[98] See, for example, Olston & Chi, 2003 or search (don't "browse") the ACM Digital Library (http://dl.acm.org/) with terms "searching, browsing."

[99] http://en.wiktionary.org/wiki/browse#English.

[100] The word "navigate" isn't perfect either but comes closer to meeting our needs as in "To move from page to page on the internet or within a program by clicking on hyperlinks" (http://en.wiktionary.org/wiki/navigate).

[101] See W. Jones, Phuwanartnurak, Gill, & Bruce, 2005 for discussion concerning the context provided by the folder.

alternatives and also the conference web page (to be reminded of dates and location). When completing an application we want not only the application itself but also a host of related information including instructions, email reminders, and copies of similar applications previously completed.

Barreau and Nardi note that location-based finding serves a reminding function not found in "logical-finding" (keyword search). As people navigate to the desired information they may notice other useful information along the way and also be reminded of other things that need to be done.

People were observed, not surprisingly, to manipulate the placement of files, icons, bookmarks, etc., to accomplish a reminding function. We do something similar when we place physical items on a tabletop or near the doorway. In the *Keeping Found Things Found*[102] book I reviewed literature relating to a more general notion of *wayfinding* as applied to information retrieval: Certainly the destination (the desired information) matters but so too does the journey.

Bergman et al. note the power of the location metaphor.[103] A sense of digital place with respect to a personal filing system is closely related to notions of familiarity, control, and organization.[104] Bergman et al. also note that the memory for how to access information previously accessed is sometimes more "in our movements" of navigation as procedural knowledge rather than "in our words" as declarative knowledge.

Navigation may be slower than teleporting, but it may also be easier and less prone to error. Navigation means breaking a larger act of finding into smaller steps, each of which often depends more heavily on recognition than recall. We then note an enduring effect from cognitive psychology research that people are often better able to recognize an item than to "recall" the name or a description for this item.[105] Moreover, it is often the case that even if we recall correctly, the computer may not recognize our way of expressing the item's name or description. We say "car" but the computer only recognizes "automobile."

Even on the Web, where many of us might happily be teleported directly to the information we want, the actual steps involve at least some navigation. We might type a few characters into the address field of our browser for a website (**recall**), but we have to navigate to get to the address field in the first place (by looking at the top of the browser window). Then we look through the listing of suggested completions (**recognition**) for the site we want.

Once we get to the website's homepage, we might scan it for a desired link (**recognition**) or we might first navigate to a site-specific search box where we then type in a few keywords (**recall**). Next we select from the returned results (**recognition**) for the pages on the website with the information we seek. Even when we've arrived at the desired page, we may still have more finding to

---

[102] W. Jones, 2007.

[103] Bergman, Beyth-Marom, Nachmias, Gradovitch, & Whittaker, 2008.

[104] Jones, W., Bruce, Jones, & Vinson, 2009.

[105] See, for example, the classic book "Cognitive Psychology" (Neisser, 1967). Or, as Justice Potter Stuart famously opined, hardcore pornography may be hard to define but "I know it when I see it" (http://en.wikipedia.org/wiki/Potter_Stewart).

do if the web page is long. We might scan the page or its table of contents for desired information (**recognition**) or we might do a within-page "find" (by typing ctrl-F) for text (**recall**) that we expect the desired information will contain.

Notwithstanding the increasing sophistication of web search services, therefore, we still navigate.

But the preference for navigation is especially strong in our efforts to re-find information in our local file system (**P1** information). Keyword search for local information—what we'll here call "desktop search"—has improved greatly since the Barreau and Nardi 1995 paper reporting a strong preference for location-based finding. Some of the predictions in a rejoinder to their findings published not long afterward[106] have come true. Index-supported search is now built into the operating systems we use on our computing devices and (mostly) works without our need to administer. Even so, recent studies suggest that for the return to personal files, people still navigate, using keyword search as a last resort.[107]

Why do we appear to navigate to our files when keyword search might be much faster? Beyond the reasons for navigation already discussed we'll consider two additional explanations:

1. **Desktop search is still bad.**[108] Notwithstanding big improvements in desktop search, it is far from perfect. web search services may be equally imperfect, but the stakes are higher and the failings more evident when we're looking for "our stuff."

   We have only to search on patterns such as "<operating system> search sucks" both to see the dissatisfaction and some of the reasons. Macintosh, Windows, Linux—no matter their version—none escapes the vitriol of articles and blog posts on the Web.[109]

2. **First impressions matter.** One of the first actions we take for any new file is to specify its name and, unless we use a default location such as "My Documents," we also specify its folder location. A well-established "primacy effect"[110] of research in cognitive psychol-

---

[106] Fertig, Freeman, & Gelernter, 1996b, but see also Nardi & Barreau, 1997.

[107] Barreau, 2008; Bergman et al., 2008; Bergman, Whittaker, Sanderson, Nachmias, & Ramamoorthy, 2010, 2012.

[108] For a review of desktop search alternatives to those provided by Apple and Microsoft see, http://www.techrepublic.com/blog/five-apps/five-fast-windows-desktop-search-utilities/1512. For research pointing to suggested improvements in desktop search see Blanc-Brude & Scapin, 2007; Marsden & Cairns, 2003; Ravasio, Schär, & Krueger, 2004.

[109] See, for example, http://www.howtogeek.com/howto/33414/how-to-make-the-mac-os-x-finder-suck-less/; http://andywibbels.com/why-does-mac-finder-search-and-spotlight-suck-so-much/; http://www.osattack.com/windows-7/windows-7-search-sucks/; Why does the search feature on Windows 7 suck so badly?, http://forums.anandtech.com/showthread.php?t=2063356, http://www.neowin.net/news/editorial-things-that-suck-about-windows-8-on-a-desktop. There may be fundamental limits on the improvements we can expect from desktop search or, more generally, the search for the information we own (**P1**). For example, we are often looking for a specific document and won't accept substitutes or "near" matches such as previous versions. But certainly there is also still room for improvement in the search UI.

[110] Again see Neisser, 1967.

ogy is that this "first impression" for our interaction with a file is likely to be especially strong and resistant to memory loss with the passage of time.

"As we keep so shall we find," we might say. Under a "first impressions" hypothesis, preferred methods of re-finding follow from previously successful retrievals of the information and ultimately from the initial act of keeping when the information was created or encountered for the first time. People re-find files by navigating through folders and then recognizing the file name because, in a traditional filing system, people often specify the folder location and name of a file to begin with. The containing folder, in turn, is part of a larger organization, the knowledge of which is repeatedly strengthened in our internal memories as various files in the organization are created and accessed.[111]

By the same reasoning, people pay special attention to properties of an email message such as sender or subject because these properties are used initially to screen and prioritize email messages. These same properties are later likely to be recalled during a retrieval attempt[112] and, when supported by the computer, prove very effective in a keyword search.[113] Why not similarly do a keyword search focused on file name and folder location? This is often difficult to do in desktop searches without resort to an "advanced search" option for file and folder names.[114]

The first-impressions hypothesis prompts a shift backward in time to the initial encounter with an information item and to the actions taken during an initial keeping stage of PIM. Support for tagging and annotating information items remains basic and fragmented.[115] Perhaps, with unified support for tagging and the application of searchable annotations, we might finally realize

---

[111] People often organize, for example, by projects (Boardman & Sasse, 2004) possibly with project folders organized under more general areas such as "Home," "Work," "School," etc. (For an account of my own personal organization see: http://keepingfoundthingsfound.com/blog/my-pim-part-i-keeping-and-organizing-find-again-later).

[112] Elsweiler, Baillie, & Ruthven, 2008.

[113] In support of this first impression hypothesis is a longitudinal, within-subjects re-finding study from our KFTF group indicating that participants who navigate to files may also keyword search for emails and that this interaction between information form (file vs. email) and preferred method of return (navigation vs. keyword search) was more pronounced for participants who had better support for indexed search. (The study was completed in 2009 and involved users of Mac or and both Vista and XP versions of Window).

[114] In documentation for search in Windows 8, we can read that "To search for a file based on properties such as the date it was last modified or what kind of file it is (such as "Picture"), first tap or click the Search Tools tab and use the options in the Refine group, and then enter your search terms in the search box. For example, if you want to search only file names and not file contents, tap or click Other properties, choose Name, and then enter your search term" (http://windows.microsoft.com/en-us/windows-8/search-file-explorer). There is even some concern that folders are being "deprecated" as an object of search in their own right. (See for example, http://superuser.com/questions/433098/how-to-search-for-a-folder-from-the-windows-8-start-screen).

[115] However, there is some research to suggest that, given proper support, tagging may be faster than filing (Voit, Andrews, & Slany, 2012).

a "placeless"[116] means of keeping that would readily mesh with keyword-search as the predominant means of re-finding.

However, absent a requirement to specify file locations manually via use of folders (or to accept the default) we'd need much better support for an alternate means of storage management. Even then, we might still find ourselves using folders for other reasons. People report, for example, that they use folders as way of summarizing their information (i.e., as information in their own right) and that folders give them a better sense of control.[117] It would appear that the semantics of the folder model are deeply entrenched in how we work with our information, and these are now strengthened by web-based services such as Dropbox, Google Drive, and SkyDrive.

And yet, as our collections of digital information continue to grow, the time required to navigate will also increase (albeit more as logarithmic function of the total number of items in a collection).[118] As our digital collections age, our own memory of "where" we put an item also ages.[119] Re-finding then becomes less certain, and our efforts to retrieve may be more an act of discovery than return. Also, desktop search will continue to improve. For these and other reasons, we may rely increasingly on keyword search as a method of finding files and other information in our own digital stores.

We may use search as our method of re-finding without even knowing it. A better desktop search system might, for example, support new combinations of keyword search and navigation. Keyword search, rather than teleporting us to our information, might be a way to "parachute" into the right region of an information space, similar to our use of web search now to get to the right website. Once in the right region, we might then navigate (or use keyword search locally) to reach the targeted item. In real situations of information access—web-based or not—the target may, in fact, not be a specific file or web page but rather a fuzzier region of information.

The integration of search and navigation can go further. With a given context established for our query, such as "Now I'm going to work on next week's presentation," certain alternatives might

[116] Dourish, Edwards, LaMarca, & Salisbury, 1999. Under a placeless scheme of information management all of our documents might be in one, very large collection albeit with each document richly represented through tags and attribute/value combinations. Smaller collections would then be fluidly, dynamically constructed on-demand through a description of the desired set of documents.

[117] In the W. Jones, Phuwanartnurak, et al., 2005, study, among the reasons participants expressed for continuing to use folders (even if information could be easily retrieved through search) were a sense of trust, control, and visibility. "Folders help me see the relationship between things." "Folders remind me what needs to be done." In some cases, the folder, not its individual contents, were the primary object of a retrieval attempt.
More recently, Bergman, Gradovitch, Bar-Ilan, & Beyth-Marom, 2013, still find a strong preference for folders over tags in the organization of P1 information. Also, when participants were encouraged to use tags, they still (in agreement with Civan, Jones, Klasnja, & Bruce, 2008) tended to use only a single tag. Moreover, a retrieval task showed slower retrieval and lower success rate for tag use.

[118] Bergman et al., 2010, 2012.

[119] In empirical investigations into the use of search in the "Stuff I've Seen" prototype more than half the searches (> 54% of the total) targeted items retrieved a month or more ago (S. Dumais et al., 2003).

be highlighted in place in order to speed our navigation to a desired item. In a display of folders, for example, a "presentation" folder might be given a different color or a larger font to indicate that it is "recommended" in the current context.

A larger point here is that we should separate search-as-interaction from search-as-technology.[120] Search-as-interaction involves a dialog between person and computer. The basic interaction hasn't changed that much in several decades (even if search speed, scope, and results precision have improved dramatically): type some words into a search box; get back a set of results; repeat as needed.

Search-as-technology, on the other hand, is constantly changing and expanding to involve a host of technologies for locating (enumerating, crawling) information, analyzing for index terms, building the indices, processing user utterances, mapping onto index terms, presenting results, and so on. Search-as-technology blends into technologies for data mining and for machine learning.

In a better world of PIM, search-as-technology would be embedded and work "behind the scenes" to help us to manage our time and attention. Search-as-interaction can still give us the option to describe desired information directly (e.g., by typing into a search box or speaking or gesturing). But supplementing the descriptions we enter ourselves—and working even in their absence—are searches situated in a larger context. Elements of the context that might be usefully factored into the search include the current time and our current location, the "digital location" of a designated project or interest area, and a history of previous interactions between us and the computer.

7.2   PERSONAL POTENTIALS OF SITUATED SEARCHING

The search box isn't large and we typically don't type more than one to three words to describe what we want.[121] Web search services work well because they don't need to give us a results list with references to *all* of the information relating to a particular query. Services only need to give us *some* of the results. Computations of document priors such as Google's famous page rank algorithm[122] help to place the most likely referents topmost for simple queries.

A generic approach (e.g., ANDing query terms and ranking results by document priors) works well for queries where there really isn't much ambiguity, or if there is ambiguity, where a high percentage of us (say 95%) are likely interested in the same interpretation. This works well for common queries such as "Facebook" or "Academy Awards" or "PageRank."

---

[120] For a longer discussion of the distinction between search-as-interaction and search-as-technology see Chapter 11 in W. Jones, 2007.

[121] Though recent studies suggest that mean query length may be gradually increasing, a substantial majority of queries (2/3 or more) are three words or fewer in length. See Arampatzis & Kamps, 2008; Shah, 2010; Taghavi, Patel, Schmidt, Wills, & Tew, 2012.

[122] Brin & Page, 1998. See also, http://en.wikipedia.org/wiki/PageRank.

But in other cases, ambiguity may be much greater and the split between alternate interpretations much more even. Susan Dumais gives the example of "SIGIR,"[123] which for her expands, first and foremost, to "Special-Interest Group on Information Retrieval" but for someone else may expand to something completely different. For Stuart Bowen Jr., SIGIR means, first and foremost, "Special Inspector General for Iraq Reconstruction."

In such cases, the user on average is likely to be less happy with the quality of results. These could reflect only one interpretation of SIGIR or the other, making either Susan Dumais or Stuart Bowen unhappy. Or results could be a blend of matches for each interpretation, in which case the "unhappiness" with results is more equally shared.

How can search do better? By looking "outside the box"[124] to add greater specificity to the search query. This means, in general, adding considerations of context. Under what circumstances is a search being initiated? How is it situated?

Figure 7.4: Which "SIGIR" do we mean?

Consider some things situational that can help to improve the quality of search results:

- **Time**, macro-level. The temporal nearness of an event might increase the weighting of one interpretation over others. For example, search results might favor an interpretation of "SIGIR" as an information retrieval conference if the associated annual information retrieval conference or a submission deadline for this conference will occur soon.

- **Location**, macro-level (city, country). We may see that the language for a web search service changes as we travel from country to country. More locally, given a search for "Starbucks," we may see results for Starbucks locations in our current city.

- **Time and location**, micro-level. Search from a palmtop equipped with some way of determining location can be even more situated with respect to time and location. We've already grown accustomed to using our palmtops to look for nearby shops and restaurants, and even friends who are nearby "now." We can expect searches that are even more current with respect to time and place to answer questions such as "Which restaurants nearby have a table for four within the next 30 minutes" or even, "I'm willing to spend

---

[123] Lecture given to INFO 320 course, Nov. 6, 2012.

[124] Dumais & Teevan (personal communication, 2009) describe a variety of techniques for enhancing the explicit query through an "outside of the box" inclusion of contextual information. The phrase is also used in GeekWire, 2011, and also in http://www.marketingvox.com/bing-continues-search-outside-the-box-with-xbox-voice-search-050186/.

$50 for a meal for me and my date. Which restaurants 'now and nearby' want to bid for my business?"[125]

- **Digital location.** Search can also be situated with respect to digital location. Text and other indexable information that is "nearby" (e.g., in the active window(s) or near the insertion point) might be used to improve search results. Such situational information might be used to disambiguate terms like "bank" or "jaguar."[126]

Taking this "outside the box" thinking even farther, we might look for situations where we can eliminate the box (i.e., the explicit query). Search services are now experimenting with ways to present "see also" lists of web pages or search queries based upon the analysis of content in an email or search results listing currently in view. Services that provide suggestions "freely" (without being asked) still do so at a cost to us—as measured by use of screen space, for example, which otherwise might be used in ways less distracting to us. Such a system might "pay for itself" by reminding us of items we would otherwise overlook. But the service walks a fine line between distracting and unnerving us ("Now what is it doing!?") and being mostly ignored.[127]

7.2.1 SEARCH AS A RELATIONSHIP

Search is further situated through factors relating to the person doing the search, his/her search history, background, interests, aspirations, etc. **Search as a relationship** is a direct extension of an understanding that search is properly considered a dialog between person and search engine that extends over several exchanges of query and response.

Bates[128] characterized search with a "berry picking model" in which the current query is partly affected by the results of the previous query so that, in a session, our focus can be seen to wander between the sub-topics of an area (much as we might be enticed from bush to bush by bigger, riper blueberries). Belkin et al.[129] proposed search interfaces that allow people to modify and refine their queries as their information needs evolve. Marchionini[130] also considered the role that search technology can play in support of an iterative *information seeking* process.

---

[125] See for example, http://www.geekwire.com/2013/startup-weekend-uw/. For scholarly articles on the use time, location, and other contextual factors, see for example, Biegel & Cahill, 2004; Hong, Chi, Budiu, Pirolli, & Nelson, 2008; Johnson, 2007; Kim, Lee, Oh, & Choi, 2009.

[126] For studies into the use of digital location for context see, for example, Reiner Kraft, Maghoul, & Chang, 2005.

[127] S. T. Dumais, Cutrell, Sarin, & Horvitz, 2004, describe an Implicit Query (IQ) prototype that analyzes the content of an email message under composition in order to build a query. Results returned by the query are displayed in a side panel. For example, if the words "holiday party" have just been typed into an email message, IQ might return a listing that references a web page, documents, and other email that are also about the holiday party. See also, Budzik, Hammond, & Birnbaum, 2001; M. Czerwinski et al., 1999; Henzinger, Chang, Milch, & Brin, 2003; Kraft, Maghoul, & Chang, 2005; Rhodes & Maes, 2000.

[128] M. J. Bates, 1989.

[129] N. Belkin, Marchetti, & Cool, 1993.

[130] G. Marchionini, 1995.

More recent efforts to support search as a dialog include Phlat[131] and Feldspar.[132] There is a related observation that we all, in our own ways, like to tell stories.[133] In fact the tags generated from a story for an item (e.g., a picture taken or document written) might be better than those we would generate directly.[134] By extension, the "narrative" we tell about the information we are seeking might form the basis for a better query than those we generate directly today.[135]

Search as a dialog would then seem to extend naturally to search as a relationship. We see attempts in this direction already with offerings such as "Siri."[136] However, we can also remember failed attempts to build relationships with our computing devices (think "Clippy"[137]). More effective may be the way our relationships to other people are leveraged through social media websites both in the initial indexing of information (via comments on photographs, web pages, and blog posts) and also in the discovery and retrieval of this information. This is a topic for Chapter 10 in Part 3 of this book.

The potential to improve search results through personalization is large and still mostly unrealized.[138] I am reminded of the time long ago when I shared a month-long "road-trip" with a college friend. Toward the end of the trip, I might say one to three words (the length of a typical query) to express a thought only to have the sentence completed by my friend. Now consider the time many of us spend with our computing devices and key applications. Can we expect a similar ability to complete and even anticipate our thoughts?

There are privacy concerns. Who sees our history of searches? Who knows about our background interests and aspirations? If we have concerns of privacy and potential bias in search results we may choose to opt out of personalizations.[139] Ultimately, we might hope for services that let us keep our personalizations more securely in local storage but shared selectively and only via the current query.[140]

---

[131] Cutrell, Robbins, Dumais, & Sarin, 2006.

[132] Chau, Myers, & Faulring, 2008.

[133] Hsu, 2008, see also, http://keepingfoundthingsfound.com/blog/can-stories-help-us-organize-and-make-sense-our-information.

[134] Marshall, 2009.

[135] Goncalves & Jorge, 2003.

[136] http://en.wikipedia.org/wiki/Siri_(software).

[137] http://en.wikipedia.org/wiki/Clippy.

[138] Ma, Pant, & Sheng, 2007; Pitkow et al., 2002; J. Teevan, Dumais, & Horvitz, 2005; J. Teevan, 2006a; Jaime Teevan, Liebling, & Ravichandran Geetha, 2011.

[139] For more on how Google's personalization works, see: http://searchengineland.com/google-now-personaliz-es-everyones-search-results-31195 (and also, http://mashable.com/2012/01/25/google-cookies/). For how to turn off Google's personalization see http://blogs.wsj.com/digits/2012/11/04/how-to-turn-off-googles-person-alized-search-results/.

[140] See, for example, X. Shen, Tan, & Zhai, 2007, for an discussion concerning how a client-side personalized search system can be used to achieve "Level IV" privacy protection.

7.2.2 ARE WE TALKING ABOUT PERSONALIZED SEARCH OR THE SEARCH FOR PERSONAL INFORMATION?

Which are we talking about in the context of PIM—personalized search or the search for personal information? So far, we've been talking mostly about the personalization of a web search. But even here, focus is on at least two senses of personal information: **P6—information that is relevant to us and our current needs and P5—information we've experienced before**. A large percentage of web page visits are a return to a previously visited web page.[141]

Conversely, as the information stored locally or otherwise under our control (**P1**) continues to grow, the search for this information may often be less about re-finding information already experienced (**P5**) and more about discovery of information (**P6**), as in "What do I have on this already?" Or search results may accomplish a little of each—we find what we were looking for and are pleasantly surprised to find additional items in the results list that we had forgotten about.

Other senses of personal information also come into play both as an object of search and a means of enhancing search. For example, given the existence of an item-event log (i.e., log) of some sort, we can begin to realize synergies between the items in our store (**P1**) and the events of the log (**P5**). We might, for example, search for and locate a photograph we remember taking at our daughter's "soccer game" but the query matches not because of information in the photo per se but because of information in another associated item, such as the calendar event of the "soccer game" specifying time and location.

Conversely, pictures we take might serve as very useful landmarks in a temporal ordering of search results.[142]

We can also consider search in relation to the three senses of personal information that have to do directly with privacy and information flow:

P2, information about us (but often controlled by someone else). Search can help us answer questions such as: What information "about me" is "out there"? Where? In what form? Available to whom? How accurate is it? Medical information, the assessed value of our homes, credit record scores, search preferences … it's all out there. To find and track this personal information we again use search. We "google" ourselves. Or we set up an alert that informs us when something about us is added to the Web.[143]

Speaking as someone with a common name, a personalization to add context to a search for "information about me" (**P2**) is essential. My recent experiences with "Google Alerts" targeting new

---

[141] By the estimates from some studies, 80% or more of our page views are to web pages previously seen by us (Eytan Adar, Teevan, & Dumais, 2009; Cockburn, Greenberg, Jones, McKenzie, & Moyle, 2003; Cockburn & McKenzie, 2001; Greenberg & Cockburn, 1999; McKenzie & Cockburn, 2001; Tauscher & Greenberg, 1997a, 1997b). For a review of web search engine support for finding and re-finding information see R. G. Capra, 2006; R. Capra & Pérez-Quiñones, 2005.

[142] See for example, work by Ringel, Cutrell, Dumais, & Horvitz, 2003, who note a "statistically significant time savings for searching with the landmark-augmented timeline compared to a timeline marked only by dates.

[143] See for example, http://mashable.com/2008/12/29/brand-reputation-monitoring-tools/.

information about "William Jones" made it very clear to me that I need a way to provide a more specific personalized query, such as "The William Jones who is sometimes mentioned as a professor at UW and who received his doctorate from Carnegie-Mellon."[144] Beyond efforts like this to improve the query precision is a more challenging problem: Much of what we might like to review about ourselves is in databases to which we don't have access.

P4, information that we share. P4 is an extension of **P2**. The information we post to a website or email or tweet may not be directly about us, but if it's provided by us it reflects upon us. Some of the information in **P4**—blog posts, articles, photographs, reviews, etc.—may persist on the Web and serve as a kind of portfolio. If we're on the job market or mean to market ourselves as a consultant, then the **P4** information we "push" plays a big role in getting ourselves noticed. We want to impress, convince, ingratiate, etc. We want to be seen. Is the information we provide having the desired effects? Who "likes" the text, photos, and videos that we post? Who is tweeting about us? Who is visiting our websites? Similar considerations apply if we're in the dating market.

As noted in the previous section, we care about a personal search engine optimization (SEO) as a converse of search—i.e., we want to be "searchable." We want our web properties to come up first in response to the targeted queries reflecting the areas of expertise we claim to have. We are also interested in web analytics[145] as a way to know better who is accessing our information and under what circumstances.

Even as we want others to find us through search, we are also using variations in search. Variations in search can help us to track the ways in which the information we provide is spreading across the Web. Are people talking about us and the information we post? Are we being quoted? With proper attribution? Or are we being plagiarized? We look to search technologies for help in detecting copies, near copies, and excerpts from any of our documents, photographs, etc.[146] We may even embed digital watermarks in the information we post in order better track it when it's copied.[147]

---

[144] In recognition of this problem, the Semex prototype invested considerable effort in reference reconciliation (Cai, Dong, Halevy, Liu, & Madhavan, 2005; Dong, Halevy, & Madhavan, 2005).

[145] http://en.wikipedia.org/wiki/Web_analytics.

[146] Search the Web with "plagiarism detector" to see a host of services, free or otherwise, such as http://plagiarism-detect.com/ and http://www.plagtracker.com/. For more background see http://en.wikipedia.org/wiki/Plagiarism_detection. For a more scholarly treatment of plagiarism see, for example, Boisvert & Irwin, 2006; Potthast, Stein, Barrón-Cedeño, & Rosso, 2010.

[147] http://en.wikipedia.org/wiki/Watermark_(data_file). See for example, Jin, Pan, & Zhang, 2010; Zhao & Lu, 2005.

7.2.3   WHAT TO DO WITH INFORMATION THAT SEEMS USEFUL… ONLY NOT NOW?

To complement the outflow of information there is the information that is directed to us from others (**P3**) or simply comes our way. **P3** blends with **P5** to comprise that portion of the information we experience and that grabs our attention for some reason. We notice the re-opening of a restaurant on the way home from work (newly painted and with "Grand Opening" signs outside). Or we hear an interview on the radio about a new book. **P3/P5** includes the magazine article that catches our eye and we start to read in the doctor's office.

The blend of **P3/P5** includes ads, computer alerts, incoming emails, texts, and people who give their business cards at a gathering. The blend includes the many interesting snippets and links of potential relevance to us that grab our attention as we surf the Web or scan through a search results list.

P3/P5 even includes thoughts or to-dos we write to ourselves concerning a project or area of interest other than the project we're working on.[148] We may scribble a note on paper or send ourselves an email, but what to do with these "scraps?"[149]

In some cases, we simply want the incoming information to be blocked—junk email, offensive websites, or marketing phone calls. In other cases, our response is "yes, but not now." The information looks to be useful, even important, but we don't have time to deal with it now.

What to do with this information so that not only can we retrieve it again later but, even more important, so that we'll remember to do so?

This is a classic problem of "keeping found information found" for later use.[150] We might email ourselves. But this only adds to our email inbox with little assurance that we'll find or even notice the information later when there is a time for its use. Some of us still use bookmarks. But do we remember to use them later on?[151]

Many of us maintain file folders to group information by projects[152] we mean to complete as well as by longer-term areas of interest topics, people, goals, etc.[153] As of this writing, I have about

---

[148] Many of our interruptions and task switches in a day are, in fact, self-initiated (Mary Czerwinski, Horvitz, & Wilhite, 2004).

[149] For a study into how people manage "information scraps" see Bernstein, Kleek, Karger, & Schraefel, 2008. For an evaluation of a prototype for quick capture of notes to self, to-dos, and other "scraps" see Van Kleek et al., 2009.

[150] W. Jones, Dumais, & Bruce, 2002. For a more general investigation into how people keep or otherwise manage encountered information see Erdelez, 2004.

[151] Tauscher & Greenberg, 1997a, estimated that less than half of the bookmarks people create are ever used. In a re-finding study, W. Jones, Bruce, & Dumais, 2003, participants, when cued to return to a specific website, would only use a previously created bookmark pointing to the page roughly 50% of the time, electing instead to access the web page by other means (e.g., web search or navigation from other web pages).

[152] For project-based approaches to the organization of information see Bergman, Beyth-Marom, & Nachmias, 2006; W. Jones, Bruce, Foxley, & Munat, 2006; W. Jones, Bruce, & Foxley, 2006; W. Jones, Klasnja, Civan, & Adcock, 2008; W. Jones, Munat, & Bruce, 2005; Kaptelinin, 2003; Raskin, 2000.

[153] Bergman et al., 2006; Boardman & Sasse, 2004; W. Jones, Bruce, Foxley, et al., 2006.

25 active project folders.[154] Folders contain a mixture of Word and PDF files, email messages and pointers to web pages. Many project folders are further organized into subfolders for tasks and some into sub-subfolders for subtasks. Separately, I have an additional 344 folders on topics of general interest to me such as "JavaScript" and "HTML5." These folders include pointers to PDFs (kept separately) and web pages.

I frequently run across an email or a web page relating to one or more of my project folders or topics of interest. I can generally navigate directly to the proper folder to place the item or a reference to it, but doing so takes time! And it's a disruptive shift of attention from my current work.

In the Keeping Found Things Found group, we developed a desktop "QuickCapture" applet available for download and installation with Planz.[155] More recently, a team of students working on an independent study with me produced "Noot," a simple quick capture applet available from the Chrome Web Store.[156]

QuickCapture and Noot are prototypes, and each has its rough edges. A more fundamental limitation is that they don't work well when users reach beyond a set of recently used folders (representing projects or topics) to "tag" information to a less recently accessed folder. Users are then left with a much slower process of folder navigation.

How to do better?

FolderPredictor[157] as its name suggests, attempts to predict a small set of folders that users are most likely to select for a File Open or File Save As operation. But predictions depend upon a mediating structure of tasks as provided through a TaskExplorer application. Also, predictions depend upon some ability to infer the current task, via TaskTracer and to infer shifts in tasks via

---

[154] Allen, 2001, http://www.gtdtimes.com/2010/02/15/managing-projects-tips-from-david-allen/, defines a project as a desired outcome requiring more than one action step to achieve. I subscribe to a modified version of this definition: a project is an effort requiring more than a single session (of at most 20 to 30 minutes) to complete. Some of my projects may take fewer than 30 minutes total to complete but effort involves several steps in sessions distributed over time.

[155] Download and install both Planz and QuickCapture through the following link: http://kftf.ischool.washington.edu/planner_index.htm. Planz is an application that provides an outline, word-processing overlay to the folders of the file system (William Jones, Hou, Sethanandha, & Bi, 2009; William Jones, Hou, Sethanandha, Bi, & Gemmell, 2010). QuickCapture is invoked as a pop-up by pressing the "Windows" (flag) + the "c" key. The selected text in the item of the active window for supported applications (currently MS Word, MS Outlook and Firefox) will appear in the pop-up and can be placed within a selected folder for viewing in Planz. By default, a link is also created to the item the item in the active window which can be clicked to access the item again either form Planz or via file system shortcut placed under the selected folder.

[156] See https://chrome.google.com/webstore/detail/noot/lcgibakoajajepfladapcgppmmmpiipn. Noot was completed by Master of Science and Information Management (MSIM) students Joshua C. Manoj, Rashmi Shekhar, and Varun R. Mendan. Noot works with a folder hierarchy as shared through Dropbox. Users can select one or more folders which are then used to tag the excerpt plus any additional text provided by the user and to link back to the web page currently in view in Chrome.

[157] Bao, Herlocker, & Dietterich, 2006.

TaskPredictor.[158] File Open/Save As operations may (at least sometimes) signal a shift. But the nature of **P3** information (directed our way from outside) is that shifts are abrupt. How to handle the arriving emails of the inbox? Or the web information we happen upon (on pages designed to grab our attention)?

A solution may lie in search technologies that match based on a content analysis of the encountered information and the information grouped under candidate folders. Work on a MailCat prototype in 1999[159] demonstrated the feasibility of a search-based approach to assist in the classification of encountered information.

The MailCat prototype focused on support for classifying incoming email into existing email folders. Centroid vectors were constructed ahead of time for each candidate folder based upon a variation of the TF*IDF term (term frequency * inverse document frequency) weighting analysis as applied to a training subset of the emails already in the folders. Centroids as classifiers were matched to a vector generated for other emails in a test set using a modified version of the cosine similarity measure. Both TF*IDF weighting and cosine-based matching are commonly used in what might be termed "classic" information retrieval.[160] Based upon a testing subset of existing emails from six different users, the folder of an email was one of three folders predicted by MailCat 80 to 98% of the time.

Search technologies we apply today to the classification of incoming information may differ considerably from those used in MailCat:

➢ There is, for example, likely to be considerable noise in the terms extracted whether in an analysis of an encountered item or an analysis of candidate folders and their contents. Noisy terms mean false matches that annoy and, worse, distract from the folders we want to find. Noise might be "squeezed" out of a term to folder matrix using latent semantic analysis (LAS).[161]

➢ The structure of an encountered item's content and its surrounding context might be used to good effect to differentially weight extracted terms for a query. Likewise, the structure of candidate folders might be used to differentially weight the terms extracted in association with candidate folders.

---

[158] The difficulty of detecting shifts in task with Task Predictor is discussed by J. Shen, Li, Dietterich, & Herlocker, 2006, "The new task may confuse TaskPredictor… This suggests that it may be appropriate to disable TaskPredictor.WDS for some period of time after a new task is initialized. It also shows that even the Hybrid method is not able to identify all cases where it should not make a prediction."

[159] Segal & Kephart, 1999. See also Dredze, Lau, & Kushmerick, 2006, for a method more specific to email and the use of "reply-to" threads. And see Brutlag & Meek, 2000, for a discussion on the challenges of text classification of email messages.

[160] See, for example, Salton & McGill, 1986.

[161] See http://en.wikipedia.org/wiki/Latent_semantic_indexing and http://en.wikipedia.org/wiki/Latent_semantic_analysis. Or for more scholarly treatment, see S. T. Dumais, 2004 and Deerwester, Dumais, Landauer, Furnas, & Harshman, 1990.

➤ The UI for classifying encountered information might support additional ways to enhance the query:

○ We might wish, for example, to highlight a selected portion (or several) in an encountered item and to have highlighting stick—not just for web pages but also for emails, tweets, and documents. Terms extracted for highlighted information could then be given extra weight in the query.

○ Similarly, we may want to add a few words to explain the connection between encountered information and the project or topic to which we wish to associate this information. (We can't assume the connection will always be obvious later). Terms for these words too might be given extra weight.

But no matter the "upgrades" in search technology, we can expect that several aspects of the MailCat approach will stay much the same:

➤ **Encountered item = query.** The encountered item provides the basis for a query which is then used to locate relevant folders.

➤ **Folders = "documents."** Each candidate folder—its name, contents, surrounding context, etc.—is used as the basis for a centroid. Each centroid then serves as a candidate classifier for encountered information. More simply, we might say that a "document" is constructed for each candidate folder to summarize folder contents and to provide a target for the query.

➤ **Learn from the choices made.** The weightings in a term-to-folder index (i.e., the index built to speed searching) are adjusted over time as we continue to place or "classify" new encountered information, i.e., our search facility learns from the choices we make.[162]

➤ **Integrate as an extension to existing UI.** The appearance of a search-based keeping facility for our deliberate classification of encountered information is probably best handled as an option integrated into existing ways of handling encountered information. This was the approach taken, for example, with both MailCat and FolderPredictor. In each case, the guesses of the keeping facility were integrated into existing dialogs (e.g.,

---

[162] For example, the Memory Extender (ME) system "learned" based upon a user's selection of files (W. Jones, 1986a, 1986b).

In general, an adjustment in weights (e.g., from terms to folders—whether for emails or files—based upon the user's current action (e.g., File Open or File SaveAs) is an incremental variation of supervised learning. http://en.wikipedia.org/wiki/Supervised_learning. Supervised learning is one of several forms of machine learning (http://en.wikipedia.org/wiki/Machine_learning). For more scholarly articles on machine learning, text classifiers, and applications in HCI and PIM see Bennett, Dumais, & Horvitz, 2005; Carpineto & Romano, 2012; Domingos, 2012; Fails & Olsen,Jr., 2003; Stumpf et al., 2007, 2009; Ware, Frank, Holmes, Hall, & Witten, 2002.

for an email "Move to Folder" or File Open/Save As). If we're not satisfied with the guesses shown, we're free to do whatever we would normally do.

The folder centroids are constructed to serve as targets (or "attractors") for query expressions of information directed our way (**P3**). But these may then, in turn, serve as queries in their own right to locate information of potential relevance (**P6**) and also as filters for a general classification of our experiences (**P5**):

➤ **Search for new relevant information (P6)** as this relates to an area as expressed in a folder. Now the tables are turned and the centroid is being used as a query in its own right. The search might be widened to target not only the Web but also information stored locally (**P1**) with the thought that in many cases information relevant to a project, task or topic lies "nearby" but forgotten.[163]

➤ **Sift, sort, and categorize the information experienced by us (P5).** Beyond the information that is directed explicitly toward us and that grabs our attention (if only briefly) is a continuous stream of information experienced by us throughout our waking day. We might well imagine that centroids serve as filters. Incoming information items above some threshold are simply placed in association with the folder represented by the centroid. These associations might lie in a "grey" area as suggestions pending our review and approval.

The use of folders has often been placed in opposition to searching and their demise predicted as search continues to improve.[164] However, in the discussion above, folders and search work together synergistically. If folders eventually fade, they may do so mostly in name in only as we come to think beyond the paper-based metaphors that have guided (and constrained) so much of our interface to our computers. We might then abandon other terms such as "label," "tag," "section tab," and "notebook" which are similarly inspired by paper metaphors.

And then maybe we'll think instead in terms of "areas of interest" or "project places" which fit into the larger landscape of our PSI (personal space of information) as playfully rendered through interactive spaces in the spirit of Figure 5.1.

But no matter the terminology we will be using or the surface representations we will be working with, my guess is that the objects underneath will be directly descended from today's fold-

---

[163] Uses of a folder centroid in searching bears some resemblance to smart folders as supported on a Mac (http://www.cultofmac.com/48911/100-tips-19-what-are-smart-folders/; http://mac.tutsplus.com/tutorials/productivity/how-to-use-smart-folders-in-os-x/) and, more generally, to the concept of virtual or search folders (http://en.wikipedia.org/wiki/Virtual_folder). However, the centroid as query is not defined explicitly by the user (who may have difficulty articulating constraints of the query). Instead, the centroid is derived from folder contents (and so implicitly defined by the user). As we shall see, search results, in turn, can be selectively incorporated as new contents of the folder. These contents, in turn, can prompt an update of the folder's centroid.

[164] See for example http://www.economist.com/node/4368267 or, for more scholarly discussion, Dourish et al., 2000, 1999; Fertig et al., 1996b.

ers and will have similar semantics concerning, for example, the effects of a "move" or a "delete." We may even still be using the term "folder."

Even so, the sense of what folders can do for us will change profoundly. These next-generation folders, in turn, will change the nature of our searches.

➢ **Situated searches.** In this section, we have considered various forms of *situated searching* as a way to improve a search query by factoring in implicit constraints from the context "outside the search box." But now we are also talking about *situated searches*: A search (= query + current results) persists over time and "lives" with its folder. Search results are updated on demand or periodically (e.g., daily or as the search query is modified). The search query, in turn, is continuously adjusted to reflect changes in the composition of the folder. The search "learns" from our explicit choices (i.e., "yes, this should be included in the folder;" "no, this doesn't belong here").

The query itself may be a set of weighted, word-level terms. Or the query may be much more structured. Consider a "Trip to Boston" as a high-level folder containing sub-folders for "plane," "hotel," and "dinner." Each subfolder might have an associated structured query. The "plane" folder query specifies that we are only interested in non-stop redeye flights arriving Thursday morning with a return flight placing us back in Seattle by dinnertime on Saturday. Results should be sorted by price. The "hotel" folder query specifies that we want a room with a king sized bed in a hotel that is walking distance (1 mile or less) to the convention center and has an on-site workout facility. The "dinner" folder query might express an interest in getting "bids" from restaurants near the convention center with fixed-price menus of $40 or so (+/- $10) and reservations for two available at 6, 6:30, or 7 on Friday evening.

Now supervised (machine) learning takes on a new aspect. Our ultimate selection of plane or hotel or restaurant may reveal, for example, preferences which might be applied to future queries for other trips. We didn't think to specify, for example, but the availability of a window seat matters—especially on redeye flights. Or perhaps our pattern across trips in our choice of hotel reveals a strong reluctance to stay with a particular hotel chain (based upon previous bad experiences).

Searches situated by and grouped together by folder structure may also help us to see larger patterns "at a glance." Our choice of restaurant depends, partly, on the hotel choice, for example, and the choice of reservation depends, partly, on flight schedules.

> **Search as a three-fold function.** The centroid derived for a folder serves at least three functions:

1. The target for explicit keeping of an encountered item, which is useful but "later, not now."

2. The query of a conscious retrieval attempt. ("Find more items like the ones in this folder.")

3. A filter (one of many) for passive categorization of incoming information.[165]

> **Search as many relationships.** We've considered search-as-a-relationship as a natural progression from search as a single query/response to search as a session dialog. Search-as-a-relationship means factoring in many considerations about us that go beyond the immediate information need—our demographics (age, sex, ethnicity, etc.), our past search history, our profession, educational level, current situation, etc.

But we are better regarded as many different people. In a given day we may be "the person who wants to learn JavaScript" and "the person who needs to finish his taxes" and also "the person who wants to plan a hiking trip to Glacier." We often switch from one "role or goal" to another abruptly, often as prompted by information directed toward us (**P3**).

Even as the computer approaches an elusive goal of "total capture" as discussed in the "Technologies to Save" chapter (Chapter 6), it is still not likely to be able to divine our switches from one goal, role, project, task, topic, etc., to another. But if a folder should happen to represent the materials and workspace for a particular area (e.g., "worksheet and materials related to taxes") then we may very well communicate the shift explicitly by opening the relevant folder (possibly as assisted by search). The search associated with each folder is then a relationship and its query changes over time to reflect changes in our relationship with the project or area of interest represented by the folder.

> **Situated serendipity.** Serendipity—"An unsought, unintended, and/or unexpected, but fortunate, discovery and/or learning experience that happens by accident"[166] or "the faculty or phenomenon of finding valuable or agreeable things not sought for."[167]

Many of us have had the experience of resolving to do something—"lose weight" or "go back to school part-time to get a master's degree" and then coming across relevant

---

[165] See N. J. Belkin & Croft, 1992, for a discussion concerning the dual nature of queries for passive filtering and active retrieval.

[166] http://en.wiktionary.org/wiki/serendipity.

[167] from Merriam-Webster Online, http://www.merriam-webster.com/dictionary/serendipity.

information, seemingly, by chance. Serendipity? Divine providence? We may delight in the thought that "someone is looking after me." But another explanation is that the information was always there or in an orbit placing it periodically in our path. We were simply too busy with other information to notice.

People are more apt to notice a connection between goal and enabling items if they have previously articulated a plan for goal achievement.[168] The common sense explanation is that, in the course of this planning, features of the items (e.g., descriptive terms in an email or web page) are called to mind and their association to the goal strengthened. If we later encounter a relevant item, we're more likely to think of the goal and, thus, to recognize the item's relevance.

Paradoxically then, the "serendipity" we happily experience is seldom purely by chance. Armed with this insight, a number of researchers have looked for ways to improve our odds of discovering useful information "serendipitously."[169] One way to do this may be through search results delivered in the context of a folder for a project to which we are currently attending.

To summarize, search—especially as situated in a larger context—has enormous potential to aid us in the management of information that is "ours" in each of the senses in which information can be personal. Search can help us to find information that is "owned by" us (**P1**)—the right version of a document, for example, that may reflect weeks of work. Search can help us to locate information about us (**P2**) on the Web especially as search technologies make more sophisticated use of the context surrounding references to names (e.g., "William Jones"). There is a natural segue from information about us (**P2**) to the information we send or share (**P4**). Search can help us to determine the impact this information is having (good and bad). Search can help us to track the uses others are making of this information (with and without attribution).

Search can help us to filter and categorize the information directed toward us (**P3**) and, more generally, search can help us to sift and sort the information experienced by us (**P5**) and that flows by us constantly in each waking moment.

Situated searches can persist as a permanent part of our information landscape to help us locate information of potential relevance to us (**P6**) and our current information need. These searches—situated in connection with folders and other structuring items—may even help to improve our chances of serendipitously coming across useful information "by chance."

---

[168] See, for example, Patalano & Seifert, 1997.
[169] For efforts to improve the chances of "serendipity" see, for example, André, Schraefel, Teevan, & Dumais, 2009; Beale, 2007; De Bruijn & Spence, 2008; Thudt, Hinrichs, & Carpendale, 2012.

Folders, situated searches and the interplay between the extensional and the "intensional"

As we consider situating searches with folders (representing projects, tasks, and enduring areas of interest), we are combining the *intensional*[170] with the *extensional*.[171] The extensional of a folder is in the items it contains—its subfolders, files and links (shortcuts, aliases). The intensional is in a search's persistent query, which may be initialized as a centroid representation of folder content, i.e., as keywords, phrases, attribute/value pairs that are characteristic of and distinguishing for the items of the folder (and perhaps with folder names thrown in for good measure).

Both representations are imperfect, incomplete. Each can get better through its interplay with the other.

The query, whether used actively by the user in a search or more passively to "filter in" promising matches, helps the user to identify new candidates for inclusion in the folder, thus improving the extensional representation. Conversely, the user's addition or modification of folder content, whether via the search or more directly, can provide input to a learning algorithm that fine-tunes the query, thus improving the intensional representation.

In one case, the direction is "top-down" from an intensional representation to extensional exemplars that match. In the other case, the direction is "bottom-up," from exemplars to an intensional representation of features that are characteristic for the items that are in (or ought to be in) the folder.

The query can be structured as, for example, it needs to be in the trip examples involving situated queries for plane, hotel, and dinner reservations. We might also develop structured, persistent queries to express the desired attributes of a job, an employee, or a date for Saturday evening.

And then, given a system that can learn from our choices over time, we may be faced with discrepancies between the "intention" we express and the actual pattern of our choices. We may say we are an "equal opportunity employer," for example, but our actual choices may reveal persistent biases in age, gender, or ethnic background.

Whether a useful interplay between the intensional and the extensional works in practice for searches situated with folders remains to be seen. Certainly, we're more hopeful for a folder

---

[170] See case #5 for intensional in the OED (http://www.oed.com/view/Entry/97473?redirectedFrom=intension#eid). See also http://en.wikipedia.org/wiki/Intension and also a charming piece by William J. Rapaport on Intensionality vs. Intentionality (http://www.cse.buffalo.edu/~rapaport/intensional.html).

[171] See case two of "extensional" in the OED (http://www.oed.com/view/Entry/66937?redirectedFrom=extensional#eid), see also http://en.wikipedia.org/wiki/Extensional_definition.

named "articles on HTML5" or "people I would consider dating" than we are for a folder named "stuff." But even for a folder named "stuff" there may be detectable patterns in folder content to be exploited by search technology.

We also get encouragement by noting some of the many other instances in life where there is an interplay—and, yes, a "tension"—between the extensional and the intensional:

➤ In text-based menu systems, alternate branches in a hierarchy of choices can either each be represented by descriptive names (an intensional representation) or via one or a few exemplars (an extensional representation) or a combination of both.[172]

➤ The venerable Oxford English Dictionary (OED) (cited throughout this book) provides not only the definition(s) for a word (intensional) but also a large number of examples illustrating the word's use (extensional). Moreover, examples ordered by time reveal historical patterns in a word's use.

➤ When asked to define a basic-level category such as "bird," we might do so either using an intensional definition ("a kind of animal that has feathers and flies") or an extensional definition ("includes robin, sparrow, crow"). Empirical evidence on, for example, the speed to identify a category exemplar is consistent with a *prototype theory* in which members of a category are differentially weighted, e.g., a robin is more "birdlike" than an ostrich.[173]

➤ Of relevance in education, though less apparently so at first, is the enduring tension between "*constructivist* models that emphasize the active construction of knowledge by learners" (i.e., through encounter with exemplars and individual learning episodes) and "*transmission* models that assume that students acquire knowledge by having it transmitted to them by a teacher or a text."[174] The constructivist approach holds that students learn best when they actively induce the principles of a domain (the intensional) through direct experience and a consideration of (many) examples (the extensional). Roughly, the reverse happens in a transmission approach: Students are taught the principles directly. Opportunities to apply or observe these principles in practice may (or may not) follow.

---

[172] See, for example, S. T. Dumais & Landauer, 1984; Lee & Raymond, 1993.

[173] See, for example, Rosch, Mervis, Gray, Johnson, & Boyes-Braem., 1976; Rosch, 1978. Also the following is good entry point: http://en.wikipedia.org/wiki/Prototype_theory.

[174] Schwartz & Bransford, 1998, p. 476.

7.3   CAVEATS AND DISCLAIMERS

And now, we need to rain on this parade of personal potential for search (situated and otherwise) with a few caveats and disclaimers:

Will search make us "stoopid"? A pinpoint access to small chunks of information via targeted search may encourage us to adopt a skimming style of reading: We teleport from one web page to the next and, further, we search locally within a page stopping only long enough to read a sentence or two before jumping to the next chunk of information. Carr[175] expresses a general concern with web use and its effect in reducing our capacity for, or at least our patience with, extended concentration and thoughtful contemplation—the kind needed, for example, to read a whole article, pausing to reflect as we do so, rather than to hurriedly skim a few sentences here and there.

There are many refutations to Carr's concerns about web use.[176] The argument, for example, that search, web access, and especially, their combination—search on the Web—promote a more superficial, skimming style of information processing can be turned on its head. Yes, we can search (skim, scan) through large amounts of information—much more information than, with comparable investments of time and effort, we might work through using the conventional paper-card catalog in a brick-and-mortar library. But the better to focus more quickly on those articles and other items of information most deserving of our focused time and attention. Moreover, we can readily return to an item, repeatedly as needed, in order better to understand its information and from a variety of perspectives.

Watch what you ask for. A search may give us what we ask for but not necessarily what we need to know. This can promote a confirmation bias: Our queries come to tightly circle a body of information in support of one position; meanwhile, other information supporting a more balanced position is out of reach, waiting to be "unlocked" using other keywords.

Marchionini[177] argues for a new kind of interface in support of exploratory search to move the search process "beyond predictable fact retrieval." Many of us practice an informal kind of exploratory search as we formulate new queries from terms returned in the results listing for a previous query.

Think you have it all? Think again! A more serious problem in our use of search is that we often greatly overestimate "recall." Here we mean recall as a measure, not of our ability to articulate features of the desired information, but rather recall as an information retrieval measure of search quality.[178] In a classic information retrieval study by Blair and Maron,[179] participating lawyers and

---

[175] N. G. Carr, 2011; N. Carr, 2008.

[176] For a refutation of Carr's argument see Holt, 2011 and also http://en.wikipedia.org/wiki/Is_Google_Making_Us_Stupid%3F. For a charming discussion in the spirit of a Socratic dialog, see Jonathan Grudin, 2011.

[177] Gary Marchionini, 2006.

[178] For a more formal definition of recall in an information retrieval or search context see http://en.wikipedia.org/wiki/Precision_and_recall.

[179] Blair & Maron, 1985.

paralegals estimated that their searches were returning 75% or more of the documents relevant to a case when, in fact, based upon a retrospective review, the actual percentage was less than 20%.

High recall is generally not important for web search since we typically access far more information on any given topic than we have time to consume. High recall becomes much more important, however, under other circumstances where a complete set of relevant information is necessary. A lawyer wishes to have a record of all (or at least a high percentage of) cases relevant to a case she is pleading. A doctor wishes to have a complete record set for a given patient. You or I might wish to have a complete set of photographs taken on a family vacation.

Awareness is at least a part of the antidote. If recall is important, better keep searching. Another part of a solution involves structure in the form of folders, tags, or attribute values (e.g., for patient ID, social security number or case ID) and the consistent use of this structure at the point of keeping. The effect of structure, when consistently used, can be to transform one finding task to locate many disparate items into another finding task to locate a single larger item (e.g., a folder or the set of all items matching on an attribute value).

Versioning and copies. Which one is the "right" one? Many of us practice file-level versioning. As we pass a document back and forth via email or as we create different variations of a presentation (for different audiences) we save versions and variations as separate files. A search then produces a large number of "close clones" for a desired document. Using the wrong version (incorrect, out of date) can sometimes be disastrous. But comparing documents to determine which one is "right" can be tedious and time-consuming.

Again, a partial solution comes through better structure in the form of keeping strategies that follow a naming strategy to signal variations in a document and that place versions "nearby" (e.g., in the same folder) so that close matches can be sorted by "last modified."

7.4   THE PIM TRANSFORMED, THE PIM THAT REMAINS

In the section on the personal potential of situated searching, we considered searching with respect to each of the six senses in which information can be personal. Here we summarize the impact of searching technologies with respect to each of the six activities of PIM. Activities of PIM are illustrated in Figure 7.5 (repeated from Figure 2 of Chapter 2 in Part 1).

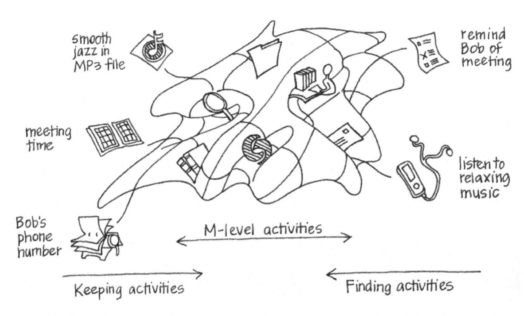

Figure 7.5: Information management activities can be viewed as an effort to establish, use and maintain a mapping between needs and information. ("M-level" can alternately mean "mapping-level" or "meta-level.") Based on an illustration by Elizabeth Boling and a variation of a figure that first appeared in Jones, *Keeping Found Things Found: The Study and Practice of Personal Information Management*. Copyright ©2007, Morgan Kaufmann Publishers.

7.4.1 FINDING/RE-FINDING

We understand that finding is dimensioned by each of the senses in which information is personal:

> ➤ Re-finding is by definition a return to information we have already experienced (**P5**). We may frequently target the information we "own" (i.e., that is controlled by us) on the storage of our devices or that is under one of our accounts on the Web (**P1**). However, as our memories fade, so too does the boundary between re-finding and what we might call "re-discovery" of information that we'd forgotten but that, even so, is relevant to our current need (**P6**). Information of different senses can complement as in, for example, the case where our time-stamped notes provide entry points into the shared video recording of a lecture or meeting.

➢ Finding as a PIM activity also applies to the three senses of personal information having to do with our privacy and our "publicy." Finding is then done in the context of the meta-level activity to manage privacy and the flow of information. We use search to find (as best we can) information about us (**P2**) whether this might be pictures that include us as posted on the Web, comments about us, and, especially, the records that others maintain concerning our health, finances, buying habits, searching habits, marital status, and so on. We track not only information about us but also information that we post, push, send to and share with others (**P4**). Who is using this information? What effect is it having? Do we get proper credit?

➢ Across all finding activities, searching can make good use not only of the query expressed explicitly "inside the box" but also of additional constraints expressed implicitly via the larger context in which the search is situated. Searching is situated with respect to attributes (macro and micro) of time and location. Searching is also situated with respect to digital location, current task/project and, potentially, an understanding derived from a longer-term relationship with the person doing the searching.

7.4.2   KEEPING

Keeping, too, occurs in a larger context of meta-level activities to manage our privacy and the flow of information. Search helps us to "keep on track" or "keep our train of thought" even as we're assaulted, almost continuously during our waking hours, by information directed our way (**P3**) in various forms ranging from drop-in visitors at work to unsolicited telephone calls to advertisements to, even, nicely authored web pages that grab our attention and "consume" us (and our time, attention, energy, and, potentially, money) far more than we might wish for.

Searching helps as a first line of defense through the application of filters that screen out the spam, the phishing attempts, the junk email, etc. We expect these to get continuously better through the application of feedback implicit in our choices ("yes, this is junk"; "no, that was an email I should see").

Beyond this, search can help by properly routing the many pieces of incoming information that are useful only not now. Search can make it easy, even automatic, to place incoming information into groups so that it is ready for our consideration when the time comes. Search can help us to stay focused on the current task secure in the knowledge that incoming information is being properly "routed." In those cases, where we need to set aside the current task (e.g., in order to capture a thought or to-do related to another task), search can help minimize the disruption.

7.4.3   THE META-LEVEL REACH OF SEARCH

Key to the fast, interactive search of any reasonably sized information collection is the construction of an index. As search indexes are built and subsequently updated, each information item to be covered by the index (in subsequent searching) must be analyzed for indexable content. This content analysis can extend across all information owned by us and under our control (**P1**) and, further, to:

- **P2,** information about us that we're able to locate on the Web.

- **P3,** information directed toward us via digital channels of communication (e.g., email, internet phone, texting, instant messaging, targeted ads, etc.).

- **P4,** information provided by us through websites we maintain, emails we send, comments we post, etc.

- **P5,** information experienced by us as recorded to increasing levels of fidelity.

The content analysis needed to complete an index then provides a solid basis for support of meta-level activities of PIM. Support is complemented by the data maintained in an item event log (i.e., log), which serves as a time- and location-stamped record of our interactions within information items (e.g., files, emails, web pages and, in general, anything addressable via a URI). The combined application of item-by-item content analysis together with this log of all our information interactions will help us to answer key questions toward a profound transformation of meta-level activities of PIM.

7.4.4   MAINTAINING AND ORGANIZING

➢ Which items (folders, files, links) are we no longer using and so might be safely archived? Archival may mean a shift to cheaper storage but, most important, archival means moving the information away from our attentional surfaces so that it no longer distracts or obscures more important information.

➢ Which items are duplicates or near-duplicates of one another? If a piece of information such as an email address or reference is wrong, how many items need to be corrected?

➢ Which items (think especially photographs or video recordings) are in older formats and should be updated to a current format?

➢ Based upon an analysis of content and usage patterns, how might items be usefully grouped instead of or in addition to existing groupings (i.e., as established by folders, tags and other grouping items)? A variety of clustering techniques[180] might be applied

---

[180] For a general survey of clustering techniques, see, for example, Jain, Murty, & Flynn, 1999. For an example of their application see Zhou, Frankowski, Ludford, Shekhar, & Terveen, 2007.

in order to suggest new groupings or even completely new organizations (but with final approval still in the hands of the person). Content-based clustering may improve through application of techniques such as latent semantic analysis (as discussed previously in this section).[181]

Search applications can't make decisions of maintenance and organization by themselves—we must decide what to do. But as we make decisions, we can use search technologies to greatly improve our ability to see into an ever-increasing amount of digital information under our management. Moreover, once we articulate policies of maintenance and organization, search technologies can help toward an automated enforcement of these policies. For example, all files and folders falling below a minimal level of use (recent and overall) might be automatically archived during a periodic sweep to update or re-build search indexes.

7.4.5   MANAGING PRIVACY AND THE FLOW OF INFORMATION

Search will help us with the management of both incoming information and outgoing information. Some filtering of incoming information can be based mostly on content: Should this email message go to a "junk" folder? …to an "FYI" folder? For other decisions, such as whether we should be interrupted in our current activity, search's content analysis may provide input to other analyses that factor in additional information about the person and the current situation.[182] Search also has the potential to monitor the outflow of information. We might like to know, for example, when the information that we've posted to the Web is copied by someone, especially if copying is done without attribution. While content words may not be individually distinguishing, they may become distinguishing in combination with one another as part of a document fingerprint. In this way, a copy that's superficially altered from the original may still be identified through searches that key on distinguishing combinations and sequences of content words.

7.4.6   MEASURING AND EVALUATING

A search indexing utility opens and inspects, perhaps on multiple occasions, all of our email messages, sent and received, all of our documents, created and saved, and all of the web pages we have visited. The resulting index is needed for fast search. The index and the indexing process might also be used to help us answer other questions:

---

[181] See http://en.wikipedia.org/wiki/Cluster_analysis. Clustering based on content alone has a long history and yet its success is still marginal. An analysis of content may produce a high percentage of clusters that are not useful or make no sense. This is partly explained by the high percentage of "noise" in an item's content. Also, items may overlap in ways that are accidental and not particularly useful. Content-based clustering may also be supplemented by techniques that factor in patterns of item access and usage (J. Shen et al., 2006).

[182] When to interrupt the user? For applications of a Bayesian network approach to this question, see Horvitz & Apacible, 2003.

- What words do I tend to use (overuse?) in the documents that I write? …in the email that I send? Are there other words I might learn to use instead?

- What words do I tend to use interchangeably? Can this information be used to augment a personal thesaurus that might be used, as needed, to expand the scope of a search?

- When I use ambiguous terms like "browsing" in a query, what sense(s) do I generally mean? Should senses be added to a personal dictionary and used, as needed, to narrow the scope of a search?

- What topics do I consistently search for on the Web?

- What topics are reflected in the articles (usually PDF documents) and web references that I keep on my hard drive?

- What characterizes the email to which I'm most likely to respond? Least likely to respond?

7.4.7   MAKING SENSE OF AND USING THE INFORMATION

The technology of search can greatly assist us in our efforts to make sense of our information. We can expect increasing innovation, for example, in the results display in particular, when results are focused on a particular content type such food recipes or flight information (see Figure 7.6). Some innovations in results display will be less dramatic but no less effective at helping us both to find the old and to notice the new.[183]

Making better sense of our information and being smarter, more effective as a consequence may also be a qualitative result of dramatic improvements in the reach, speed, and effectiveness of search multiplied many times over. We find information now via the Web in a matter of seconds that only 20 years ago or less would have necessitated a lengthy phone call or a trip to the library. On many occasions we would have simply done without.

The ready availability of large amounts of information on virtually any topic we can think of is not without its downside as discussed in the "Caveats and disclaimers" section. We suffer from information overload and, sometimes, from "analysis paralysis." We skim. We may focus more on remembering "how" to get back to the information than "what" the information is about. But, as Holt argues, the good outweighs the bad. In any case, we're not going back.

Figure 7.6: A Hipmunk display of flight search results makes it easy to compare price, flight duration, and departure/arrival times.[184]

[183] Jaime Teevan, 2008.
[184] Taken from search on Hipmunk.com done on Sept. 19, 2013 (http://www.hipmunk.com/flights/ SEA-to-PAR#!dates=Sep17,Sep23&pax=1).

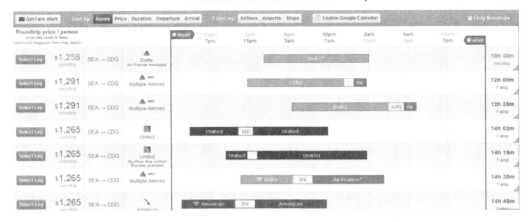

7.4.8   THE TECHNOLOGY REMAINING

Technologies to search, especially as applied to ever greater amounts of digital information afforded us by technologies to save (i.e., to capture and store information) will greatly transform our activities of PIM ranging from minute by minute activities of finding and keeping to meta-level activities to maintain and organize, manage privacy and information flow, measure and evaluate, and, especially, make sense of and use our information.

In both saving and searching, we depend upon structure. Structure is the third leg of our technology platform for PIM.

But what is structure? How is it represented? How can structure be represented so that it is not locked ("siloed") within our applications? Can our structures truly be ours, accessible to be worked with, and used in many ways, across any number of applications? These are questions for the next chapter of Part 2.

CHAPTER 8

Technologies to Structure Our Information

Even as we've considered technologies to save and to search in previous chapters, we've also considered structure.[185] Any search that we do is structured by its scope. For example, in our efforts to re-find, we may be searching within a specified folder or we may be searching for email only. The scope of any web search is implicitly "stuff that my search service searches for." We shouldn't fool ourselves that we're searching the whole Web.[186]

And then we use the structure of the information we're searching through to further constrain the results returned by a search. We don't, for example, want any email containing "Harry" but only those emails "From: Harry."

In a web search, even a restrictive search is likely to return far more results than we have time to consider. Again, structure helps and, in fact, is indispensable. Google's famous PageRank algorithm, for example, uses a recursive analysis of in-link structure to rank search results.[187]

Structure also provides a basis for navigating to information, either as a complement to search or as a primary method of information access. And structure helps people to recognize a desired item in search results.[188] People can scan email subject lines returned by a search query or sort a list of documents such that those most recently modified appear first.

Most important, search through any large corpus depends upon the structure of an index. A search index is an "inversion" in which the documents of a corpus are grouped by terms extracted from an analysis of document content. When search terms match index terms, a listing of documents for a term can be generated quickly without a need to search exhaustively through all documents of a corpus. Without the index, our searches become a non-interactive "batch job" that we wait hours or even days to complete.

---

[185] A blog post by Alex Payne, "The Case Against Everything Buckets" (https://al3x.net/2009/01/31/against-everything-buckets.html), nicely argues for the use of structure as realized through our local "free" file system. The post cautions against "Everything Buckets" that promise us can save and search (e.g., our notes, to-dos, web references, etc.) without a need to structure. The post notes that "everything" applications (e.g., Evernote) are backed by some database—often proprietary. The structure realized through such an application is much less easily shared than are structures realized through a local file system. The post was referenced in a later post by Adam Pash where it prompted considerable discussion (http://lifehacker.com/5666954/avoid-everything-buckets-aka-why-i-cant-get-into-apps-like-evernote, scroll to the comments at the end).

[186] See for example, http://www.quora.com/What-percentage-of-the-web-does-Google-index-and-how-has-it-changed-over-time.

[187] See http://en.wikipedia.org/wiki/PageRank; and also Bryan & Leise, 2006.

[188] J. Teevan, 2006b.

We've also implicitly considered structure as we considered technologies to save our information. An item-event log (i.e., log), for example, is structured as a sequence of events where each event includes time, location, address for information item and an action taken (e.g., "open," "close," "create," "delete," "move," "rename," etc.). No matter what the fidelity of our "lifelog," whether a sequence of URIs, pictures taken at regular intervals or full-motion video, the log as a whole is quickly too long to review in its entirety. We need some structure in the form of time- and location-based entry points, for example, if we're to focus and selectively sample (e.g., for purposes of recollection, retrieval, etc.).

In other words, we can't help talking about structure even in chapters where the focus has been on technologies to save or to search.

But in this chapter we consider technologies to structure in their own right.

What are these technologies to structure? The corresponding question is answered by example for save and search. Technologies to save include devices we might wear or mount for capturing information. Technologies to save include new ways to store ever more information, ever more cheaply, for ever longer periods of time.

As an application of search technology we think right away of the web search box and the sometimes seemingly magical return of the information we seek. Behind the UI are methods for building indexes, methods for matching query terms to index terms, and methods for the ordering and display of results. Index building includes methods to crawl for content and methods to analyze this content for index terms.

Technologies to save mean that massive amounts of data can be stored digitally as the raw materials of search. Properties and patterns of this data are made visible for structural expression (automated or optional) through search technologies. Index-building is a process of automatically structuring our information. We also actively structure as a follow-on to a search as, for example, when we bookmark a search result or when we save a document we've found to a local folder for later use.

Lots of structuring, in other words, is happening already—enabled by technologies to save and completed by technologies to search.

What then remains to discuss in a chapter on technologies to structure?

A lot.

But first, what is structure?

8.1   STRUCTURE, STRUCTURE EVERYWHERE ... NOR ANY BIT TO SHARE [189]

Structure "... from Latin *structura* ('a fitting together, adjustment, building, erection, a building, edifice, structure'), from *struere*, past participle *structus* ('pile up, arrange, assemble, build')." Structure is both a verb ("To give structure to; to arrange.") and a noun (e.g., "A cohesive whole built up of distinct parts... The underlying shape of a solid... The overall form or organization of something.").[190]

The concept of structure is important across disciplines and art forms from biology, chemistry,[191] and physics to music,[192] literature, and poetry[193] and then to sociology,[194] organizational psychology,[195] and, of course, mechanical engineering and architecture.

Structure accomplishes a grouping and interrelating of heterogeneous elements. Through structure comes an emergence of properties we could not predict from a separate consideration of component elements. "The whole," as the phrase goes, "is greater than the sum of the parts."[196]

Structures for information come in many forms and at many levels. The data of a relational database is structured into tables with rows of attribute values. The content of an XML document is structured into a hierarchy of elements where a given element may contain attributes and sub-elements.

The structure in some information items is the product of a formal schema or template—a structure in its own right. In other cases, the structure is implicit. Part 2 of this book is a little of both: A structure of chapters, one each for input/output technologies and technologies to save, search and structure. Some chapters, in turn, have a section concerning "caveats and disclaimers" relating to the chapter's technology area. The six activities of PIM and six senses in which information is personal have also provided a structure of sorts for an assessment of impacts for each chapter's technologies.

---

[189] With apologies to Samuel Taylor Coleridge, http://en.wikipedia.org/wiki/The_Rime_of_the_Ancient_Mariner.

[190] Definitions are taken from the Wiktionary (http://en.wiktionary.org/wiki/structure).

[191] We can be very glad, for example, that the structure of water leads to an unusual property that its density decreases when cooled below 4 °C. See http://en.wikipedia.org/wiki/Properties_of_water, http://chemistry.about.com/od/chemistryfaqs/f/icefloats.htm, http://wiki.answers.com/Q/Why_does_ice_float_in_water.

[192] Consider, for example, the traditional four movement structure of a "classical" symphony (http://en.wikipedia.org/wiki/Symphony) in which at least one movement is composed in sonata-allegro form, which is itself typically structured into sections of exposition, development, and recapitulation (http://en.wikipedia.org/wiki/Sonata_form).

[193] For a list of poetry forms (an structures) see http://thepoetsgarret.com/list.html. See, for example, the structure of a villanelle (http://en.wikipedia.org/wiki/Villanelle).

[194] There is for example, Durkheim's theory "Structural/Functionalism" (http://www.wavesofwords.4t.com/theory-webpage.htm).

[195] There is discussion, for example, of an appropriate level of structure in organizations. Optimal structure varies with the organization, its charter and competition. See for example, J. P. Davis, Eisenhardt, & Bingham, 2009; Ogollah & Bolo, 2009; H. A. Simon, 1971.

[196] This emergent magic of structure is nicely described by Chaisson, 2002. See also Pullan & Bhadeshia, 2000; Herbert A. Simon, 1962.

Information structures can be "strong," providing skeletons for the flesh of content. But then we also note that the boundaries between structure and content are not fixed. What appear to be "blobs" of content at one level reveal, on closer inspection, a structure (or structure in several overlays) holding together smaller blobs of content within.

Information structure can give consolidated expression to data patterns lying otherwise diffuse, hidden, and dormant. A search index does this, for example. Structure makes the implicit explicit.[197]

But the full expression of an information structure itself may be mostly hidden from our view. We see that some text is underlined and in a special color and that, if we click on it, a web page comes into view. Unless we're in an editor to "view source" for the page's HTML, we don't see the anchor tag and the "href" attribute that defines the hyperlink.

We structure as we use folders, tags, sections, "albums," and a host of other structuring forms. We structure as we place, order, highlight, and otherwise format our information. We follow conventions of structuring even in our choice of words, their ordering and the selection and ordering of characters within. Consistencies of word choice, ordering, and spelling, in turn, provide the basis for the index structures that are so essential to search. Structure builds on structure.

We often speak as if we needed more structure, in our lives and with our information, as we use phrases like "I should get more organized" or "My information space is kind of a mess right now."

But if we look at our information structures, we could easily conclude that we have too much structure already.

More accurately, we have too many disparate structures. Each application, each tool we use for the management of our information, comes with its own forms for structuring. Table 8.1 lists forms for structuring for several popular applications.

Table 8.1: Each application we use comes with its own ways to structure	
Application	**Forms for structuring**
Microsoft Outlook	Email folders
Microsoft OneNote	Notebooks, Sections (top), Pages (right-hand)
Evernote	Notebooks, Tags (in a hierarchy)
Remember The Milk	Lists, Tags
Facebook	Groups, Albums, FriendLists

As we work with various applications, whether desktop or, increasingly, web-based, we structure in similar but slightly different ways using different forms for structuring.

Different applications may use the same name but "mean" very different things. Consider "tags" in Evernote vs. "tags" in OneNote. Evernote tags can be structured into a hierarchy. Tags in OneNote, on the other hand, can each be given a font, a color, and an icon but cannot be structured into a hierarchy.

---

[197] Implicit (entangled, twisted together). http://en.wiktionary.org/wiki/implicit.

We should not be surprised, therefore, that the information structures we build, as we use these different forms for structuring, are varied and inconsistent with one another. Our structures are fragments—shards, we might say—imperfectly reflecting the more coherent, integrative expression we might like to give to our information.

If only we could.

The services of the desktop file system provide at least basic unifying support across desktop applications for the "file" and "folder"[198] as information items with existence independent of any given application. Included with this support are basic operations to create, delete, move, re-name, etc. We lose this unifying support as we shift to web applications and use the storage these web applications provide.

But we shouldn't kid ourselves that the organization of our information was so good back in the old days—the days a decade or so back when we couldn't so easily push information into web-based apps and when the file system (including various storage devices) was all most of us had for persistence of digital information.

If we look at our personal folder organizations today, we're likely to see a great many abandoned systems of information organization.[199] We start one system of organization, only to leave it in favor something else.

Worse, we may switch back and forth between two or more systems for organizing. We're then reluctant to decommission one organization in favor of another. Which one? And what a pain to move everything! But then we're uncertain where to find old information. And we're uncertain where to keep new information. Maybe we decide to keep the information in several places inside different organizations. But then... if we change an item even slightly—with a comment or a highlight, for example—we're left with different versions. Which to use later? Which is the right one?

This diversity of similar—but not the same—structures, especially as "siloed" in different applications, is part of a bigger problem of *information fragmentation* as briefly discussed in Part 1 of this book.

People persistently express a desire for greater integration, as an antidote to fragmentation, with comments such as "*ideally I would like a unified system, I wouldn't have all these different databases and all these different check lists and manuals.*"[200]

In particular, people want to organize project-related information together but end up duplicating and maintaining related structures across different applications (e.g., file managers, email

---

[198] Karger, 2007.

[199] See Erickson, 1996, for personal account of the challenges in creating and maintaining an system for organizing personal information.

[200] See, for example, Bruce, Wenning, Jones, Vinson, & Jones, 2010, for the results of a longitudinal study into the ways people manage information related to a project they wish to complete. Participants, after relating locations of information related to a project and reviewing the various applications used in the management of project-related information, were asked to reflect upon their "ideal system."

clients, web browsers and a wide range of web applications).[201] Most of the structures people use lie buried in their applications and cannot readily be re-used or even easily examined.

With the emergence of collaborative tools, these fragmentation problems are replicated and exacerbated for collaborating teams who have to create and maintain shared structures—a complex task we consider further in Chapter 10's (Part 3) exploration of *group information management* (GIM).

In our field studies in the Keeping Found Things Found group, the participants we interview are frequently critical of their organizations. As we ask people to give us "tours" of their organizations of personal information we often hear comments like "I'm really messy" or "I really need to take some time to get this stuff better organized."[202] Sometimes people even interrupt the interview to move or delete a folder that "really shouldn't be there."

Paradoxically though, we also hear people expressing embarrassment for being too organized or, more accurately, these people express embarrassment for the percentage of their time and energy that is required to maintain their organizations. We're "damned if we do; damned if we don't."

We shouldn't be so hard on ourselves.

Our structures, even if we invest considerable time and effort to make these consistent, will still lie scattered and siloed in various applications. And our investment in desktop folder structure,[203] based on past experience, may later be abandoned only to add to overall clutter. Whether based on the desktop or the Web, the tools for viewing and working with information structure are poor. Without better tool support, the organizations we devise may be more trouble than they are worth (i.e., more trouble to maintain than we save in costs of keeping and finding).

Suppose our information—content and structure—were "first class"? What might this mean?

For one thing, this might mean that structures are no longer buried within different applications. Structures, instead, would have an existence independent of any given application.

But then what is information—especially digital information—without supporting applications?

We then need to stipulate, in addition, that, for information structure to be given first class treatment, it needs to be shared between, and viewed and manipulated through, a large number of applications.

To be clear, sharing in this manner is *not* a serial export/import of our information from one application into another... Export/import might have worked well enough back in a day when packages of our information—a document or a presentation or a figure—were the primary object

---

[201] For accounts of how project-related information can be scattered by the very applications we use to manage this information see Bergman et al., 2006; Boardman & Sasse, 2004.

[202] See, for example, Bruce et al., 2010; W. Jones, Phuwanartnurak, et al., 2005, for reviews of empirical studies done in the Keeping Found Things Found group.

[203] Again, I use the term "desktop" in connection with applications, information, and information structures that are managed through the operating system of a laptop or desktop computer.

of our efforts and where these packages were passed along from one application to the next in the manner of an assembly line (often with printing to paper as a final step).

There is nothing first class about our information in an export/import assembly line. Notwithstanding the noble goals of initiatives such as the Data Liberation Front,[204] the export of information from one application into another remains a troublesome, time-consuming. and "lossy" process. Information structures in particular are apt to be mangled or left behind altogether. And in an age where power comes from a persistence and projection of our information, through our devices and interconnected on the Web, an assembly line focus on a single information item will no longer do.

We invoke again the metaphor used in Chapter 4 (Part 1)[205] of our information as house... or a garden.

And then we return to an original definition of *application* as in "the act of applying or laying on." We apply a variety of tools to a vegetable garden: First a shovel, then a hoe, then a rake, then the hose for watering. Similarly, Chapter 4 (Part 1) considered how information for an activity (a project) might be worked through a variety of tools. Different tools, for example, might help us to organize this information according to an evolving story told first in the future tense (what are we going to do?), then in an extended present tense (what do we need to do now or soon?) and then in the past tense (what did we do?)

Let an application be a tool we "apply" to our information—the right tool for the right job[206] —rather than a thing to which we "submit." Tools work with our information in place.

But that place is defined by structure—a structure to be shared with the applications we use and, selectively, with other people. And with ourselves over time.

We'll consider how this might happen later. But first, what is the personal potential of shared structure (and a concomitant ability to share information "in place")? What are the benefits?

---

[204] http://www.dataliberation.org/.

[205] William Jones, 2012.

[206] Our information structures accomplish a componentization of our information that can be contrasted with and is complementary to efforts toward a componentization of the software we use in our applications for information management. See, for example, http://en.wikipedia.org/wiki/Component-based_software_engineering. The dynamic assembly of reusable software components into a larger application has often proven to be demanding of computing resources—and the patience of users. See, for example, http://en.wikipedia.org/wiki/OpenDoc#Problems. If we can use our information structures to focus more selectively on a "chunk" of information (e.g., a paragraph, a photo, a single figure, or table) then less assembly may be required to realize the applications needed to work with this information.

Taking back our information, #1. Focus on the grouping item.

This is the first in a series of insets on the theme, "Taking back our information." Drawing upon the work of the Keeping Found Things Found initiative,[207] the series describes an approach toward gaining greater control over the information that is personal to us in any of the six senses in which information can be said to be personal.

Why bother?

Motivation on the one hand comes from the pain of a present situation where our information is scattered across a range of devices and applications. The fragmented nature of our information makes each of the six activities of PIM more difficult. Where to keep useful information for later use? How to find this information later? Similarly with meta-level activities. How to maintain and organize information that is so widely scattered? How to manage privacy and the flow of information when we haven't a clue where our information is? How to measure and evaluate our practices of PIM when these seem so disjointed—partly on our laptops, partly on the Web, partly though a host of highly specialized apps on our palmtops and, still, partly through paper? Most important, how to make sense of our information when we have difficulty even assembling relevant information (e.g., for a decision we must make or a task we must otherwise complete) into a single view?

Motivation on the other hand comes from the power of a future situation in which we are able to work with and use our information much more effectively than today. Our information on the Web serves as proxy for ourselves, speaking for us on routine matters (e.g., current status, job availability, time and place of parties we're organizing and so on). Our information on our palmtops frees us from a need to be physically "here" or "there"; we can be digitally present in any number of places no matter the physical distance. We look to a future where we are much less constrained by acts of clerical necessity and have greater freedom to pursue those creative "CAPTCHA" activities that make us uniquely human.[208]

Taking control of our information means, first and foremost, taking control of our information structures. Control the structures and the content will follow.

---

[207] For more on the Keeping Found Things Found initiative see http://keepingfoundthingsfound.com/ and http://kftf.ischool.washington.edu/.

[208] The reference is to CAPTCHA (Completely Automated Public Turing test to tell Computers and Humans Apart) (see http://en.wikipedia.org/wiki/CAPTCHA and also http://www.captcha.net/). As we register for this or that service on the Web, many of us have likely encountered the CAPTCHA test to type in the letters of a distorted image. The test remains valid even today as a way to distinguish people from computers and heaven help us if algorithms eventually give computers to the ability to "see" the letters as well. For an entertaining and thought-provoking exploration into what it means to be human in an age of ever smarter computers see Christian, 2012.

But, as the "Structure, structure everywhere…" section explores, information structure comes in many forms. Where to start?

Consider a focus on the "grouping item."

The *grouping item* is a kind of information item whose primary purpose is to group together and provide access to other information items. Folders, tags, "section tabs," and "pages" (for Microsoft Outlook), "albums" and "groups" (for Facebook), and "notebooks" as defined (differently) in several applications are each examples of grouping items.

Alternatively, any information item can be regarded as a grouping item. When we do so, we consider the item primarily for its function to represent and provide quick, easy access to other information items (including other grouping items). An ordinary web page, for example, has its own content but also, via its hyperlinks, provides ready access to other web pages and their content.

Grouping items are called by different names in different information management applications. Evernote, for example, provides for "notebooks," "notebook stacks," and "tags." Microsoft OneNote, an alternate note-taking application, provides for "notebooks," "section groups," "sections," "pages," and "sub-pages." A file system like that used in Microsoft Windows or on the Macintosh provides for directories or "folders." Even indexing and search utilities such as Lucene[209] can be seen to create a kind of grouping item in the form of a term + links to documents in which the term has been found or to which the term is otherwise associated.

Grouping items differ from one another in many respects such as the manner of their creation and the manner of and restrictions in their use. For example, folders are created by people (except, of course, for all the other folders that are created by desktop applications in the course of their installation and use). Index terms and their lists of associated documents, on the other hand, are created by an indexing utility (though people can exert indirect control over the indexing process through choices made with respect to indexing components such as the word stemmer and the word separator).

Notwithstanding these and other notable differences, all grouping items share the following features in common:

➤ A basic "noodle" structure (see Figure 8.1) consisting of a node + outgoing links.

---

[209] http://lucene.apache.org/.

➢ Links point "directly" (i.e., via an address such as a URI that is quickly and unambig-uously resolved) to other information items including, when the application allows, to other grouping items. For example, a folder points to its subfolders and files. An Ever-note tag points to other Evernote tags and to notes that have been "tagged" by the tag.

➢ The grouping item is addressable by one or more URIs. Through these URIs the node of a grouping item can, in turn, be addressed by other grouping items.

➢ The grouping item often has a name or a label by which it is represented in displays.

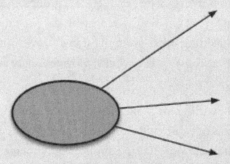

Figure 8.1: The explicit structure of a grouping item is a "noodle" (node + outgoing links).

We use grouping items in one form or another throughout a typical day. Consider these ex-amples:

➢ To decide which hotel to book, Gordon copies text, pictures, and links from the Web for several alternatives, placing information as notes on a OneNote page. Alternatively, he might take notes in Evernote, giving each the tag "hotels-Boston."

➢ Rashmi is working to complete a complicated application process that requires her to fill out several different forms. She seeks first to place all forms in one place—perhaps in a folder or even as printouts on a physical desktop. She does this to gain a clearer sense of the effort involved and to be sure she has "everything in one place."

➢ In his search for the current version of a document, Oscar navigates to a folder contain-ing several versions as separate files. He then sorts these by "last modified" date before selecting the most recently modified of these.

➢ Ursula doesn't have a direct address for a targeted web page but she knows that a hyper-link to this web page is the second of two that can be found in the "upper right-hand corner" of another page.

➤ Piao wants to contribute to an email discussion. To do so, he needs both to locate the most recent post and also to locate previous posts so that he can reflect their content in his response. If he is using Gmail, this grouping is already done for him. But he doesn't know how to do this in Microsoft Outlook so, instead, he opts to see "related messages in this conversation" and he does a reply-all to the most recent post.

➤ Susan is planning her wedding. Nearly six months prior to the event, she creates a "wedding" folder in her file system in which she places files and also URLs (as shortcuts) that relate to different aspects of her wedding. As her tolerance for "clutter" is reached, she begins to organize items into subfolders for different aspects of her wedding such as "wedding dress," "honeymoon," "reception," and "wedding vows." On the eve of her wedding, the folder structure nicely resembles a problem decomposition for her wedding with grouping items (folders and subfolders) representing sub-areas ("honeymoon") and specific tasks ("decide on wedding dress").

The folder, the OneNote page, the web page, the subject line used in common among the email messages of a conversation—even the physical desktop—are forms of a grouping item. In each case, the grouping item, including its set of associations to other information items, provides an important context for the activity at hand—whether this is selecting the right document, the right hotel room, the right hyperlink, responding to the most recent email post in a conversation or, more generally, getting a sense for and making sense of the information at hand.

Taking back our information, #2. Observations and speculation about the grouping item.

A grouping item provides fast, usually certain access to the items it groups.

A grouping item provides key context. Even in the two examples of the previous inset where focus was on a single link—to the latest version of a document or to a specific web page—the selection could not be made absent a larger context provided by the grouping item that includes a representation of alternate files or links.

The grouping item supports a stepwise navigation to the desired information that both simplifies the activity of finding the desired information and also helps us to more easily determine the relevance of this information once found.[210]

The context provided by the grouping item becomes especially important in cases where the activity is less well defined and we are trying to "see what we have here."

---

[210] See Bergman, Whittaker, Sanderson, Nachmias, & Ramamoorthy, 2010; Jones, Phuwanartnurak, Gill, & Bruce, 2005; Teevan, Alvarado, Ackerman, & Karger, 2004.

Two additional observations can be made about the grouping item. Each observation prompts speculation concerning the study of the grouping item as a way to understand better how people categorize, conceptualize, and, generally, make sense of the information at hand.

Grouping items are an external expression of internal goal-derived categories and "ad-hoc concepts"

How do people use categories and concepts to represent their world in meaningful, useful ways? Much of the work originally done to address this important question had[211] a "semantic" focus on categories such as "bird" or "dog" that we learn early in life, use every day and that seem almost to be "built into" the way we view and interact with our world.

More recently, there has been work to demonstrate the practical importance and widespread use of *goal-derived categories,*[212] i.e., categories that are created ad hoc in support of the completion of a project or the solving of a problem. "Things to pack for the ski trip" and "Hotels to stay at in Boston" are examples of goal-derived categories. The formation of goal-derived categories appropriate to a given set of circumstances is an important and *teachable skill.*[213] Can this formation also be supported through tools that support the creation of grouping items and through an underlying representation of the structure in these grouping items?

More generally, people form and make use of concepts ad hoc (i.e., as needed for a particular task or situation) for which they can articulate no formal definition. An ad hoc concept or category may represented, instead, extensionally through exemplars we are able to list or can recognize if shown. As Justice Potter Stewart famously said when facing the challenge to define "hard-core pornography," "I know it when I see it."[214] We may have ad hoc concepts for "things to do before I go to bed" or "things to look for in a work situation." Many interpersonal conflicts arise from discrepancies between people with respect to a concept such as "things to expect from a friend."

Ad hoc concepts are manifest in our grouping items[215] and so too are challenges to define these concepts in ways that would support their consistent use over time and amongst the

---

[211] See Collins & Quillian, 1969; Rosch et al., 1976; Tulving, 1983.

[212] Barsalou, 1983, 1991; Chrysikou, 2006.

[213] Chrysikou, 2006, showed improved problem-solving performance after training to construct goal-derived categories.

[214] http://www.oyez.org/justices/potter_stewart/, found through http://en.wikipedia.org/wiki/Potter_Stewart#cite_note-oyez_stewart-10.

[215] "Concept" relates to "conceive" which derives from "Middle English conceiven, from Old French concevoir, concever, from Latin concipere ('to take'), from con- ('together') + capio ('to take')." (http://en.wiktionary.org/wiki/conceive). A concept is a "taking together" of things (ideas, to-dos, features, etc.).

members of a group. For want of shared definition or description of purpose, for example, the pages of a team wiki—a form of grouping item—may become a hodgepodge. Or the burden to maintain these may be borne by the one person in the group who "understands" the organization of the wiki and the meanings (purposes) of its various pages.[216] But exclusive maintenance by one person is no guarantee that grouping items and their underlying concepts will continue to make sense over time. As we approach a folder we haven't used in a while we may often ask "what (on earth) was this for?"[217]

Grouping items have latent, implicit structure, and emergent properties

The grouping item has structure explicitly represented in its outgoing links. At the same time, as we perceive these links (as mediated by the sights or possibly the sounds of a tool) these links may seem to relate to each other and to node-level information in ways less easily described explicitly. "Semi-groupings" may "pop out" as perceived patterns in the information being viewed. Our perceptions of emergent groupings are influenced, for example, by the relative location of links in a display or by display properties of their appearance such as their color, size, or shape.

In the spirit of *spatial hypertext*,[218] we may manipulate our perceptions of these semi-groupings as, for example, when we place notes close to one another on a page in Microsoft OneNote. Such a manipulation is often a first step toward a more explicit chunking of links under a finer-grained partition of grouping items. A grouping of links to web pages related to a "term paper on search" might, for example, be further divided into sub-groupings of links to web pages for "Lucene," "faceted search," "stemming and word-breaking," etc. It is often the case that these subgroupings emerge and can then be made explicit only after an initial process of discovery that happens in the larger context of the initial grouping.[219]

The creation of grouping items and the naming of these is then an essential step in the *problem setting* (i.e., the definition of the problem space) that precedes *problem-solving*. Before we figure out which hotel best meets our travel needs in Boston, we first create a "hotels in Boston" folder affording ready access to information concerning hotel alternatives. Schon[220]

---

[216] Burrow, 2004; Jonathan Grudin & Poole, 2010; Phuwanartnurak, 2009.

[217] W. Jones, Phuwanartnurak, et al., 2005.

[218] Buchanan, Blandford, Thimbleby, & Jones, 2004; Gamberini & Bussolon, 2001; Marshall & Frank M. Shipman, 1995; Shipman, Hsieh, Moore, & Zacchi, 2004.

[219] As a complement to the bottom-up process of chunking (or composition), new grouping items achieving a finer-grained partition are also generated through a top-down process of decomposition. We may do this, for example, when we break a larger project such as "Plan trip to Boston" into smaller tasks more appropriately placed on a checklist (e.g., "make the hotel reservation," "book the flight").

[220] Schon, 1984, p. 4.

defines problem setting as "a process in which, interactively, we *name* the things to which we will attend and *frame* the context in which we will attend to them."

Making use of a chemical metaphor we might call the grouping item a "molecular" unit of structure. In contrast, the link, association, or proposition (such as those formed by a subject-predicate-object statement) is an "atomic" unit of structure. The notion of emergence has implications for efforts (such as the Semantic Web initiative discussed further in the "Personal potentials of shared structure" section) that aim for a more atomic level of structural representation. Some properties of a link and its referent—such as "most recent version"—can only be confirmed in the larger context of a grouping item. Even more so, relationships and emergent groupings of links require the larger context of a grouping item. The grouping item is the shared subject for a collection of propositions or a collection of links pointing to information (e.g., "Hotels in Boston" or "things to do this weekend").

The "noodle" alone is not enough

From the two observations of this inset it is apparent that the structure of a grouping item is only partially described by the explicit structure of a node + outgoing links. The properties of the node and each of its outgoing links—for example, display properties such as size, shape, color, display location—may also help us to perceive additional structures. We can call these "gestalts."[221] But then we realize that in our efforts toward a metadata representation of grouping items, a stark "noodle" representation of the grouping item is not enough. We also need to provide room for tool-specific (more generally, "namespace-specific") properties both at the level of the node and each of its outgoing links.

How? How can we realize both a tool-independent "noodle" metadata representation of the explicit structure of a grouping item and also leave tool-accommodating room for additional properties of the node and its outgoing links that are so critical to our efforts to understand and manage our information? And then, given this metadata representation, what can we do with it? These are topics we consider in the next inset in the "Taking back our information" series.

---

[221] See, for example, http://en.wikipedia.org/wiki/Gestalt_psychology#Emergence.

8.2   PERSONAL POTENTIALS OF SHARED STRUCTURE

We share lots of information structure already. One very prominent example of global sharing is, of course, the World Wide Web.[222] As noted in Chapter 4 (Part 1),[223] the Web has so profoundly changed the lives of most of us that we may find it hard to imagine what life was (or would be) without it. This holds true even for those of us (for me, for example) who spent much of their lives without the Web.

The Web functions through shared structures and shared conventions of three kinds: 1. A shared protocol (HTTP[224]) for the exchange of information—as web pages. 2. A shared syntax for generating web page addresses as Uniform Resource Locators (URLs[225]). A URL is a text string that provides information needed to locate a web page for return (via HTTP). 3. A markup language—HTML (HyperText Markup Language[226])—used to express the content and structure of web pages including the hyperlinks of these pages.

As a result of this sharing of structure and convention, we're able to view a web page retrieved from anywhere in the world via a variety of devices and in several different web browsers. Pages linked together define a global structure that may eventually link together nearly all of the world's human-generated information. The Web is obviously a huge success. And, even so, as noted in Chapter 4 (Part 1), we are only just beginning to realize its potential.

8.2.1   VISIONS OF THE SEMANTIC WEB

If we get this much benefit from a relatively modest investment in shared structures, what might we realize from even more shared structure? The tags of HTML, for example, deal mostly with the display of information with some limited semantics in the form of, for example, its treatment of hyperlinks (via anchor tags each with an href attribute taking a URL as a value).[227]

What if the structure of a web page could also communicate the "meaning" of its information in a format that could be "understood" and acted upon by "machines"—your computer or mine or some server somewhere in the cloud?

---

[222] Wikipedia provides a very nice introductory article on the World Wide Web with good pointers to additional information (http://en.wikipedia.org/wiki/World_Wide_Web).

[223] *The Future of Personal Information Management*, Part I (William Jones, 2012).

[224] http://en.wikipedia.org/wiki/Hypertext_Transfer_Protocol. Or see http://www.w3.org/Protocols/HTTP/AsImplemented.html for the original definition as used in1991.

[225] http://en.wikipedia.org/wiki/Uniform_resource_locator. See also one of the original specifications of the URL, http://www.w3.org/Addressing/URL/url-spec.txt. Conventionally, the URL has been classed as a sub-type of the Uniform Resource Identifier (URI) (http://en.wikipedia.org/wiki/Uniform_resource_identifier). However, the "contemporary view" is slightly different: (http://www.w3.org/TR/uri-clarification/).

[226] http://en.wikipedia.org/wiki/Hypertext_Markup_Language. See also http://www.w3.org/TR/1999/REC-html401-19991224/ and for HTML5 see http://www.w3.org/html/wg/drafts/html/master/.

[227] http://en.wikipedia.org/wiki/Hyperlink.

Enter the Semantic Web[228] as a seemingly natural—some might even say "inevitable" (it is often called "Web 3.0")—progression in the shared structures of the Web.[229]

In the words of Berners-Lee, Hendler, and Lassila, "The Semantic Web will bring structure to the meaningful content of web pages, creating an environment where software agents roaming from page to page can readily carry out sophisticated tasks for users."[230]

As early as 1998, Berners-Lee provided a "Semantic Web Road Map… with the goal that it (the Web) should be useful not only for human-human communication, but also that machines would be able to participate and help."[231]

He observed that "One of the major obstacles to this has been the fact that most information on the Web is designed for human consumption, and even if it was derived from a database with well-defined meanings (in at least some terms) for its columns, that the structure of the data is not evident to a robot browsing the Web."

Why not express information both ways: for people in a web page display and, in a more structured format, for "machines."

A major part of Berners-Lee's road map and still a key component of the Semantic Web is the encoding of virtually any assertion of interest as a subject-predicate-object statement using the Resource Description Framework or "RDF" for short.[232] RDF assertions are often (but not necessarily) serialized for persistent storage using XML (Extensible Markup Language).[233]

Building on RDF/XML is the RDF Schema (RDFS)[234] for defining the basic elements (building blocks) of ontologies[235] for use on the Semantic Web. The Web Ontology Language

---

[228] For a more formal description of the Semantic Web and access to specifications for its major components see http://www.w3.org/standards/semanticweb/. For a more accessible overview with additional pointers to Semantic Web components and applications see http://en.wikipedia.org/wiki/Semantic_web.

[229] The hypertext community has also generated technologies for information structuring, including taxonomic hypertext (Millard, Moreau, Davis, & Reich, 2000), open hypermedia (Østerbye & Wiil, 1996), spatial hypertext (Marshall & Shipman, 1995), structural computing (Nürnberg, Leggett, & Schneider, 1997), and Xanalogical structure (Theodor H. Nelson, 1999).

[230] Berners-Lee, Hendler, J.A, & Lassila, O, n.d., p. 1.

[231] Berners-Lee, 2005.

[232] For more on RDF see the "RDF Primer" of W3C (http://www.w3.org/TR/rdf-primer/) and for a hands-on experimentation, try the W3schools.com RDF tutorial (http://www.w3schools.com/rdf/). For an overview with pointers to additional information try http://en.wikipedia.org/wiki/XML.

[233] Formal specifications for XML can be found with W3C (http://www.w3.org/XML/). But for a hands-on tutorial see http://www.w3schools.com/xml/. And for a more accessible overview with pointers to follow-on information, try http://en.wikipedia.org/wiki/XML.

[234] For the formal specification of RDFS see http://www.w3.org/TR/rdf-schema/; for a more informal overview with several good references for greater exploration see http://en.wikipedia.org/wiki/RDFS.

[235] For an overview on ontologies in the context of the Semantic Web effort see (Horrocks, 2008). For an example of an ontology see Sowa's work, http://ontology4.us/english/Ontologies/Upper-Ontologies/Sowa%2520Ontology/index.html. For one person's efforts to render his personal ontology see http://personalontology.wordpress.com/.

(OWL)[236] then builds upon RDF and RDFS to provide a family of languages for the authoring of ontologies.[237] Ontologies in turn specify objects/concepts of interest in an area (e.g., "event," "location"), properties of these and relations between them. RDF expressions can be selectively retrieved using expressions (in RDF) conforming to the SPARQL query language.[238]

Taken together, what do these and other initiatives of the Semantic Web provide? Berners-Lee et al. describe the power of "agents": *"The real power of the Semantic Web will be realized when people create many programs that collect web content from diverse sources, process the information and exchange the results with other programs. The effectiveness of such software agents will increase exponentially as more machine-readable web content and automated services (including other agents) become available. The Semantic Web promotes this synergy: even agents that were not expressly designed to work together can transfer data among themselves when the data come with semantics."* [239]

Elsewhere, Berners-Lee describes the power of the Semantic Web in terms of data integration: *"To appreciate the need for better data integration, compare the enormous volume of experimental data produced in commercial and academic pharmaceutical laboratories around the world with the frustratingly slow pace of drug discovery. Life-science researchers are coming to the conclusion that in many cases no single lab, library or genomic data repository contains the information necessary to discover new drugs."* [240]

Interest in the Semantic Web has spawned a number of projects over the years including DBpedia,[241] an effort to extract structured data from Wikipedia for general use, Friend of a Friend (FOAF)[242] to describe the relationships between people and their "things" and GoPubMed,[243] a structured search engine for biomedical texts designed to significantly improve the speed and effectiveness of information retrieval for medical professionals (in comparison to information retrieval using Pubmed as a baseline).[244]

At a more personal level, Wesabe was designed to turn a jumble of personal "bank statements, credit-card accounts and so on"[245] into information we might use (e.g., "where is my money going month by month?," "When will I have enough savings to retire?"). Alas, Wesabe "is no more."[246]

---

[236] For formal specifications relating to OWL see http://www.w3.org/TR/owl2-overview/; for a more informal overview with pointers to additional information see http://en.wikipedia.org/wiki/Web_Ontology_Language.
[237] http://en.wikipedia.org/wiki/Ontology_(information_science).
[238] http://en.wikipedia.org/wiki/SPARQL.
[239] Berners-Lee et al., n.d., p. 5.
[240] http://www.economist.com/node/8134382.
[241] http://en.wikipedia.org/wiki/DBpedia. See also http://en.wikipedia.org/wiki/Freebase.
[242] http://en.wikipedia.org/wiki/FOAF_(software).
[243] http://en.wikipedia.org/wiki/GoPubMed.
[244] For an explanation for how semantics and an assessment of meaning can improve search effectiveness see Haller, 2010.
[245] http://www.economist.com/node/9716955.
[246] http://wesabe.com/.

8.2.2   FROM THE PUBLIC TO THE PERSONAL

In the spirit of the Semantic Web and often using its components (e.g., RDF and OWL) a number of research initiatives have explored the benefits of shared structure as these might be realized by individual people in their practices of PIM.

Research efforts divide roughly by focus, whether primarily on representation or application. On the representational side and related to efforts toward "personal knowledge management" as discussed in Chapter 1 (Part 1),[247] are a number of efforts over the years that have focused on support for the creation and use of **personal knowledge bases** and **personal ontologies**.[248] Motivation is expressed by the following excerpt, "*People often use powerful tools to manage the documents they encounter, but very rarely to store the mental knowledge they glean from those documents.*"[249]

Whether or not knowledge is a "thing" to be represented directly and externally from its applications is questionable,[250] but certainly one dominant theme of these efforts is the imposition of greater structure on information: "*The personal ontology attempts to encompass a wide range of user characteristics, including personal information as well as relations to other people, preferences and interests. The ontology may be extended through inheritance and the addition of more classes, as well as class instantiation according to the needs of user stereotypes or individuals.*"[251]

Related to these efforts are the more application-oriented efforts to realize a semantic desktop:[252] "People gather information on their desktop computers, but current systems lack the ability to integrate this information based on concepts or across applications. The vision of the *Semantic Desktop* is to use Semantic Web technology on the desktop to support *Personal Information Management* (PIM). In addition to providing an interface for managing your personal data it also provides interfaces for other applications to access this, acting as a central hub for semantic information on the desktop."[253]

There is some research to suggest that semantic desktops can help, giving users a more satisfying experience in their interactions (especially with personal information of the first sense, P1)

---

[247] William Jones, 2012.

[248] See, for example, Catarci, Dong, Halevy, & Poggi, 2007; Chaffee & Gauch, 2000; Dieng & Hug, 1998; Haase, Hotho, Schmidt-Thieme, & Sure, 2005; Horrocks, 2008; Huhns & Stephens, 1999; Katifori et al., 2008. See also Völkel & Haller, 2009. PIMO (http://www.dfki.uni-kl.de/~sauermann/2006/01-pimo-report/pimOntologyLanguageReport.html; http://www.semanticdesktop.org/ontologies/pimo/) is an effort to support the construction of ontologies in the context of Nepomuk (http://en.wikipedia.org/wiki/NEPOMUK_(framework), http://nepomuk.semanticdesktop.org/), a semantic desktop effort.

[249] Davies et al., 2006

[250] See "No knowledge but through information" (William Jones, 2010).

[251] Katifori et al., 2008, p. 3.

[252] http://en.wikipedia.org/wiki/Semantic_desktop. See also http://www.semanticdesktop.org/. For more scholarly treatment, see Chirita, Gavriloaie, Ghita, Nejdl, & Paiu, 2005; Decker & Frank, 2004; Groza, Handschuh, & Moeller, 2007; Sauermann & Heim, 2008; Sauermann, 2005a, 2005b; Sauermann et al., 2006; Sauermann, Bernardi, & Dengel, 2005.

[253] Sauermann & Heim, 2008, p. 467.

and improving user efficiency.[254] However—and this applies to any prototype evaluation—we must season the results of one evaluation with a few grains of salt since evaluations under ideal, laboratory conditions for the prototype may not translate to real-world conditions of ongoing use where people may face daily challenges of maintenance and use long after the "luster" of the prototype has dimmed.

Haystack[255] is one of the better known efforts to bring the power of the Semantic Web down to a personal level to help people manage their information. Haystack creates a URI "to name anything of interest."[256] And then all information is represented via the RDF standard.

Elsewhere, Karger[257] describes the benefits of unification (e.g., as a achieved through a uniform use of RDF) in terms of the sharing of structured information between applications: *we can argue that the functionality of sending email should not be locked up in the address book, but should instead apply to any person we encounter in any application—calendar, photo album, and so on.*

And through a sharing of structured information between applications comes greater opportunity for integrative visual displays of information: *One motivation for unification is that a user may need to observe several distinct information objects in order to draw conclusions about them. Looking at them one at a time can be slow and difficult, particularly if we must return to each several times.*

The difficulties Karger identifies with our current situations of PIM are real enough—as are the benefits of a solution to reduce these difficulties. We have likely all experienced problems in the sharing of information—especially structured information—between applications. Related to this, we've likely experienced the difficulty of bringing all of our information into a single coherent view so that we can "make sense of things" in order to make effective use of our information.

What isn't established is the necessity of the Haystack approach, i.e., unification via RDF. Also not established is the *sufficiency* of the RDF approach given the many practical difficulties of its use, which we explore further below.

8.2.3   UNFULFILLED PROMISES

The potential of the Semantic Web overall, and its applications to PIM in particular, would appear to be enormous. But now, over 15 years after the Semantic Web roadmap, the Semantic Web initiative is still mostly promise, having produced little in the way of practical solutions of widespread use beyond the research laboratory. McCool, cofounder of the large-scale RDF project TAP, notes a three-fold lack of deployment—of information, services, and applications and this "despite substan-

---

[254] See, for example, Franz, Ansgar, & Staab, 2009. Of course, evaluation is not only used to demonstrate the value of a prototype or its approach. Evaluation can also be very useful in directing the design and refinement of a prototype. For an example of such an evaluation as applied to the Gnowsis Semantic Desktop prototype see Sauermann & Heim, 2008.

[255] E. Adar, Karger, & Stein, 1999; Karger, Bakshi, Huynh, Quan, & Sinha, 2005a; Quan, Huynh, & Karger, 2003.

[256] Karger, Bakshi, Huynh, Quan, & Sinha, 2005b.

[257] Karger, 2007.

tial research funding in the US and European Union (EU).[258]" McCool concludes that "Because it's a complex format and requires users to sacrifice expressivity and pay enormous costs in translation and maintenance, the Semantic Web will never achieve widespread public adoption."

In a letter to the editor posted in the Communications of the ACM in response to Horrock's article on ontologies,[259] Aït-Kaci notes that "Whether the various languages proposed by the W3C are able to fly beyond toy applications has yet to be proved, especially in light of the huge financial investment being poured into the Semantic Web."[260]

Successes are no better in efforts to apply Semantic Web components in tools of PIM. For example, although code for the original Haystack prototype has been open-sourced, there no longer appears to be active work on the prototype. Karger reflects that "I'm still a believer in the Haystack vision, but in practice we found it difficult to convince people to abandon their long-cherished pim tools in favor of a half-baked research tool."[261]

Based on their own efforts to provide support for non-expert users to work with personal ontologies, Katifori, et al.[262] observe that "some users had problems when familiarizing themselves with the ontology model–they found it in some cases overwhelming. ... it seemed that the full complexity of an ontology ... may be difficult for the end user to comprehend."

McCool[263] notes that "The ontological data model makes representation of any nontrivial factual information difficult because it can't represent context of any kind." He goes on characterize the Semantic Web as a kind of "shadow web" that is entirely separate from the Web we use every day.

Singh[264] notes that "if there is one lesson to be learned from the long history of databases, it is that it is practically impossible to describe data well enough for it to be used in arbitrary applications."

Doctorow[265] goes further, characterizing efforts toward a rendition of meaning in a "world of exhaustive, reliable metadata" as "a pipe-dream, founded on self-delusion, nerd hubris and hysterically inflated market opportunities." Among the "seven insurmountable obstacles between the world as we know it and meta-utopia" he notes, for example, that "people lie" and that "There's more than one way to describe something."

But not even Doctorow suggests dispensing with metadata altogether. He recognizes, for example, the obvious value of in-link analyses of hyperlink structure, as practiced by search services,

---

[258] McCool, 2005.pp. 88 and 86.
[259] Horrocks, 2008.
[260] Aït-Kaci, 2009.
[261] http://haystack.csail.mit.edu/blog/2010/10/20/why-all-your-data-should-live-in-one-application/.
[262] Katifori et al., 2008.
[263] McCool, 2005, p. 88.
[264] Singh, 2002, p. 1.
[265] http://www.well.com/~doctorow/metacrap.htm.

as a kind of derived or implicit metadata. What else? How might structures be shared—whether to communicate meaning with our machines or, less grandly, simply to do useful things?

8.2.4 MORE SPECIFIC, MORE APPLIED, IN-LINE, "SMALLER"—YES; BUT SIMPLER?

Some argue for an abandonment of the Semantic Web initiative altogether.[266]

Others argue for its simplification. In his own writings on "linked data," Berners-Lee[267] provides some general guidelines toward the publishing of structured data that might have wider use:

1. Use URIs as names for things.

2. Use HTTP URIs so that people can look up those names.

3. When someone looks up a URI, provide useful information using the standards (RDF*, SPARQL).

4. Include links to other URIs so that they can discover more things.

McCool[268] believes in the need for more drastic simplification of the Semantic Web initiative drawing lessons from the success of the Web as a drastic simplification of earlier hypertext initiatives: *"My proposal is to do for the Semantic Web what Tim Berners-Lee … did for Project Xanadu, the original hypertext project."*

Noting the irony here, we might say that the Semantic Web needs someone in pragmatic spirit of the Tim Berners-Lee of the early 90s to correct for the complexities introduced by the visionary Tim Berners-Lee at the start of the new millennium. McCool goes on to argue for an approach that would permit an embedding of "named-entity" information directly in HTML markup—and so eliminate the need for a "shadow web" of semantic data maintained separately from the Web.

---

[266] See, for example, Sean B. Palmer explanation of his decision to "ditch it" after eight years of effort on the Semantic Web (http://inamidst.com/whits/2008/ditching).

[267] http://www.w3.org/DesignIssues/LinkedData.html. See also http://en.wikipedia.org/wiki/Linked_data, http://www.w3.org/TR/2013/WD-ldp-20130730/, http://en.wikipedia.org/wiki/Linked_Data#cite_note-DesignIssues-2 http://www.w3.org/wiki/LinkedData and Heath & Bizer, 2011.

[268] McCool, 2006, p. 96.

There is a general call, voiced by McCool and many others, for more targeted, practical, "real" (or less contrived) applications to illustrate the value of the Semantic Web.[269] Karger[270] argues for "Less Semantic, More Web" noting that "The introduction of structured data can drive that revolution forward, but only if we continue to think about how end users will use that technology."

Singh[271] argues that "best hope for the Semantic Web is to encourage the emergence of communities of interest and practice that develop their own consensus knowledge on the basis of which they will standardize their representations. For example, such standards have emerged in narrow areas of personal information management, e.g., with the vCard standard." From such standards may come, gradually, selectively, the shared structures needed for at least a partial fulfillment of the Semantic Web dream.[272]

---

[269] Similar arguments can be made in relation to technologies for information structuring generated by the hypertext community including taxonomic hypertext (Millard et al., 2000), open hypermedia (Østerbye & Wiil, 1996), spatial hypertext (Marshall & Shipman, 1995), structural computing (Nürnberg et al., 1997), and Xanalogical structure (Theodor H. Nelson, 1999). While a compelling case can be made for each of these initiatives, none (to my knowledge) has scaled beyond prototypes or very small-scale deployments. More recent work has explored ways to realize some of the goals of these hypertext initiatives in ways that constraints and required services to a minimum (K. M. Anderson, 2005).

[270] http://haystack.csail.mit.edu/blog/2013/06/10/keynote-at-eswc-part-3-whats-wrong-with-semantic-web-research-and-some-ideas-to-fix-it/.

[271] Singh, 2002, p. 2.

[272] See also community efforts toward a wiki-style authoring and shared use of a knowledge base such as Wikidata (http://www.wikidata.org/wiki/Wikidata:Main_Page) and Semantic MediaWiki (http://en.wikipedia.org/wiki/Semantic_MediaWiki; http://www.semantic-mediawiki.org/wiki/Semantic_MediaWiki). (And for comparisons between the two initiatives see http://semantic-mediawiki.org/wiki/FAQ#What_is_the_relationship_between_Semantic_MediaWiki_and_Wikidata.3F).

Figure 8.2: Efforts to represent meaning through structure have produced a complexity of different initiatives and formats.[273] Used courtesy of Vuk Milićić, http://milicicvuk.com/blog/2011/07/21/problems-of-the-rdf-syntax/.

The call for representations of meaning done in-line (i.e., as part of an HTML or XHTML representation for a web page) has been answered by not one but several new formats. Each may be simpler (easier for people to read and write in) than RDF/XML. However, in aggregate, new formats have added to overall complexity. Understanding similarities and differences among the formats is difficult, even for people experienced in the area. The three primary formats for in-line representation of meaning are:

- **Microformats**—a re-purposing of tags/attributes already available in HTML/XHTML prior to HTML5 (i.e., HTML 3 and later).[274]

- **RDFa**—a method of expressing RDF information in-line. RDFa was first proposed in 2004 for use with XHTML but its newer version (RDFa 1.1) is now compatible with HTML5 as well.[275]

---

[273] Image downloaded from http://milicicvuk.com/blog/2011/07/21/problems-of-the-rdf-syntax/.

[274] http://en.wikipedia.org/wiki/Microformats. See also http://knowledge.wharton.upenn.edu/article.cfm?articleid=1247 ("What's the Next Big Thing on the Web? It May Be a Small, Simple Thing—Microformats" for a discussion that motivates not only Microformats but also RDFa and Microdata formats).

[275] See http://en.wikipedia.org/wiki/RDFa and http://www.w3.org/TR/xhtml-rdfa-primer/#html-vs.-xhtml.

- **Microdata**—the most recent of the three formats, developed specifically in the context of HTML5 and as an alternative to RDFa.[276]

In-line formats have been used in several applications and initiatives. We have, for example:

➢ **Schema.org**—a joint effort by Google, Microsoft Bing, and Yahoo[277] to define schemas that websites might optionally use in order to pass along structured data (along with free text) to search engine web crawlers. Schemas are available to structure information for many different circumstances and in many different areas (e.g., events, organizations, places, products, medical).[278] For example, the "Event" schema provides attributes for "duration," "location," and "performer." Following the structure defined by a schema, web crawlers are able to preserve property/value pairings in support of more structured queries by people (e.g., "Show me everything happening nearby this weekend"). Schemas and instances of their expression are based in the Microdata format.[279]

➢ **COinS** (ContextObjects in Spans)[280]—a method of including bibliographic (citation) metadata in a web page for purposes of inclusion in a bibliography. If the page in view in our browser includes information written in the COinS schema, we may see a small icon to the right of the URL in the browser's address well. We can click to include citation information in the reference database of a reference manager that supports COinS (e.g., Zotero, Mendeley, Research Gate, etc.). In this book's completion, I have found COinS to be incredibly useful. It has saved me enormous amounts of time I would otherwise spent in a laborious, error-prone entry of citation information by hand. COinS is a win for citer and the citee (i.e., the people whose work is being cited—insuring that information concerning the work is complete and correct). COinS information is currently written in Microdata format.

➢ **vCard/hCard.** vCard[281] is a file format standard for the electronic exchange of business card information (i.e., the information found on a typical business card including name, contact information, picture portrait, etc.). "vCards are often attached to e-mail mes-

---

[276] http://en.wikipedia.org/wiki/Microdata_(HTML). For more technical detail, see http://www.w3.org/TR/microdata/, http://microformats.org/wiki/microdata and http://www.whatwg.org/specs/web-apps/current-work/multipage/microdata.html#microdata.

[277] http://en.wikipedia.org/wiki/Schema.org/ http://schema.org/.

[278] see http://schema.org/docs/schemas.html.

[279] Although the website expresses the intention to track RDFa and Microformats for possible support later (http://schema.org/docs/faq.html#14). See also documentation on Google's support for "rich snippets" (http://googlewebmastercentral.blogspot.com/2009/05/introducing-rich-snippets.html)—also expressed using Microdata format.

[280] http://ocoins.info/; see also http://en.wikipedia.org/wiki/COinS and http://epub.mimas.ac.uk/openurl/KEV_Guidelines-200706.html#sect5_4.

[281] http://tools.ietf.org/html/rfc6350.

sages, but can be exchanged in other ways, such as on the World Wide Web or instant messaging."[282] hCard is a microformat that is used to embed the structured property/value information of a vCard into a web page.[283]

RDFa, Microformats, Microdata—how do these in-line formats for the expression of meaning compare with one another? Which one(s) should we use? When? And how do these formats relate to the Semantic Web initiative? Are these new formats simply a pragmatic detour whose path ultimately leads back to the fulfillment of the visions originally expressed for the Semantic Web? Or do new formats presage a gradual abandonment of the Semantic Web?

These are all good questions to which only the briefest attention can be given here. In his careful comparison of the three formats, Manu Sporny[284] notes that only RDFa has a clear mapping to RDF.

Chris Sliver Smith[285] observes that "Microformats have been established the longest of the three protocols, and used by the search engines the longest. Google and Yahoo! both introduced hCard microformat on their own webpages by marking up local listings with it" and that "Microformat's initial advantage was that it worked seamlessly in existing HTML code, so using it within a page didn't require any special tags that might overly restrict one's version of HTML nor cause a page to be invalid code. The downside is that it primarily required using particular naming conventions of class attributes."

The use of Microformats and a need to support these will likely persist as long as there are still web pages written in HTML 3 or 4. But moving forward, the extensibility built into the design of the Microdata format and its place as part of the HTML5 standard would seem to position Microdata format as the successor to Microformats. For example, Google now recommends the Microdata format for the representation of "rich snippets" and other structured data[286] (although RDFa and Microformats are also supported).

Microdata appears also to be winning the "format battle" with RDFa. Jason Ronallo[287] notes, for example, that "Google has supported RDFa in some fashion since 2009, and over that time

[282] http://en.wikipedia.org/wiki/VCard.

[283] http://en.wikipedia.org/wiki/HCard, for a more technical description, see, http://microformats.org/wiki/hcard.

[284] "An Uber-comparison of RDFa, Microdata and Microformats, The Beautiful, Tormented Machine," http://manu.sporny.org/2011/uber-comparison-rdfa-md-uf/. See also http://en.wikipedia.org/wiki/Semantic_HTML http://programmers.stackexchange.com/questions/166612/schema-org-vs-microformats, http://blog.foolip.org/2009/08/23/microformats-vs-rdfa-vs-microdata/, http://ablognotlimited.com/articles/microformats-html5-microdata, http://stackoverflow.com/questions/14307792/what-is-the-relationship-between-rdf-rdfa-microformats-and-microdata, http://stackoverflow.com/questions/2986918/microformats-rdf-or-microdata, http://blog.teamtreehouse.com/writing-semantic-microformats-amp-microdata-in-html-markup and http://evan.prodromou.name/RDFa_vs_microformats. For a concise but incomplete history of microformats (as of my access on August 10, 2013, history stops at 2005) see http://microformats.org/wiki/history-of-microformats.

[285] http://www.semclubhouse.com/microformats-rdfa-or-micro-data/.

[286] https://support.google.com/webmasters/answer/99170.

[287] Ronallo, 2012.

has discovered a large error rate in the application of RDFa by Webmasters. Simplicity is a central reason for the development of Microdata and the search engines preferring it over RDFa."[288]

Even so, the format battles continue with the more recent introduction of "RDFa Lite."[289] Sporny argues that "RDFa Lite contains all of the simplicity of Microdata coupled with the extensibility of and compatibility with RDFa."[290] Others, however, point to problems inherent in RDF and the extreme ambiguities concerning how to "correctly" express meaning through RDF.[291] These problems persist no matter whether "a" or "a Lite" is appended.

Which format will win? Or will two or more coexist for better (we can choose) and worse (continued complexity and confusion concerning which to use)? Will the winning (surviving?) format(s) lie on a path toward eventual realization of the Semantic Web visions? Even in a book about "The Future" (of PIM) I won't hazard a prediction.

But we can speculate concerning how formats will be used and what this will mean for us. We take inspiration from growing list of schemas provided by schema.org (and supported by Bing, Google, and Yahoo) or we can consider the kinds of structured information we might work with following the hCard example.[292]

Web pages might embed structured information concerning calendar events (e.g., upcoming concerts, school plays, soccer matches, etc.), products such as palmtop devices (price, storage capacity, connectivity, etc.) and recipes (ingredients, preparation time, calories, etc.). We in turn could promote ourselves (e.g., on the job market or the "dating market") through the structured information we push (e.g., education, hobbies, job history, languages spoken, etc.).

And then we can consider some specific examples where a sharing of "meaning" (structured information, metadata) might bring real benefits:

> **Form filling.** We will own (P1) a "this is my life" resume of structured information to represent job history, credit card information, hobbies, preferences, family background, medical history, etc. Information can be structured according to shared standards (e.g., an elaborated version of the "person" schema of schema.org or the hResume microformat[293]).

---

[288] Read "The New York Times Blunders Into Linked Data, Pillages Freebase and DBPedia" (http://go-to-hell-man.blogspot.com/2009/10/new-york-times-blunders-into-linked.html) for an example of the "wrong" use of RDF. The article also illustrates the intricacies of RDF and imparts, I think, a greater understanding for how easily mistakes can be made in its use.

[289] http://www.w3.org/TR/rdfa-lite/.

[290] http://manu.sporny.org/2012/mythical-differences/.

[291] See, for example, the series of posts by Vuk Miličić (http://milicicvuk.com/blog/2011/07/19/ultimate-problem-of-rdf-and-semantic-web/, http://milicicvuk.com/blog/2011/07/21/problems-of-the-rdf-syntax/, http://milicicvuk.com/blog/2011/07/16/problems-of-the-rdf-model-literals/).

[292] http://en.wikipedia.org/wiki/HCard. See for example, the listing of "Specific Microformats" at http://en.wikipedia.org/wiki/Microformat#Specific_microformats.

[293] See http://schema.org/Person and http://en.wikipedia.org/wiki/HResume, respectively.

If the standard is widely supported, we have greater freedom to switch between services such as Amazon or Expedia, knowing that the same information can be used and that we don't need to do a time-consuming (and error-prone) re-entry of information. More generally, the completion of all manner of forms—for travel reimbursement, medical claims, job applications, etc.—should become much faster, easier, and less prone to error. We can push updates concerning our status to others who maintain information about us (**P2**). We can push information about ourselves out to others (**P4**) in ways that more clearly establish our relevance (e.g., to a prospective employer).

We're also more likely to take the time to get the information right (or at least right for us and our aims), knowing that we need do so only once. This information is selectively, securely communicated to others on a need to know basis. Obviously, this information is extremely personal so it is good that it is under our "lock and key."

➢ **Bidding for us and our resources (money, time).** We can expect searches for relevant information (P6), especially for goods and services, to be much more effective. Meaning expressed through structure (metadata) will support searches for relevant information that are more precise ("only hotels within a mile of the convention center please and under $200 per night"). Just as important, shared meaning (e.g., of and through attributes like "price," "bed type," "on site fitness center") will give us a basis for making sense of the results returned. We can elect to display and sort by attributes that help us to compare and contrast the results returned. Using the search for an airplane flight as an example, we might elect to display cost, date, travel time, number of plane changes, for the flights that are returned by a search.

Different from today's support through services such as Expedia and Kayak is the possibility to pick and choose for different components to a search. Pick one application for assistance in the specification of the query; pick another for the actual completion of the search; and pick a third for results display. For example, I really like the results display provided by Hipmunk. If only I could combine with a search (or searches) that returned the best possible matches for my query.

Shared meaning though structured information gives us a basis for issuing our own personal advertisements or our own "contracts" for bidding. We might post (**P4**) our interest in planning a vacation for "sometime in June" with appropriate restrictions for total cost, duration, location, etc. Let providers bid for the money we're willing to spend. Have all bids organized into a spreadsheet for display and sorting by the features we care about.

As we considered the personal potential of shared structure at the start of this section, we drew inspiration from the vision of the Semantic Web. The Semantic Web is envisioned as a structured expression of meaning—for nearly everything of interest—to be shared globally between machines as well as people. What could the realization, if only partial, of the Semantic Web vision mean for each of us in our personal practices of PIM? Scenarios described "agents" operating on our behalf and capable of doing a wide range of things to make our lives easier, more productive, and—dare we say?—happier.

But the path toward fulfillment of the Semantic Web has been anything but straight. Detours have brought us to Microdata and RDFa Lite as the likely the top two formats, moving forward, for the structured representation of meaning. Whether these detours eventually lead back to a fulfillment of the Semantic Web is not clear.

Experiences so far would seem, at the very least, to challenge the notion that meaning can be simply expressed as RDF subject-predicate-object triples or that these triples can be meaningfully shared—whether between people or computer-based applications—absent the sharing of a larger context. We note, for example, that the successes listed above for sharing of structured information—schema.org, COinS, and vCard/hCard—each depend critically upon the use of schemas.

Schemas express expected attributes, their names and the types of values these attributes can be assigned. A schema establishes a namespace—"title" in the context of vCard means something distinctly different than "title" in the context of COinS bibliographic reference. Schemas establish a grouping for attribute/value pairs and so a subject for these pairs. In the context of such a grouping we can meaningfully generate RDF triples, i.e., attribute/value pairs of a grouping are each "about" the same entity (e.g., the person described in a vCard or the bibliographic reference described via COinS).

But micro-expressions of structured information for events, personal contacts, bibliographic references and so on fall far short of grand unifications envisioned in the context of the Semantic Web. More important for our purposes, these tell only part of the story for the personal potential of shared structure.

What's left to consider?

8.2.5   PERSONAL POTENTIAL REVISITED: THE MEANINGFUL SHARING OF STRUCTURE

We've considered the sharing of meaning through "micro" structure as expressed through subject-predicate-object triples or, alternatively, as attribute/value pairs in the larger context of a grouping to establish "subject."

But much of the information we work with resists such a fine level of structuring. What matters, instead, is a more "macro" level of structuring. We need to organize our information so that, as we work to complete a task or make a decision, the information we need is all in one place. (See the "Taking back our information, #1" inset with its discussion of the grouping item.)

In considering a macro vs. micro level of structuring we distinguish between the "sharing of meaning through structure" (in the spirit of RDF, for example) and the "meaningful (useful) sharing of structure." At a macro level, computers can help us to share structure through, for example, search and social media support but may not need to "know" much about meaning in order to provide this support—any more than, for example, Google, Bing, or Yahoo! search needs to "understand" a web page in order to give us fast access via a standard keyword search.

What are these macro structures? And what personal benefits can we realize as these structures are shared—whether between the applications we use, among the people in our lives or with ourselves over time?

A review of macro structures we might potentially share and the benefits of doing so can be organized by one of the two yardsticks we've been using to assess PIM—the six senses in which information can be personal. We'll start with the sixth and work our way backward.

P6, information that is relevant to a current or future need. How can the sharing of structure help us with the information in this "6th sense" of the personal? **P6** comes from a variety of sources but it's easiest to think of **P6** in the context of our search for information on the Web. An intriguing finding by Qu and Furnas[294] is that our searches on the Web are often more for structure, e.g., in the form of definitive, well-organized articles, than it is for mere "bags of facts." Subsequent searches are then often guided by the structure extracted from such an article.

Those of us who have, at one time or another, been given the task of writing on a topic—especially one with which we are not familiar—can surely relate to this finding. We often look for a good, well-cited (or "well-linked") review on the topic. The headings and subheadings of a review article may then each be the basis for follow-on searches. These may also (with some modification by us) form the outline of our own report and also the structure that we use to organize search results we wish to keep.

If structure, more than content, is sometimes the object of a search, what implications can we draw? Search services might, at least as an option, rank matching items higher if their internal structure is more elaborated. Beyond this, couldn't the structure (especially as expressed in the HTML/XHTML) be extracted as first class to be used in its own right as part of our own organization of information and also (with attribution and modified to meet our needs) as part of the structure of our own report?

P5, the information experienced by us. I happened to sit on a plane about a year ago next to a woman in her 90s who had been a dancer at the Latin Quarter[295] in New York City during World War II. She had fascinating stories to tell. But I've forgotten their details… and her name. If only I'd written the details of my encounter down while these were still fresh in my mind. How many of us wish we were more disciplined about keeping a diary or a journal? Yet we never seem to

---

[294] Qu & Furnas, 2005, 2008.
[295] http://en.wikipedia.org/wiki/Latin_Quarter_(nightclub).

find the time. Part of the problem in a digital age of information is that we're not sure where to put our reflections. In a special-purpose "digital diary" app? Which one would we trust? On Facebook? Many of us may not want to be that public with our personal thoughts and reflections.

We may be more inclined to record our daily experiences—our stories—if these can serve not only as content but also as enhancement to shared structures with multiple uses:

- Stories might be told as an overlay to the item event log.[296]

- Stories might in particular be a way of organizing the pictures we take.

- Stories are a framework in which to weave in additional information—our thoughts, to-dos, or links to additional information (to the Wikipedia article on the Latin Quarter for example).

We often tell our stories with different audiences in mind. Some stories are told for our bridge or poker buddies. Or the members of our book club. Others may be told for colleagues at work. Still others are told for our children or our spouses.

Stories linked to our intended audiences on the one hand and to pictures and video clips on the other may provide a more solid basis (structure) for sharing. Many of us are unsure what to do with our pictures. Or with whom these should be shared. Sharing individual pictures can be something of a mish mash anyway. Stories provide a basis for organizing pictures and other information items (e.g., videos, web page links) and for systematically sharing these. ("that's a story I'll tell only my spouse;" "this is a story I'll tell my friends and colleagues[297]").

An intriguing thought behind the sharing of structure in these examples is that we might be better about keeping a diary and better about being more organized in general if only we could get more leverage from our efforts. Even the busiest of us might invest the time in structures for our information if only these could be shared more widely (with our applications and with other people) and used in more ways.

P4, the information we share with others. As we share our experiences with others, we move from **P5** to **P4** (information sent to/shared with others). Shared structure for **P4** information can come in forms other than a story. The classic is the structure of a resume. A search for "resume templates" returns many useful links.

But increasingly the information we use to sell ourselves and our services persists on the Web. We use principles of SEO to draw people to our site. Shared structure now comes in the form of templates we might use to improve the attractiveness of our site and its ranking in search results

---

[296] As discussed in the section on saving and also in Chapter 3 of Part 1 to this book.

[297] Selective sharing in this manner might use features of existing services such as Google+ (e.g., "circles") and Facebook (e.g., "friend lists") (See for example, http://timwhitlock.info/blog/2011/08/circles-vs-friend-lists/, http://www.webpronews.com/facebook-sharing-2011-08, http://www.zdnet.com/blog/facebook/facebook-engineers-bring-google-circles-to-facebook/1885, and http://www.googleplusdaily.com/2013/02/differences-google-plus-facebook.html#.UgfR2ZK1GSo)

(for the search phrases we target). Also, shared structure may come in the form of standard layouts for the web pages on our site so that visitors, familiar with the standard, can more quickly find the information they seek. (We don't want visitors to "time out" on our sites in frustration for not being able to find what they're looking for.)

P3, information directed to us from others. In the chapter on technologies to search we considered the potential for a filtering of incoming information directed our way from others (**P3**) and, more generally, the information we experience (**P5**). This is done via situated searches—searches that are placed in association with a folder (or tag or other grouping item) that represents a project or area of interest for which the search is tuned to return relevant results. But how are these folders organized? And what might the folders and their organization say about the diet of information we receive? Are we getting a balance of information and viewpoints on controversial topics? Is the information we receive on professional matters balanced by information relating to finances? Fun things? Family? We can imagine sharing template structures (and supporting applications) that help us to achieve a greater balance. Working through the structures we use and the information so organized, a "Work-life balance" application might give us an assessment concerning the "weight" of information under different branches of the tree (e.g., for work, play, family, friends, community involvement, etc.).

P2, information about us (especially as kept by others). Structure in the case of **P2** information might help us most by simply giving us an overview of all the different people and organizations that keep information about us and the members of our family. Such as structure might include categories for finances (income and expenses), legal, school/academics (for us or our children), and medical (for us and each member of our family).

P1, the information we own. Shared structure as applied to the information we own (and is under our control) might come in the form of "Getting Organized" templates.[298] Also, as structure is given first class treatment, we can expect that any number of websites might provide structure for us to copy and paste as a local structure (realized by folders or otherwise) that we can apply to our own information. This was the possibility discussed above for **P6** information and so now we've come full-circle—from information relevant to us to information we own. The structures we extract can be made ours to manage our information.

Consider, for example, a small sampling of many "how to" sites available now and providing a range of step-by-step procedures:

- How to get into a top college or university[299]

- How to buy a house[300]

---

[298] See for example, http://www.howtogeek.com/howto/15677/zen-and-the-art-of-file-and-folder-organization/ and http://www.pcmag.com/article2/0,2817,2385612,00.asp.

[299] http://www.ehow.com/how_138030_top-college-university.html.

[300] http://michaelbluejay.com/house/index.html.

- (So you wanna) run a marathon?[301]

- How to get a job[302]

Each comes with a structured set of steps (and sub-steps and even sub-sub-steps). This structure has value not only as breakdown (decomposition) of a procedure into manageable steps, but also as a way of organizing the information we collect or generate along the way toward our own personal fulfillment of a goal. A step toward buying a house, for example, is often to find a lender. This step can do double duty as a grouping item (such as a folder) in which to place lender information and paperwork associated with the loan application.

More generally, **P1** is where we bring together the information that is personal to us across all the senses of personal. If information content is stored elsewhere and not under our control then at least the links to this information can be kept locally for our awareness. And the structures we impose can be local to be viewed and worked upon through tools that work with structure.[303]

Summarizing this section we can say that the personal potential of shared structure (and the information content so structured) is considerable. Shared "micro"-structures can greatly improve the ease and accuracy in the exchange of information about events, bibliographic references, and people. Micro-structures can form the basis of persistent queries or, alternatively, "requests for bid" made available on the Web to providers of goods and services. Micro-structures can also help us to organize the results that come back. Key to the useful sharing of microstructures, however, is also a sharing of associated schemas and namespaces to avoid inconsistencies and "collisions" in the use of names (for attributes and predicates).

Shared macro-structures—whether in the form of stories told, step-by-step "how to" guides, comprehensive reviews, personal SEO templates, or systems of personal organization—have the potential to help us with our information, in each of the six senses in which our information is personal.

But this section, especially in its review of the troubles with the Semantic Web, also points to several caveats and considerations we need to be aware of as we use and share information structure. These are discussed in the next section.

---

[301] http://www.soyouwanna.com/site/syws/marathon/marathon.html.

[302] http://jobsearch.about.com/od/findajob/tp/tensteps.htm.

[303] As we invest more in the structuring of our information we may find application from tools such as IMapping (http://semanticweb.org/wiki/IMapping) which were originally developed in the context of research connected to the Semantic Web initiative.

Taking back our information, #3. Representations of structure that are tool independent and also tool-accommodating.

In order to take back our information, we need, first and foremost, to take back our information structures: Reclaim our structures and the content will follow. This is done by giving structures—especially those defined through various forms of the grouping item—a first-class representation. A first-class representation of structure is one that is:

1. Tool-independent but also

2. Tool-accommodating, i.e., representations need to provide room for different applications to work with a structure, each in its own way and to persist relevant data.

In this special insert, we consider how representations can be both tool-independent and tool-accommodating through use of an XML schema called "XooML."[304] For a complete definition of the current version visit the keepingfoundthingsfound.com website.[305] XooML has also been described in several papers.[306]

The following things are true for XooML and the XooML approach:[307]

➤ **XooML is a simple application of XML.** We chose XML over reasonable alternatives such as JSON and RDF for two basic reasons:

○ We like the "document focus" of XML. Documents are assembled from XML fragments (e.g., conforming to the XooML schema). Digital documents displayed online can provide a dynamic, interactive surface for our interactions with information. Document = application. In the spirit of HTML5 any web page can be considered to both a document and an application.

○ XML supports namespaces and, most important, does so in a decentralized way (no central registry). Namespaces are key if the representation of structure is to be tool-accommodating.[308]

[304] XooML (pronounced "zoom'l") stands for Cross (X) Tool Mark-up Language. XooML was briefly discussed in this book in Chapter 4 (Part 1, in section 4.1, see especially Figure 4.2).

[305] http://keepingfoundthingsfound.com/xooml.

[306] William Jones, Anderson, & Whittaker, 2012; William Jones & Anderson, 2011; William Jones, 2011.

[307] People involved in the development of XooML and related work over the years include: Dawei Hou, Deen Sethanandha, Sheng Bi, Zhiyong Xie, Jasper Bleijs, Lizhang Sun and Cody Stebbins.

[308] We do use JSON for the communication of information to and from applications that use XooML. There has been discussion over the years about introducing namespace conventions to JSON. If this occurs, we may consider a XooML-approach using JSON. For more on the discussion to support namespaces in JSON see http://davidchuprogramming.blogspot.com/2011/10/jsonnet-issue-does-not-support.html, https://www.p6r.com/articles/2010/04/05/xml-to-json-and-back/, http://www.mnot.net/blog/2011/10/12/thinking_about_namespaces_in_json.

➢ **Focus is on the grouping item,** as described in previous insets. A given XooML fragment models the simple node + outgoing-link structure of a grouping item. In recent work, we've focused especially on file folders but XooML can be used to represent the structure of any form of grouping item (e.g., tags, "albums" of pictures, "notebooks" of notes, and so on).

➢ **Structures are "mirrored" for first-class treatment.** A critical principle of the XooML approach is that people shouldn't have to change and their information shouldn't have to move in order for structures to become first class. We may rather like the folders, tags, albums, notebooks, etc., that we have or, at least, we may have gotten accustomed to using them. Mirroring is done via *itemMirror* drivers. Drivers, running from the client side, all work according to a single *itemMirror* object model but these vary on their "back end" depending upon the *storing application* and the API it supports for access to the grouping item (e.g., various Windows APIs, various Mac OS APIs, Graph API, the Dropbox API, POSIX, RESTful APIs, etc.). *itemMirror*—the object model, drivers, and overall approach in relation to XooML—is further described in the next insert.

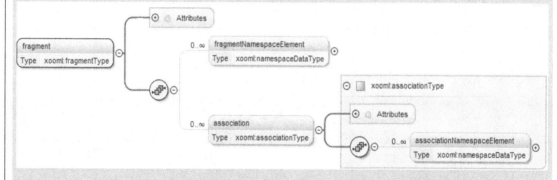

Figure 8.3: A XooML schema provides for a tool-independent representation of the structure of a grouping item as a fragment (node) plus 0 or more associations (links). XooML is also tool-accommodating through the provision for NamespaceElements. An application can store data specific to its work with the structure within namespace elements—both at the fragment level and for each association of a fragment.

The "essentials" of the XooML schema are depicted in Figure 8.3. A fragment, representing the node-link structure of a grouping item, consists of:

➢ tool-independent (fragment common) attributes +

➢ zero or more tool-accommodating (fragment namespace) elements +

➤ zero or more associations

This pattern partially repeats for each association which also consists of:

➤ tool-independent (association common) attributes +

➤ zero or more tool-accommodating (association namespace) elements

The schema supports a representation of structure that is both:

➤ **Tool-independent**—a fragment (node) can have zero or more associations (links) and

➤ **Tool-accommodating**[309]—at both the fragment level and the level of each association, "XooML-speaking" applications can store data specific to their work with the structure within namespace elements.[310]

A few variations in the use of XooML are worth noting:

1. **Support a metadata standard.** A collection of applications might all work with the information in a namespace element. For example, applications self-described as supporting Dublin Core might each work with elements (at both the fragment and association levels) accordingly identified (e.g., xmlns:dc="http://purl.org/dc/elements/1.1/"). Other tools might work with iCalendar namespace bundles (e.g., with xmlns:ic="urn:ietf:params:xml:ns:icalendar-2.0").

---

[309] The "tool-accommodating" extensions provided for in the XooML schema (as namespace elements) are designed to make it possible for any number of applications to work with the same structure. The more applications that can do so, the more "first class" the representation of structure. But there is a more basic reason to provide for application-specific namespace elements (at both the level of a fragment and at the level of an association): There always will be an aspect of our information interaction that is dependent upon and fundamentally intertwined with the specific tools that we use. Furthermore, this tool-dependent aspect of the information interaction cannot be fully explicated in a way that allows for its preservation separate from the tools.

[310] Namespace elements are uniquely identified via a URI (assigned as the value of the xmlns attribute). For more on namespace conventions of XML see http://www.w3schools.com/xml/xml_namespaces.asp (for a tutorial), http://stackoverflow.com/questions/1181888/what-does-xmlns-in-xml-mean (for some nice examples of use), http://www.w3.org/TR/REC-xml-names/ (for W3C definitive source), and http://www.ibm.com/developerworks/xml/library/x-nmspace.html (for a detailed developer-centered but very accessible overview). We might say that through the data stored in namespace elements (as interpreted by the application),the grouping item (or any of its associations) can differential in the manner of stem cells to assume the behavior of different item types such as to-dos, appointments, contacts, references, etc. This is the notion of "notions" as described in Chapter 4 (Part 1, "Sometimes a small notion"). Alternatively, namespace elements can be seen to provide a basis for flexible use of many different schemas as argued for by Karger (http://haystack.csail.mit.edu/blog/2013/06/05/keynote-at-the-european-semantic-web-conference-part-1-the-state-of-end-user-information-management/, http://haystack.csail.mit.edu/blog/2013/06/06/keynote-at-eswc-part-2-how-the-semantic-web-can-help-end-users/).

2. **Make bibliographic references, tasks, and to-dos.** As an extension to variation #1, namespace sub-elements needn't be restricted just to "surface" information for display (e.g., position, color, shape, etc.). Elements can contain information needed for an association or a fragment to work (appear and behave) as a task, an appointment, a bibliographic reference, etc.[311] For example, an iCalendar attribute bundle could provide the necessary data for a fragment or an association to behave as an event (ic:vevent) or a "to-do" (ic:vtodo).

3. **Use associations or whole fragments?** As #2 suggests, the namespace bundle needed to make an association work in a special way (e.g., as a task, an appointment, a reference, etc.) could just as easily be placed at the level of the fragment as a whole. Fragment or association? The answer depends upon whether we wish for the "thing" involved to behave as a grouping item in its own right—i.e., capable of linking to other items and, in turn, capable of being linked to.[312]

4. **Support RDF.** Namespace bundles can also be used in support of RDF (i.e., using namespaces with the following assignment: xmlns:rdf="http://www.w3.org/1999/02/22-rdf-syntax-ns#"). The grouping item mirrored might then serve to group together SPO triples pertaining to the same subject.

5. **Represent a multidigraph.** Fragments as nodes, link one to another via an association attribute, associatedXooMLFragment (an association-common attribute). Two or more associations of a fragment can link to the same fragment or even to the fragment itself. As such, fragments in aggregate have the flexibility to represent a multiple digraph or

---

[311] We might say that through the data stored in namespace elements (as interpreted by the application), the grouping item (or any of its associations) can differential in the manner of stem cells to assume the behavior of different item types such as to-dos, appointments, contacts, references, etc. This is the notion of "notions" as described in Chapter 4 (Part 1, "Sometimes a small notion"). Alternatively, namespace elements can be seen to provide a basis for flexible use of many different schemas as argued for by Karger (http://haystack.csail.mit.edu/blog/2013/06/05/keynote-at-the-european-semantic-web-conference-part-1-the-state-of-end-user-information-management/, http://haystack.csail.mit.edu/blog/2013/06/06/keynote-at-eswc-part-2-how-the-semantic-web-can-help-end-users/).

[312] In this respect, folders as a grouping item are especially plastic. Given the right information within its associated XooML.xml file (in namespace elements), a folder can be made to appear in many different ways.

multidigraph.[313] XooML has the flexibility needed, for example, to model the hyperlink structure of the Web as a whole.

6. **Represent a hypergraph.**[314] In example #4 and with reference to graph theory, an association is an edge (link) with three vertices (nodes): one each for the subject, predicate, and object of the proposition. More generally, an association, through the additional attributes of a namespace element, can link to any number of nodes.

In the XooML approach, our information stays where it is. Leave the information organized into the folders of our local file system or the synchronized folders of a web-based storing application like Dropbox. Leave the information in the albums of Facebook or the notes of Evernote or the tasks of Remember The Milk. XooML-speaking applications work with our information "as is" via APIs supported by the storing applications (i.e., the applications through which the information is currently stored).

The XooML approach doesn't presume that these existing applications will (ever) change. Nor does it presume that we will ever move our information from these applications. Nor does XooML's success depend upon the adoption of new standards or the dominance of some new unifying storage "vault." The XooML approach allows, instead, for an incremental approach in which integration happens through the supported APIs of existing applications and through a gradual accumulation of XooML-speaking apps built or retrofitted to "speak XooML" in order to work with our information through these existing applications.

But how? How can apps be built or modified to speak XooML... correctly? clearly? consistently? And how much work are XooML-speaking apps required to invest in order to speak not only XooML but also the API of a storing application? The answer, in short, is "not much." But this is a topic for the next inset in this "Taking back our information" series.

---

[313] For more on multidigraphs see http://en.wiktionary.org/wiki/multidigraph (for simple definition), http://networkx.github.io/documentation/latest/reference/classes.multidigraph.html (for more formal definition) or http://en.wikipedia.org/wiki/Multigraph#Directed_multigraph_.28edges_without_own_identity.29 (for a nice explanation for how multidigraphs relate to other graph forms). Or, for even more on graph theory, try Bollobas, Bela; Modern Graph Theory, Springer; 1st edition (August 12, 2002). ISBN 0-387-98488-7. XooML is simple but extremely flexible as a means for representing structure. However, in the context of graph theory, its flexibility is not without limit. We note, for example, that XooML is not well-suited to represent undirected multigraphs nor, equivalently, to represent a graph in which links are bi-directional. On the other hand, efforts over the years to support bi-directional links in hypertexts (e.g., Project Xanadu, http://en.wikipedia.org/wiki/Project_Xanadu) have had difficulty gaining widespread adoption whereas the very distributed, decentralized Web, even with its one-way hyperlinks that frequently break ("404 Not Found") is succeeding brilliantly.

[314] For more on hypergraphs see http://mathworld.wolfram.com/Hypergraph.html (for simple definition) or http://en.wikipedia.org/wiki/Hypergraph (for more elaborate explanation and references).

8.3　CAVEATS AND CONSIDERATIONS

Following the structure of chapters for saving and searching, this section would be titled "Caveats and disclaimers." But we've considered a number of disclaimers already in the context of the chapter's review of the Semantic Web. In short: The grand vision of the Semantic Web as a global, interconnected, machine-readable representation of meaning may never be realized nor efforts to extend the Semantic Web into the realm of PIM.

If some form of a grand integrative representation of structure for meaning is eventually realized, it will most likely happen from the ground up. Efforts to represent structured information, in-line in the HTML/XHTML representation of web pages, and to share this information, have been successful and have proven very useful. Whether these islands of structure—for contact information, bibliographic references, events and so on—are eventually linked into larger, grander representations of meaning remains to be seen.

This section keeps a focus on caveats (warnings, concerns, exceptions). But then, in a more constructive vein, caveats are grouped by considerations that apply to any initiative to make more effective use of information structure—whether the initiative is grand and global or limited and local (as in "I need a better system for organizing my stuff").

8.3.1　CONSIDERATION #1: WHAT IS THE SMALLEST UNIT FOR A "MEANINGFUL" SHARING OF STRUCTURE?

Efforts to share meaning in structure can occur at two distinctly different levels. Call these:

➢ An "**atomic**" level in the form of the beguilingly simple subject-predicate-object (SPO) triples of RDF.

➢ A "**molecular**" level in "micro"-nuggets of information conforming to a schema such as the contact information of a vCard/hCard, the bibliographic information of a COinS citation or the "events," "organizations," "people," etc., as specified through schema.org.

There is a seemingly similar question to that of Consideration #1: What is the smallest unit for the structured representation of meaning? But this question is actually quite different and out of scope for a proper treatment here. The answer to this second question may very well be 3-tuple of a SPO statement as represented through RDF. But some might argue that our "atoms" for the representation of meaning through structure need to be larger or that, conversely, they might be smaller still—i.e., that we might possibly create a structured representation of meaning out of 2-tuples (pairs).

The question of Consideration #1 is what is the smallest unit that can be meaningfully shared, amongst ourselves and with our applications? In his blog post "The Ultimate Problem of

RDF and the Semantic Web,"[315] Vuk Miličić contests the frequent characterization that "RDF is just triples" as an "illusion." But RDF is, at its essence, an expression of information in simple subject-predicate-object statements, i.e., as SPO triples. *Triples* are the unit for the expression of meaning. The illusion then may be in ever thinking we can infer or share meaning at the level of the SPO triple.

An example illustrates. If I happen across the statement "John's cell phone number is +1 888-888-8888" then, even if "+1 888-888-8888" is a perfectly working phone number and even if I'm clear which John is being referred to (in an actual RDF statement, "John" would be identified by a URI), I might still have questions. When was this statement made? By whom? Based on what? A reliable source or my own scribbles hurriedly made on a scrap of paper? Sure, I could give the number a try anyway. But what if this is no longer John's number? What if the number has been assigned to someone else who happens to be in a different time zone? (This actually happened to me once. I found myself making apologies to a groggy, irritated stranger.)

The questions above are meant to elicit metadata (data about data, information about information) concerning the statement's *provenance*.[316] We rarely take a statement at face value in our daily lives. We want to know who is making the statement. When? Where? From the answers we can make a judgment about the statement's current validity. A forecast of "rain today" may no longer be valid if it turns out that the forecast was made last week (unless, perhaps, if the forecast was made for Seattle in the wintertime).

And what happens if two statements conflict with one another as when we have two statements concerning John's current telephone number? Do we compare metadata statements of provenance associated with each? But then, what about the metadata provenance of these metadata statements? Statements concerning when a statement was made, where, and by whom, are themselves subject to the same questions of provenance.

In simple cases where a "micro" chunk of structured information is communicated in-line, we're spared infinite regress by making reasonable assumptions. If we trust what we see in a web page's display, for example, we're also inclined to trust the structured information within. This isn't foolproof. But the assumption mostly works. We trust the hCard information we get through a person's website. We trust the COinS information that comes from a publication database or a researcher's site with its "list of publications." If a website is masquerading as that for a person or an academic institution, that is another matter entirely. More likely is that the micro-information is improperly formatted or out of date or that content for visible web content was updated but not the micro-information. Cross-checking and sanity checking are always advised. Reasoning "outside" the space of information, we might say, for example, "this can't be her current email

---

[315] http://milicicvuk.com/blog/2011/07/19/ultimate-problem-of-rdf-and-semantic-web/.

[316] "From French provenance ('origin'), from Middle French provenant, present participle of provenir ('come forth, arise'), from Latin provenio ('to come forth')." (http://en.wiktionary.org/wiki/provenance) as in the source of an artifact (e.g., place, time or history of "ownership").

address—I got a message from her sent via another email address. I wonder if the rest of the information is wrong too?"

For some formats and facilities, updates and provenance are built in. The vCard we have may be out of date but we might be able to query SOURCE to get an updated copy. Wikis provide information concerning provenance in the form of a revision history. Increasingly, we should expect (insist) that the information we work with includes at least minimal information concerning the who, when, and where of its origin and possibly including an "expiration date."[317]

In the meaningful sharing of structure, we need to work at a "molecular" level where the sharing is not of just one but of a constellation of interrelated, schema-conforming, namespace-qualified statements. The individual statements including statements of provenance, might themselves be fully expressed in RDF (or not). But the sharing is of a grouping of statements.

We also note that making statements of provenance in RDF about a statement requires a reification of the statement, i.e., the statement is given its own URI and statements of provenance refer to the statement via its URI.[318]

Reification in RDF is needed not just for statements of provenance but even to represent simple sentences such as "John gave Mary the book." We might, for example, assign a URI to the SPO triple representing that "John gave the book" and then address this statement through its URI as an object in its own right to add that "Mary is recipient" (of the act of John's giving the book).

Why bother? Well, if I want the book it matters. But then provenance also matters. If John has lent the book out on several occasions I want to be sure that the statement "John gave Mary the book" represents the current state of affairs.

Needless to say, RDF expressions, no matter how these are serialized, can get quite involved (and difficult for people to read). Source code is also hard for people to read, the rejoinder might be, and even more so compiled code. But then a counter (to this counter) is that some readability and an ability to edit directly (e.g., in a plain text editor) was a key part of the success of HTML and may be so as well in efforts toward the representation and sharing of meaning on the Web.

Levels of meaningful sharing and issues of provenance are not just the province of researchers working on the Semantic Web. We encounter a variation of the problem of provenance whenever we come across a document such as "Very important marketing report, Final Version." "Final version"? Really? We're wise to take such a statement with a few grains of salt. We're more confident that the document really is the final version if we're able view its entry in the context of a folder listing all versions of the document, sorted by "last modified."

---

[317] For discussions of an expiration date for information see, for example, http://bigthink.com/videos/should-information-have-an-expiration-date and http://sloanreview.mit.edu/article/should-information-have-an-expiration-date/.

[318] For more about the use of reification and issues of provenance for RDF statements see (Dividino, Sizov, Staab, & Schueler, 2009; Hartig, 2009; Jensen et al., 2010).

8.3.2 CONSIDERATION #2: HOW MUCH MEANING CAN BE SHARED (RELIABLY, USEFULLY) THROUGH STRUCTURE?

The question of Consideration #2 points to the heart of discussions concerning the relative merits of *ontologies* vs. *taxonomies*. What's the difference?[319]

Let's start with origins and definitions:

➤ **Ontology.** "Originally Latin **ontologia** (1606, Ogdoas Scholastica, by Jacob Lorhard (Lorhardus)), from Ancient Greek ὤν ('on'), present participle of εἰμί ('being, existing, essence') + λόγος (logos, 'account').[320]

The modern general meaning closest to our purposes is "The science or study of being; that branch of metaphysics concerned with the nature or essence of being or existence."[321]

➤ **Taxonomy.** "It derives from the French **taxonomie** coined from the Greek words **taxis** (τάξις; order, arrangement) + **-nomia** (method) from **-nomos** (νόμος; managing, law) from **nemein** (manage, distribute, put in order)."[322]

The modern general meaning closest to our purpose is "Classification, esp. in relation to its general laws or principles."[323]

Ontologies are often thought to trump taxonomies in a manner similar to the way "knowledge" is often considered by some to be a stronger playing card than "information." In the case of knowledge vs. information, why wouldn't we want to manage knowledge representing, for example, expertise in an area, rather than mere information? (Or, even better, why not some kind of "mind meld"?) Likewise, in the contrast between ontologies and taxonomies, isn't it better to represent the "nature of essence" rather merely to classify?

---

[319] A distinction is also often made between "classification" (i.e., a classification scheme) and "taxonomy" especially in the field of library and information science. See, for example, http://www.aiim.org/community/wiki/view/Classification-and-Taxonomy. What's the difference? I found especially helpful the blog post by Heather Hedden, author of *The Accidental Taxonomist*, in which she reviews distinction between uses of the two terms and summarizes: "Classification is for: where to put things/where does this document or item go. Taxonomy is for: how to describe content/what is this text, image, or other media about". By this distinction we might say that a file system is a classification whereas a system of tagging is a taxonomy. However, as soon as we introduce the support for shortcuts ("aliases", "links") to a file system, however poorly supported, we also introduce the possible use of a folder to "tag" (via shortcut) a file or folder that is not strictly "contained" under the folder—and, so, by Hedden's distinction, a folder structure can become a taxonomy.

[320] http://en.wiktionary.org/wiki/ontology.

[321] http://www.oed.com/view/Entry/131551?redirectedFrom=ontology#eid.

[322] http://ewonago.wordpress.com/tag/etymology-of-taxonomy/.

[323] http://www.oed.com/view/Entry/198305?redirectedFrom=taxonomy#eid.

If only we could. But we can't. Elsewhere, I argue that information is a thing to be managed.[324] Knowledge, by contrast, is "information in action"—to be inferred from actions and behavior—ours or an organization's. In the other direction, we acquire new knowledge for an area through a process of *instillation* rather than "installation," i.e., we learn. The information we experience must be made sense of, internalized, and integrated with the knowledge already in our heads. No such thing as a "mind meld."

All of our efforts to "capture" knowledge and to express as a thing in its own right produce information instead, albeit often in a more complicated form that is more difficult for us to understand and maintain. And then, even so, the information so rendered may not be all that consistently understandable by our computing applications either (for reasons discussed in the previous section).

But the analogy that ontologies are to taxonomies as knowledge is to information is imperfect. I'm not a philosopher and this is not the place anyway to deal with questions concerning the differences between *ontology* and *epistemology*.[325] Suffice it only to say that "ontology" as used in an informational, computational context[326] is quite different from its use in philosophy.

In an informational context, efforts to produce either an "ontology" or a "taxonomy" result in external expressions of an internal understanding, i.e., information representing knowledge. Guarino et al. note that "The backbone of an ontology consists of a generalization/specialization hierarchy of concepts, i.e., a taxonomy."[327]

But then, with some rough connection to the philosophical roots of ontology, we can agree that an ontology in an information context should, somehow, be "more" than a taxonomy, i.e., the aims behind the creation of an ontology are more ambitious and there is an attempt to convey more meaning in the structure of an ontology, in contrast to the structure of a taxonomy.

What then is an ontology that makes it "more" than a taxonomy?

A taxonomic structure is often a hierarchy or rooted tree[328] (i.e., where, informally, every node—taxon, category—except for the root has exactly one parent.[329] But this is not a restriction. We can allow for the possibility that an information item, for example, can be "classified" in more than one way. We do so when we apply more than one tag to an item or—if folders are used instead as the grouping item—when we place link (e.g., via a "shortcut" or "alias") to an item that isn't "contained" within the folder.

---

[324] See "No knowledge but through information" (William Jones, 2010). We often hear discussions of data, information, knowledge and even "wisdom". But how do these terms relate? Simply put, we might say that information is data "in motion" (i.e. communicated to someone). Knowledge then, is information "in action" (i.e. apparent only indirectly through its impact on behavior). And then, wisdom is knowledge "in perspective" (to know, for example, the limits of our knowledge).

[325] But for a reasonably accessible discussion see http://ethicalpolitics.org/seminars/neville.htm; see also the Wikipedia articles on each, http://en.wikipedia.org/wiki/Ontology and http://en.wikipedia.org/wiki/Epistemology.

[326] See http://en.wikipedia.org/wiki/Ontology_(information_science)#cite_note-50.

[327] Guarino, Oberle, & Staab, 2009.

[328] http://en.wikipedia.org/wiki/Rooted_tree#rooted_tree.

[329] See, for example, the discussion at http://en.wikipedia.org/wiki/Taxonomy_(general)#cite_note-5.

What then, distinguishes an ontology from a taxonomy?

Gruber, a well-cited authority on ontologies, offers the following definition: "In the context of computer and information sciences, an ontology defines a set of representational primitives with which to model a domain of knowledge or discourse. The representational primitives are typically classes (or sets), attributes (or properties), and relationships (or relations among class members). The definitions of the representational primitives include information about their meaning and constraints on their logically consistent application."[330]

What does an ontology look like? Portions of sample ontologies are graphically depicted in Figure 8.4 and Figure 8.5.

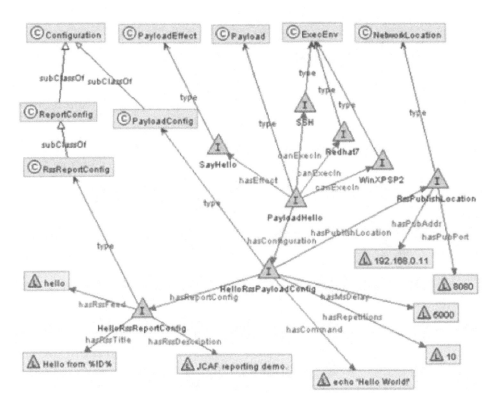

Figure 8.4: A graphical depiction of the Java Cyber Agent Framework (JCAF) ontology for payload description.[331] From Wallace, *Leveraging OWL-DL, SPARQL, and XSLT to Automate Java Agent Configuration*, 2009. Copyright © 2013 Mediabistro Inc.

---

[330] Gruber, 2009, see also http://en.wikipedia.org/wiki/Ontology_(information_science)#cite_note-50>.

[331] From http://semanticweb.com/leveraging-owl-dl-sparql-and-xslt-to-automate-java-agent-configuration_b10690.

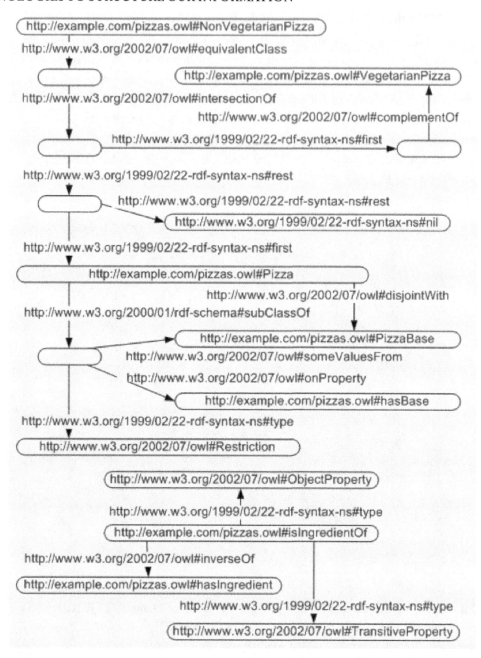

Figure 8.5: Pizza OWL ontology expressed in RDF triples.[332] OWL Example with RDF Graph. Copyright (c) 2007 Marek Obitko. Used with permission.

[332] Excerpted from http://www.obitko.com/tutorials/ontologies-semantic-web/owl-example-with-rdf-graph.html.

One thing evident in both figures and also in Gruber's definition is an emphasis not only on relating the elements (classes, categories) but also in a more precise specification of the nature of the relationship(s) between two elements. This is the "P" in an SPO triple. This is also the attribute connecting the implicit subject (e.g., of a vCard or COinS reference) to the value (as object).

The relationship between elements in a taxonomy may be characterized as one of class, containment, "copied from," or "links to" (e.g., a web page is a node in a taxonomy, with links to other web pages via its hyperlinks). But this relation is not explicitly represented in the links of the taxonomy. Links are not typed or labeled.

Does explicit representation of the relationship (the attribute, the predicate) matter? Yes. But not always and everywhere. We care whether a phone number as value is for a person's mobile phone or land line. Even more so, we care that it is a mobile phone number and not a surface address or a credit card number. Consideration #1 already established the utility of structured information in "micro"-chunks, represented in-line in HTML or XHTML web pages and conforming to a specified schema and with attribute names unambiguous within a specified namespace.

But a more general, consistent, application-independent representation of relationships is problematic. Thinking in terms, now, of SPO triples, we can observe that, though agreement concerning the "S" and the "O" may sometimes be challenging, it is certainly doable. We do the equivalent all the time when we point from one web page to another using a hyperlink. Far more problematic is consistent specification of a link type or, equivalently, the "P" of a triple. Doable to be sure. But the costs are considerable—costs to create, costs to test, costs to update later, and the costs of the inevitable error now and then in the representations.[333]

In most situations of PIM, we must question "Are these costs are ever likely to be repaid?" If our interest is mostly in a basic organization of our information according to interest areas (e.g., people, places, general topics of interest) and according to current projects, then the answer is a definite "no."

Yes, we forgo the potential for a finer-grained support from our computing devices as envisioned under the Semantic Web initiative. But we also forgo the costs associated with a finer-grained representation needed for this support.

In reference to the word "ontology" and its use in connection to information management, Bates notes that we are burdened by philosophic etymology of the word as "describing the world as it truly is, in its essence…" when "…in fact, we do not actually know how things 'really' are. Put ten classificationists (people who devise classifications) in a room together and you will have ten views on how the world is organized."[334]

---

[333] I experienced these costs first hand when, while working at Boeing in the early 1980s, I was tasked to join a team to do an on-site, hands on evaluation of CYC as part of a visit to Austin, TX. (For an entry point into more information about CYC see http://en.wikipedia.org/wiki/Cyc and also www.cyc.com).

[334] Marcia J. Bates, 2002.

In the final chapter ("To each of us, our own") of this book we will consider the development of schemes for the organization of all of our information. These schemes are meant to have sufficient durability and flexibility to last us a lifetime, in contrast to "brittle" schemes organization that we may develop with high hopes only to see these "break" under the pressure of incoming information).

These schemes are taxonomies not ontologies: Personal unifying taxonomies or PUTs. PUTs can be realized through an assembly of grouping items (see previous inserts) linking to one another and to items of information content.

Grouping items to realize a PUT may come in the form of folders, tags, section tabs, and even ordinary web pages or any combination of these.

As we'll explore through the next inset in the "Taking back our information" series, the choice of grouping item (and storing application) shouldn't matter providing that the applications we use do a small number of things the "same" way. But convincing application developers to do things the same way is a tough sell. Sameness should bring benefits not just eventually for the end user but also immediately for developers as the application is being built. This is a topic for Consideration #3.

8.3.3 CONSIDERATION #3: HOW MUCH NEEDS TO BE THE SAME FOR STRUCTURES TO BE SHARED?

How much do things need to be "the same" in order to make better use of structure? This is a question that's more often of concern to developers than to end users. As end users, we might happily reap the benefits of, for example, "RDF sameness" as described in the Semantic Web initiative but still have little reason understand or care about the way this sameness is actually implemented—unless the costs of sameness are passed along to us as a degradation in performance or as unexpected behaviors in the agents that are supposedly acting on our behalf.

Sameness matters more to developers who may be charged with using a common infrastructure in support of whatever "sameness" is meant to reign across a particular information landscape. The near uniform support we see now for copy & paste and the clipboard, though clearly a win for us as end users, came at an initial cost to application developers who were required to make modifications in their code in order to use shared ("same") support for these features.

For successes such as the clipboard, there are many other failed attempts at sameness. Consider, for example, initiatives in the hypertext/hypermedia community toward a basic sameness in the storage and semantics of hyperlinks. First came efforts toward *open hypermedia* systems in which anchors, links, and other structural elements are flexibly defined and have existence independently of the documents to which they apply.[335] The open hypermedia initiative, in turn, inspired a move-

---

[335] See for example, K. M. Anderson, Sherba, & Lepthien, 2002; K. M. Anderson, Taylor, & E. James Whitehead, 1994; H. Davis, Hall, Heath, Hill, & Wilkins, 1992; Karousos, Pandis, Reich, & Tzagarakis, 2003.

ment toward structural computing[336] as an attempt to generalize the techniques and lessons learned from open hypermedia efforts.

But a shared limitation of these efforts is a "heavy weight" requirement that participating applications make common use of basic utilities and structured storage. The work and the trust involved to do this has been prohibitive. Anderson, in reference to structural computing efforts aimed at integration, notes, for example, that an environment may require "installation of a database, … server, … support tools … clients" and that, in general, these requirements are "too steep."[337]

A little bit of sameness can go a long way toward making our interactions with information easier. In a book chapter, "Unify Everything: It's All the Same to Me," Karger[338] notes that unification can come in many different forms. He describes common support for text as one such useful unification. (And, we might say more specifically, support for ASCII and, now, variable-width encoding standards—most notably UTF-8—as a way of supporting the Unicode character set while maintaining backward compatibility with ASCII[339]).

But especially notable as a success story are the unifications that underlie the Web. As reviewed at the outset of this chapter, the Web is based on three key unifications: HTTP, the URL, and common support among browsers for the rendering of HTML. From these basic unifications has emerged a World Wide Web that may ultimately link nearly all human-generated information in one way or another. The Web grows daily in a highly dynamic, distributed, decentralized fashion. Any one of us can add to and extend the Web without "approval" from a central authority.

One downside of this relatively low level of unification and the informal flexibility it permits is that links break and we occasionally see the 404 error ("page not found"). Most of us likely consider this a fair tradeoff.

Proposed unifications such as a uniform use of RDF for the sharing of structured information between applications may still "go viral" in the manner of the Web unifications. But, notwithstanding the apparent simplicity of the basic SPO triple as a means for representing information, the evidence so far suggests that the costs of consistent, coordinated use or RDF are too heavy and the requisite changes required of participating applications too extreme for RDF to gain widespread adoption.

In the book *Keeping Found Things Found*[340] I make a distinction between unification and *integration*.[341] "With integration, pieces fit together to make a more perfect whole but still retain

---

[336] See, for example, K. M. Anderson, Sherba, & Lepthien, 2003; K. M. Anderson, 2005; Nürnberg, Wiil, & Hicks, 2004.

[337] K. M. Anderson, 2005.

[338] Karger, 2007.

[339] http://en.wikipedia.org/wiki/UTF-8.

[340] W. Jones, 2007, Chapter 14, "Bringing the Pieces Together."

[341] The making up or composition of a whole by adding together or combining the separate parts or elements; combination into an integral whole: a making whole or entire. http://dictionary.oed.com/cgi/entry/50118573?single=1&query_type=word&queryword=integration&first=1&max_to_show=10.

their identity as separate pieces. With unification, the pieces lose independence with respect to the dimension of unification."

Integration at one level can build upon unification at a lower level. We see it all the time in the form, for example, of web pages generated dynamically through a linking in of different pieces—text, pictures, videos—that still retain their separate identity (and URLs) to be used in other ways in other web pages.[342]

We aim for a greater integration of our information through the structures we share—with our applications, with other people and with ourselves over time. Sharing in turn is enabled through some unification—some sameness—in an enabling infrastructure used by applications.

But requisite sameness is a cost to application developers—a cost measured not only in changes to a code base but also in dependencies that could be an ongoing source of bugs and maintenance headaches. In general, the more sameness, the more cost. We then need to be selective and strategic in the unifications we embrace.

It's all well and good to speak of offsetting benefits in the eventual goodness delivered to the end user (and also to the developer whose application is successful with the end user). But benefits are later and costs are now. In the ideal, sameness also brings some immediate benefit—to developers—as well as delayed benefits to users. This might happen, for example, to the extent that common use of external utilities spares developers the cost of developing these utilities on their own. This is a topic for insert #4 in the "Taking back our information" series.

8.3.4 CONSIDERATION #4: HOW MUCH NEEDS TO CHANGE FOR STRUCTURES TO BE SHARED?

Just as Consideration #3 is more of a concern for developers, Consideration #4 is more of a concern for us as end users. How much must we—are we willing to—change in order to make better use of our information structures?

The question is addressed more generally in a later chapter of Part 3 to this book (the chapter titled, "PIM by Design"): How much—how quickly—are we willing to change our habits of information interaction in order to improve our practices of PIM? How soon do we need to see payback for our efforts?

These questions are especially important in a "web-widened" world where the requirement to install an application on the desktop or even as a browser plugin is often a "nonstarter"—all the more so if any money must be paid.

We return to a previous "post-mortem" comment by Karger on the difficulties of getting people to use Haystack: "in practice we found it difficult to convince people to abandon their long-cherished PIM tools in favor of a half-baked research tool."[343] I'm not so sure most of us "cher-

---

[342] This process is sometimes referred to as tansclusion—a term coined by Ted Nelson (1982).
[343] http://haystack.csail.mit.edu/blog/2010/10/20/why-all-your-data-should-live-in-one-application/.

ish" the applications we currently use. The relationship between us and our current applications is often more love-hate. I quip, for example, that "MS Word is an app that I hate to use … everyday."

Even so, a requirement that we abandon existing applications in favor of new applications—even if these are polished products rather than research prototypes—is usually a non-starter. This holds especially true if we're asked to move our information to some new storing application or to transform our information in ways that mean we can no longer work with the information through our current applications.

Much better is if information can stay where it is but also be used in new and different ways. One accounting for the tremendous success of Dropbox with consumers is that Dropbox does—almost—exactly this. Yes, we need to move information to be in or under a designated Dropbox folder in our local file system. This is a drawback.[344] But information is still in our local file system. Our information stays where it is but now, thanks to Dropbox (or, similarly, with SkyDrive or Google Drive), can be shared with others and synced across our devices.

How can we realize a comparable sharing of our information structures—so that these structures stay where they are (e.g., as folder structures in our local file system) but can now be shared not only with other people but also with a whole new set of applications? This is another question to be addressed in inset #4 of the "Taking back our information" series.

Taking back our information, #4. Taking back our information even as we leave it where it is.

The previous inset in this "Taking back our information" series described the XooML way of using XML to represent—"mirror"—the structure of grouping items (such as folders, tags, "albums," "notebook," and ordinary web pages). The XooML representation of structure is "first class" in the two senses described previously in this chapter on structure.

1. The XooML fragment is a modular, **tool-independent** representation of a "noodle" (a node + outgoing links). Since nodes can link to other nodes (or even to themselves), fragments in aggregate can be seen to form a *multidigraph* (as described in the previous insert on XooML).

2. A fragment, and each of its associations, can include any number of **tool-accommodating** namespace elements to store the data an application (or a collection of applications supporting a particular metadata standard) needs in order to give its special spin on the underlying structure.

---

[344] Dropbox requires that we move information to be under a designated Dropbox folder in our file system—a local move. Even better would be if information needn't move at all. Instead we would simply designate the folders—any folders—to be shared through Dropbox. The ability to do so may eventually be supported by Dropbox. In the meantime, workarounds are being developed. See, for example, http://www.apartmenttherapy.com/how-to-sync-any-local-folder-t-139040.

The XooML approach, in line with the "Caveats and Considerations" section, focuses on the grouping item as the basis for a meaningful sharing of information structure. As end users, we aren't required to move our information or otherwise change very much of what we do already in order to take advantage of new ways of working with our information as provided by "XooML-speaking" apps.

But where do these XooML apps come from? How difficult are they to build? How difficult is XooML to use? How well do apps work together? And how much needs to be the "same," beyond use of XooML, among XooML-speaking apps?

The short answer: itemMirror.

itemMirror[345] is an object class supported through a simple code base that can be translated into different programming languages for use on different platforms. We playfully call the code base the zootilities (as a combination of "XooML" as it should be pronounced + "utilities"). itemMirror is currently supported through JavaScript zootilities for use in the construction of HTML5 applications. However, by the time you read this we expect to have a port of itemMirror code to Objective C for use to build applications on the iOS[346] platform to build applications for iPhone, iPod Touch, and iPad devices.

As mediating software, itemMirror zootilties (or simply, "itemMirror") has both a front-end and a back-end:

➢ **On the front-end**, itemMirror "faces" developers and XooML-speaking applications with a simple itemMirror object model.

➢ **On the back-end**, itemMirror is able to work with—read and write-changes back to—the structure of various forms of the grouping item via the APIs of storing applications such as Dropbox, Google Drive, SkyDrive, Box, and even social media applications like Facebook (e.g., via Graph API). Interaction with the APIs of storing applications is through itemMirror drivers as specified through association-common attributes and described further below.

All of a XooML-speaking application's interactions with a grouping item, its storage, and the XooML fragment take place through the itemMirror objects.

---

[345] See keepingfoundthingsfound.com.
[346] See http://en.wikipedia.org/wiki/IOS and http://www.apple.com/ios/.

On the front-end: itemMirror methods

An application begins a session with a user by instantiating an itemMirror object for a "seed" grouping item. Instantiation can happen either using a known XooML fragment for the grouping item or, if such a fragment is not available, by creating one.

Thereafter, instantiate additional itemMirror objects recursively for each link of the grouping item under consideration according to app-specific settings from a previous session with the user. In the desktop version of Planz, for example, expansion happened in order to reconstruct the state of the outline view from the previous session—where each heading/subheading of an outline corresponded to a different folder/subfolder (as the grouping item). Expansion was driven by an "isCollapsed" attribute in the namespace element that Planz kept for each association of a grouping item.

Methods of the itemMirror object provide support for the following:

➤ List associations.

➤ Create an association.

➤ Delete an association.

➤ Save—i.e., save the XooML fragment back to its file.

➤ Sync—synchronize to insure that the XooML fragment accurately reflects the structure of the grouping item it is mirroring. (In cases of conflict, the grouping item wins.)

➤ Create namespace element—the app provides a namespace URI as an argument. Elements can be created at both the fragment level and for each of a fragments associations.

➤ Delete namespace element.

➤ Get and set of common attributes—both at the level of the fragment and for each of its associations.

➤ Get/set namespace element.

A promise to application developers is that an application, developed once, will work no matter what the storing application is—whether Dropbox, Google Drive, SkyDrive, Box or, even, some applications that we don't think of us as "storing" (e.g., Facebook).

On the back-end: itemMirror drivers

Key for uniform support across all storing applications are association-level attributes, specified in the XooML, that point to the code needed to read the structure of a grouping item, its mirroring XooML fragment and to handle the logic of synchronization between grouping item and fragment:

> *itemDriver*

> *xoomlDriver*

> *syncDriver*

A class project to use itemMirror[347]

itemMirror (and through itemMirror, XooML) was successfully used by a group of sixteen Master of Science in Information Management (MSIM) students as part of an independent study project the Information School at UW during the spring quarter of 2013. The class split into five teams and were asked to build end-user applications in HTML5 using item-Mirror objects.

Teams built the following apps (available to try out at http://keepingfoundthingsfound.com/itemmirror/):

- Noot, an application that used tags to categorize information

- Planz5, a way to organize information by project

- StormNote, a simple note-taking application

- Mind-mapper, a way to visualize and link information

- NoteU, an application that created an effective use of check-lists

By working with itemMirror objects—one, for example, per Dropbox folder—student applications could focus on the "front end" and the user experience, while JavaScript drivers accessed through the itemMirror objects worked directly with Dropbox to ensure that applications also worked well with each other. Apps each worked with the same folder hierarchies as

---

[347] Cody Stebbins, a junior in the Informatics program, and Lizhang Sun, a graduating student of the MSIM program, did tremendous work to complete a zootility code base in JavaScript in time for the class to use.

shared through Dropbox but each in their own way (in support of mind-mapping, outlining, note-taking, to-do list management, and quick capture).

The essential steps of the XooML/itemMirror approach are simple (see Figure 8.6):

1. Leave the information where it is (in "storing" apps and services such as Dropbox, Google Drive, Facebook, etc.).

2. Model the structure of this information using *itemMirror* objects that...

   a. support the same methods on the front-end but, ...

   b. on the back-end, work with drivers specific to a given application and its API.

   c. Drivers provide read/write access to information structures that are "siloed" in the storing app.

3. Now other apps working exclusively through these itemMirror objects might provide complementary ways of working with the information structures.

4. itemMirror objects persist their "mirrors" of structure in synchronized XML fragments according to a "XooML" schema that is both app-independent and also, using XML's namespace convention, "app-accommodating."

   a. Fragments can also support the requirements of metadata standards such as *Dublin Core* and *iCalendar*.

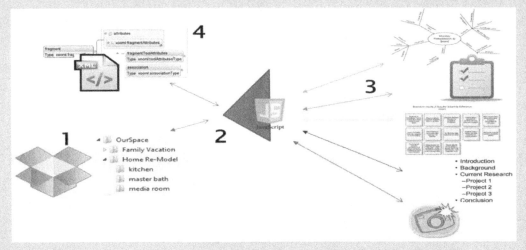

Figure 8.6: The essential steps of the XooML/itemMirror approach.

CHAPTER 9

PIM Transformed and Transforming: Stories from the Past, Present, and Future

We are nearly to the end of this Part 2 to "The Future of Personal Information Management" with its theme: "Transforming Technologies to Manage Our Information." It is time to take a broader view of the transformative power the technologies reviewed—technologies to save, search, and structure; then also the technologies for input/output. How do technologies transform our practices of PIM? And then, in turn, how might our practices of PIM transform the lives we lead?

Joseph Carl Robnett Licklider,[348] a pioneer in computing, the development of the Internet, and the human-computer interaction, did a "Time-and-Motion Analysis of Technical Thinking" in 1957 with himself as his subject. Here are excerpts from his accounting:

"About 85 per cent of my 'thinking' time was spent getting into a position to think, to make a decision, to learn something I needed to know. Much more time went into finding or obtaining information than into digesting it. Hours went into the plotting of graphs, and other hours into instructing an assistant how to plot. When the graphs were finished, the relations were obvious at once, ..."

"Throughout the period I examined, in short, my 'thinking' time was devoted mainly to activities that were essentially clerical or mechanical: searching, calculating, plotting, transforming, determining the logical or dynamic consequences of a set of assumptions or hypotheses, preparing the way for a decision or an insight. Moreover, my choices of what to attempt and what not to attempt were determined to an embarrassingly great extent by considerations of clerical feasibility, not intellectual capability."

Licklider concluded: "*...the operations that fill most of the time allegedly devoted to technical thinking are operations that can be performed more effectively by machines.*"[349]

---

[348] For shorter "web page" length biographies on Licklider with additional references see: http://en.wikipedia.org/wiki/J._C._R._Licklider, http://www.livinginternet.com/i/ii_licklider.htm and http://www.ibiblio.org/pioneers/licklider.html. Licklider wrote an influential book, *Libraries of the Future* (Licklider, 1965) which still makes for thought-provoking reading. See also the article "Man-computer symbiosis" (Licklider, 1960).

[349] Licklider, 1960, p. 4.

9.1   HOW MUCH "CLERICAL TAX" DO WE PAY?

85% of the time Licklider had available for thinking—for creative activities—went instead to the "clerical or mechanical." Call this the *clerical tax*[350] on his creative time. What about us? How much clerical tax do we pay as we work with our information?

The question matters because we spend significant amounts of a typical day in information interactions—sometimes called "knowledge work"—of one kind or another.

The Oxford English Dictionary (OED) defines *knowledge work*[351] as "work which involves handling or using information." The OED quotes Peter Drucker as saying back in 1959 that "Today the majority of the personnel employed even in manufacturing industries… are… people doing knowledge work, however unskilled."[352] As noted back in Chapter 1 (Part 1), the number of white collar jobs exceeded the number of farming and blue collar jobs in the USA back in the 1950s, i.e., at about the time that Licklider did his study.[353] Similar patterns hold true for other developed countries and, we would expect, will hold true globally as countries develop. Most of us with jobs are "knowledge workers" with "white collar" jobs. We work with information.

At play too—that is in our leisure time—much of what we do is informational whether in the form of, for example, seeing a movie, staying in touch with friends and acquaintances via Facebook, watching television, reading a book or magazine (increasingly via a digital display device), etc. We do physical activity too, of course, both for fun and health. But increasingly, these activities include an informational overlay. We wear headphones while we run or bike so that we can listen to music or a podcast, for example. Or we wear inserts in our running shoes to record how far we've run, how fast, and where. In the exercise gym, we watch television while using an exercise bike or we bike as part of a video game.

Similarly, at home as we manage our personal lives. Yes, we're more likely to be a "jack of all trades" in our homes as we do manual work such as replacing light bulbs, cooking, gardening, cleaning the house, mowing the lawn, etc. But at home too, our activities are increasingly informational. We may contract some of the manual jobs out, when we can afford to, in a manner similar to the way these activities are contracted out in a workplace. Or we may use machines (including robots for vacuuming and mowing the lawn). Some activities we'll still do ourselves because we like doing them—cooking and gardening, for example. What we are then left with to do at home are tasks involving information management. We plan meals, pay bills, plan vacations, plan for our retirement or our children's college fund—all of it is informational.

---

[350] In the *Keeping Found Things Found* book I also use the term "information friction" to refer to the small clerical/mechanical actions we must take as we manage our information.

[351] http://www.oed.com/view/Entry/104170?redirectedFrom=knowledge+worker#eid40033264.

[352] Drucker, 2009.

[353] See Naisbitt's book (1984), *Megatrends: Ten New Directions Transforming Our Lives*. The reader is also invited to review for the accuracy (nearly 30 years ago) of this book's attempts to predict the future.

Most of us likely spend several hours each day—8 to 14 hours or more—working with information in one form or another. Reductions in clerical tax rates matter. I write "tax rates" since different rates may apply in different areas of our lives and for different activities of PIM.

But let's simplify for the sake of illustration. Suppose we spend an average of 10 hours each day working with our information (at work, at home, and at play). Suppose that 50% of this time is spent doing clerical activities (i.e., activities that our computing devices might do just as well or better than we do). If we were able to reduce this clerical tax rate from 50% to 40% then we'd have an extra hour in each day.

But this understates the transformative potential of information technologies. Reductions in clerical tax rate may be much greater. If Licklider spent 85% of his time on the clerical we might envision a future in which we spend as little as 5% of our time on the clerical. The savings then works out to 8 hours per day—i.e., the time spent in a working day on a typical job. It is then as if each of us were able to take early retirement.

Alas, unless our "agents" are able to make money on our behalf, we'll keep working. But the nature of what we're able to accomplish with our information—at work, at home, at play—will also be transformed by the technologies we've reviewed here in Part 2. We don't just have quantitatively more time for the creative, but our creative activities change qualitatively as well.

9.2 TOWARD A SYNTHESIS OF THE SENSES OF PERSONAL INFORMATION AND THE ACTIVITIES OF PIM

To better understand transformative potential of information technologies, let's make a speculative comparison between Licklider's world of information and our own, now nearly 60 years later as of the writing of this book and then let's try a jump into the future of 2057—100 years after Licklider's time and motion study. Reflections and predictions are prompted and organized by the six senses in which information is personal (Table 9.1).

Table 9.1: A speculative comparison between Licklider's world of personal information, ours "now," and a projected world of personal information in 2057 with respect to each of the senses in which information is personal to us.

Senses	1957	"now"	2057
P1, information owned by us	Nearly all information we keep is paper-based in the form of books, magazines, newspapers, scrapbooks with newspaper clippings, photographs. Partial exceptions for photograph slides—though these are framed in paper. Also an exception for reel-to-reel tape and home movies. Information is kept in "piles" and "files." Paper files are physically placed inside folders that are placed inside file drawers. This takes time!	Increasingly, the information we have—books and magazines we read for recreation, our medical, banking, credit card, and tax information—is not only in digital form but also online (on the Web, in the Cloud) and accessible from anywhere. The great migration of our information onto to the Web (into "the Cloud") continues.	Nearly all of our information is on the Web, interconnected, securely encrypted (when this matters), selectively shared, and serving as an extension to and spokesperson for us in a variety of situations. However, we keep copies of some portions of our information off-line under physical lock and key to hedge against Internet outages. Some information may be archived in paper or in a solar-powered mass storage device. Fly over and "zoom" into our information using gestures, eye movements, and voice.

Senses	1957	"now"	2057
P2, information about us	No computerized databases for storage of information about us.[354] Possibly some data about us kept in microfilm or microfiche.[355] Otherwise, everything about us as kept by the tax authorities, banks, credit card companies, doctors, and insurance companies is in paper form as organized via enormous numbers of filing cabinets.	Information about us is everywhere. But increasingly so too is the ability to locate and track this information.	New "Freedom of Information" laws entitle us to request and inspect nearly all information kept about us (with exceptions, unfortunately, for information kept by government law, security and intelligence agencies).[356] Moreover, we can request updates to this information when discrepancies are noted (by "bots" acting on our behalf) between our information as maintained by others and our own master copy of this information. The master copy we maintain (P1) includes all information "that matters" about us including medical records, financial statements, job history, college transcripts—everything. Information is kept in fluid, flexible micro and "macro" structures for access and manipulation from any number of applications. We can see and work with our information in many different ways—e.g., in a conventional spreadsheet, a "box model" web page or even as a "life portrait" animation.

[354] The term "data base" was first used in 1955 according to the online version of the Oxford English Dictionary: "Q. Jrnl. Econ. 69 155 A thoroughgoing character classification of federal government activities, à la J. R. Hicks, would provide the data-base necessary for this kind of stabilization policy." http://www.oed.com/view/ Entry/47411. Computer-based databases were not in widespread use until the 1960s. For a brief history of databases, see also http://en.wikipedia.org/wiki/Database#History.

[355] It's tough to tell. The reader is invited to find out the extent to which for example credit card companies used microfilm/microfiche in the mid-1950s. For a starting point, see http://en.wikipedia.org/wiki/Microfilm#History.

[356] A mandated right to inspect and even request changes to information kept by others about us is, of course, wishful thinking but not without precedent. We're able today (in many countries) to request credit reports about us, for example. And we may be able to see not only the tax assessment for our property but also our neighbors. See, for example, Chapter 16 of the book, *Personal Information Management* (Shamos, 2007). Insurance agencies, credit card companies, advertising agencies, and Google will likely fight against such "Freedom of information" laws. But providing access via web-based databases and even supporting update requests is already technically feasible.

Senses	1957	"now"	2057
P3, information directed toward us from other people (individually and through organizations).	Billboards, magazine and newspaper ads, radio, television commercials, telephone solicitation, door to door sales people selling things like Hoover Vacuum Cleaners[357] and Encyclopedia Britannica's,[358] surface mail subscriptions to magazines, newspapers and "books of the month".	Nearly everything in the 1957 column (except for the Hoover Vacuum Cleaner and Encyclopedia Britannica salespeople). Also.... cell phone calls, text messages, emails, targeted advertisements on nearly every web page we view.	**P3** and **P4** merge. We push information to the Web and pull back responses. We post CFPs (calls for proposal) or CFBs (calls for bids) and offers come back (filtered to remove spam). We sell portions of our attentional surfaces for use to advertise products and services we might use. **P3** and **P5** merge. The constant flow of incoming information includes items of information directed toward us from other people. We are notified via special eye glasses, "watch" watches, and "web windows" we stand in front of (in places public and private). Some **P3** information is blocked. Much more is sorted into our **P1** organization for review later on "when the time is right".

<hr>

[357] See http://www.youtube.com/watch?v=aLKJFSi14gk for a 50s era video of the Hoover vacuum cleaner salesman.

[358] http://www.movements.net/2005/04/21/who-killed-the-encyclopedia-salesman.html; http://www.huffingtonpost.com/2012/03/14/encyclopedia-britannica_n_1346094.html.

Senses	1957	"now"	2057
P4, information shared by us	Letters written (thin paper, all the space used, even the margins), classified ads, letters to the editor, applications filled out (on paper) and sent via surface mail. Our houses and, especially, our cars are another form of **P4**— if money is tight, we may scrimp on house to by a flashier car. Others see first us in our car before they see us in our house.	How many of us still write paper letters (a dying art?). We send emails, tweets, texts. We post to Facebook. Some of us publish. We post comments to the blogs of others. We "like". Increasingly, we have our own websites. But we also have lots of information scattered in various web services and applications. We've forgotten about many of these.	**P4** merges with **P1**. Our information stays in place and is selectively shared with others (sometimes for specified periods of time).
P5, information experienced by us	Photographs (but allow a week before prints can be developed; then save the negatives in case), home movies, reel-to-reel tapes for sound, diaries.	We carry a camera with us at all times as part of our palmtop and take a digital picture anytime we want to. "Logs" of our information interactions are kept in the form of emails, sent and received, last viewed/ last modified dates for files and the "History" facility of the web browser. **P2** and **P5** merge as others also record our informational interactions and also take pictures and videos of us.	**P5** merges with **P1**. The item event log provides an integrative automatically generated recording of all of our information interactions.

Senses	1957	"now"	2057
P6, information relevant to us	Libraries (and their paper card catalogs) with information mostly in paper form (but also microfilm/microfiche); word of mouth through friends and colleagues; magazine subscriptions.	We search on the Web through services like Google, Bing, and Yahoo. Also we ask friends and colleagues. And we browse and post questions to online discussion groups and bulletin boards.	**P6** merges with **P1**. Much of the information relevant to us is already "situated" within our information space awaiting our attention. We can actively search from laptop, palmtop, "watch" watch, and other devices we wear or carry. We also locate relevant information via "web windows"[359] mounted on physical walls at home and in public places too. Web windows are able to recognize us individually as we approach (possibly as aided by the palmtop device we carry with us in pocket or purse). Search using voice, eye movements, and gestures.

Obviously, much of what is under the "2057" column is a product of educated guessing and a little wishful thinking, too.[360] This is especially the case with the **P2** cell. Laws to mandate that companies share the information they have gathered about us and, even more so, the enforcement of these laws, will not happen except through persistent activism on our part. But we have plenty of time to make it so.

One thing in evidence in the 2057 column is the extent to which our information in its different senses merges through its integrated presence on the Web. The information we own (**P1**) includes, for example, a structured organization in which to place situated searches that serve both to locate new relevant information (**P6**) and also as filters or classifiers to sort the information directed toward us (**P3**) and, more generally, the information we experience (**P5**).

---

[359] See for example, http://www.greenstar.org/butterflies/Hole-in-the-Wall.htm, http://www.ted.com/talks/sugata_mitra_the_child_driven_education.html.

[360] Past predictions of the future prove often to be hilariously off course. But not always. See, for example, Apple's vision of the future in 1987 for hints of Siri (http://www.youtube.com/watch?v=JIE8xk6Rl1w; http://www.intomobile.com/2011/10/05/apple-concept-video-from-1987-shows-siri-style-personal-assistant/; http://techcrunch.com/2011/10/05/siri-ous-mind-blowing-video-evidence-of-apples-prophetic-past-circa-1987/. See also, http://en.wikipedia.org/wiki/Knowledge_Navigator and http://en.wikipedia.org/wiki/Office_of_the_future).

Also in **P1** is a master copy of much of the information about us (**P2**) that others are likely to maintain. We might imagine "bots" or "agents" operating on our behalf that periodically check known databases containing information about us and that also crawl the Web in search of new stores containing information about us. We're alerted to discrepancies between our version of "us" and the information others keep about us and can then decide whether to request an update or correction. In many cases updating/correction can happen automatically. Many agencies keeping information about us have a vested interest in updating contact information and information concerning changes in job or marital status. In other cases, we may need to force the issue. But at least we know.

There is also a merging of information experienced by us (**P5**) and **P1** information. The item event log we maintain to record and link to items experienced or experiential (web pages viewed, pictures and video clips taken automatically or manually) is also one basis for organizing much of our **P1** information. In the spirit of Lifestream,[361] we can retrieve information previously experienced based upon our (approximate) memories for when we've encountered the information before. Also, we can retrieve this information based upon our memories for "where" we've encountered the information before. (Our memories for "where" are often more precise and durable than our memories for "when").

And finally, there is a merging of information we direct outward (**P4**) and the information directed toward us (**P3**). Information in both cases is part of an extended space of information we own (**P1**): Our house of information. Incoming information sits in one or another anteroom as sorted through our searching/filtering facility awaiting our attention. Outgoing information may be sent via email, tweet, or Facebook post. But increasingly this information stays in place and is shared instead (with only the notice of its sharing going out to intended recipients).[362] **P2**, **P3**, and **P4** information is part of an ongoing dialog we have with other people, mediated by the Web.

Activities of PIM also merge as we approach 2057. Keeping and finding are part of a dialog that leverages the structures we've created through our activities of maintaining and organizing. Our information structures also provide a basis for the managing of our privacy and the general flow of information, outgoing and incoming. Structures also provide basis for measuring and evaluating—both our practices of PIM and our lives in general. Finally, our efforts to make sense of our information are facilitated by effective groupings of our information as viewed and manipulated by any number of applications, able to work with our information—structure and content—in place.

---

[361] Fertig et al., 1996a; Freeman & Gelernter, 1996.

[362] Situated sharing of information that stays in place could work in ways similar to the way a hosting service for software development such as GitHub (github.com) or Bitbucket (bitbucket.org) works today. Information is managed by the hosting environment and subscribing members are notified of changes.

Senses of personal information, activities of PIM … as these flow one into another, we too are better able to stay "in the flow"[363] and stay more fully, productively, and, even, restfully focused on the task at hand.

9.3 PERSONAL INFORMATION MANAGEMENT, THEN AND NOW

Leaving aside an admittedly speculative "2057" column, let's now compare the "1957" column with the "now" column to appreciate how different our world of information is from Licklider's. Consider, for example, **P1** information. Keeping digital information and keeping it organized is still a challenge and consumes time. But we are certainly saved the time of physically going over to a filing cabinet, pulling a drawer out, thumbing through hanging folders, etc. We're also spared these steps later to retrieve information from the file cabinet and then later to re-file this information again (often making errors in the process).

I'm a terrible speller and am happy that the detection of (most) spelling mistakes is now automated. I can recall only a few years back spending many painstaking minutes (adding up to hours) in the entry of bibliographic information and I'm *extremely* happy that this is now mostly automated through the support for initiatives like COinS.

I've done my own very informal "time and motion" observation of activities in the completion of this book. And I've compared to the activities in the completion of my dissertation at Carnegie-Mellon University (CMU) back in 1982.[364] Consider only one portion of the dissertation—the mandatory literature review—and compare with the comparable review of relevant work done throughout this book. The differences in the clerical/mechanical are profound.

In 1982, there was no web, no wireless, no laptops, no smartphones, etc. A search for relevant information almost always started with a trip to CMU's "brick and mortar" library. For a time, I went nearly every day. When there, I accessed physical copies of the journal issues containing articles relevant to my own doctoral work. I chained forward to other articles that appeared relevant via an article's bibliographic references. I recall occasionally chaining backward, i.e., to get "cited by" articles using the Social Science Citation index. I also heard of some relevant material through colleagues.

---

[363] Many of us have experienced occasional periods of intense—almost meditative—concentration on task. We lose awareness of self and time. The experience can be restful even though we're working hard and getting a great deal accomplished. We might think of this as a mental equivalent of superconductivity. Csikszentmihalyi uses the term "flow" (Csikszentmihalyi, 1991) (see also http://en.wikipedia.org/wiki/Mihaly_Csikszentmihalyi). A related notion is "peak experience" as described Abraham Maslow (Maslow, 1972).

[364] My doctoral research involved empirical studies and computer-based simulations of human memory and the potential for integrating themes to lessen or even eliminate the effects of "set size" and "fan"—both measures of information (over)load. For a write-up of this work see W. Jones & Anderson, 1987.

But, to a considerable extent, I located relevant work by browsing—as in the dictionary definition sense of the word ("To scan, to casually look through in order to find items of interest"[365]). I browsed through all the journals of relevance for my area. There were perhaps six or seven journals directly relevant. I likely browsed through each issue in each of these journals going back for a decade or more.

And with each reference found—of apparent relevance above a threshold—I needed to take a number of physical, "mechanical" steps in order to access a copy of the article for closer inspection:

1. Walk to the reference shelf housing issues of the journal in which the article was published. Some journals were on the other side of a reference desk and were retrieved only by filling out, on paper, a reference request form and giving to the reference librarian. In other cases, though the journal issues were in shelves directly accessible to me, the issue itself was missing. Or the issue was older and no longer in the shelves. In these cases, it might be on microfiche, or I might need to make a special inter-library loan request and then wait a week or more for the request to be filled.

2. With article in hand, I would then scan to determine if it was a "keeper"—i.e., an article of sufficient relevance that I might like to read and cite. Many were not. That is, I spent several minutes and possibly waited a week or more only to determine that the article wasn't sufficiently relevant to my work to be included in the literature review. For those that were, I generally made a copy using the library's photocopy machine. Photocopies cost money—some number of cents per page. I honestly can't recall how this was handled since as a poor graduate student I likely wanted to avoid spending my own money for a copy. I possibly was able to charge to my advisor's account or possibly I had a "key" (box) to plug into the photocopier to enable copying, count the copies, and debit some credit for my department. Regardless, the photocopying of an article took many minutes to complete. At the time, I thought the ability to make photocopies a tremendous innovation since otherwise I would need to take many more hand-written notes.

3. With copy in hand, I would often read the article from start to finish—carefully—to understand research methods used, results, and implications. I highlighted passages using a yellow marker.

---

[365] http://en.wiktionary.org/wiki/browse#English. In the "Technologies to search our information" chapter, the term "navigation" was selected in preference to "browsing" as a better term for the purposeful activity of accessing a specific desired information item through actions such as folder navigation or web surfing in which the recognition component of the finding activity is higher than the recall component. In contrast, the specification of a search through text entered into the search box places a stronger emphasis on the recall component—what are we able to recall about the information item we seek? "Browsing", however, more aptly describes what we do when looking through a table of contents for articles of interest without a specific article in mind.

4. And then, for keeper articles, I also generally made an index card listing authors, title, and other reference information along with a short hand-written description expressing what was relevant about the article and how it might fit into the dissertation's literature review.

5. And finally, when back at a terminal connected to university account, I would enter reference information by hand for later electronic formatting into the bibliography.

In short, a very large percentage of my time in the completion of the dissertation literature review was spent in clerical/mechanical activities. I had the benefits of a computer-based text editor and also could use computer-based typesetting and formatting (including for references). In other areas of the dissertation I could use the computer for data analysis and to plot basic graphs. So, in contrast to Licklider's 85% estimate, make my time with the clerical/mechanical about 65% of the total time invested in the literature review and elsewhere in the completion of the dissertation, i.e., about two thirds of my time.

How times have changed!

It has been a long time since I visited the library out of necessity to access information related to the work I was doing. Now look-up is as quick as a few words typed or pasted into the search box. Mostly I use a general purpose search service. Sometimes I use Google Scholar or the ACM Digital Library (dl.acm.org).

Logged into the virtual private network through the University of Washington means that I can generally access a PDF for a desired article without cost. I keep a large and growing collection of articles locally in my personal file system. Why not? Storage is cheap. I highlight passages in these using Adobe Reader.

For articles I mean to reference, citation information is quickly downloaded in the form of COinS information to Zotero (my current reference manager) via a simple click on a little box at the right end of the browser address well. Citations are made, in-place, in the document I'm working on via another few clicks with the help of a Zotero plug-in for Microsoft Word. With another click I can ask Zotero to assemble citations scattered though the document into a bibliographic reference list and to format these according to any of several bibliographic formats.

I've made back-ups of book drafts both by self-addressed email and also via Dropbox folder. I'll also use one or the other to share drafts with the publisher and with reviewers, copyeditors, and proofreaders.

What's my clerical tax for the writing of this book as a percentage of total time? I'll estimate around 25%.

9.4   TAX-FREE PIM?

Would we, if we could, take the clerical tax down to zero? The initial response might be "Sure! Why not?"

But we're reminded of Lansdale's paradox—as we automate, we lessen our contact with our information and so reduce the chances of accidental discovery through incidental contact. Also, some of the mechanical and the clerical may actually be restful to complete "by hand."

My personal proofreading of this book is a little of both (although I need to admit that—like many of us—I have trouble seeing my own mistakes). Researching and writing the content is the hard part. Proof reading, though increasingly delegated to my computer through facilities like "check as I type" spellchecking and grammar checking, can be restful and satisfying. I might also "delegate" to a willing friend or a paid assistant but by doing it myself I come into closer contact with the material I've written. As I proofread, new ways of expressing the content often occur to me. More important, new ways of *thinking* about the material occur to me. In other words, making (better) sense of the information is facilitated by and intertwined with the clerical task of proofreading.

But there are many more clerical tasks I'm happily rid of. The entry of reference information, for example, in a precise, fussy format (to meet the demands of one or another convention for bibliographic references) was neither restful nor illuminating. Its entry did nothing to facilitate a deeper understanding of the work being referenced.

Moreover, the discoveries and deeper understanding I sometimes gain in the course of proofreading my own work might be gained in other ways. If this book were broken into a series of blog posts, for example, and you were to post comments then we might reach a deeper shared understanding in the course of the dialog that ensued.

What's left? The mechanics of typing, for one thing. I'm a reasonably fast typist but, like most of us, I can speak faster than I can type.[366]

There is also the mechanics of moving text around. How best to order? What to delete? Also, it's easier for me to delete text if I know it's "nearby" should I change my mind. For me that means pasting into a "leftovers" file. That takes time. Streamlining the leftover process might cut my clerical tax. So too might a greater use of touch to select passages to be moved coupled with gesture or voice recognition to indicate where passages should go.

Even better might be a "readability" or "logic checker" which is to the grammar checker as the grammar checker is to the spelling checker—a higher-level analysis of text that identifies possible problems in narrative flow and, better, proposes solutions that I can "accept" or "ignore."

---

[366] See J. Grudin, 1988, for an analysis of the asymmetries in the cost/benefit of different modes of communication. Overall, most of us speak faster than we type. On the hand, we read/scan faster than we can listen via audio channel. With technologies of voice recognition we approach an ideal where sender can speak the message and the recipient can see and have all the affordances of a written transcript of this message.

And then there's the shift of attention required to go from the manuscript to the browser in order to complete a search. My word processor (Microsoft Word) provides a "look up" facility for selected text which as one option returns in-place search results in a window pane to the right of the document I'm working on. But this facility doesn't work well for me. The space for the results listing is narrow and results are difficult to evaluate. Also, any click takes me back to the browser window anyway which has no special connection to the document window.

In the spirit of the "Taking back our information" insets of Part 2, suppose the structure of this book were first class—and that I might then use any number of applications—not just Microsoft Word—to help me in the creation and assembly of its pieces. Pieces might be "cards" similar to the paper notecards I used in my dissertation work in 1983 (or, like the cards of the commercially successful Hypercard application[367] of the 1980s).

With structure now first class, I might still opt to see a Page Layout view in Microsoft Word just as I do today with cards assembled into a scrollable document that appears much as it will appear in "final form" formatted in PDF or for printing. But I might use the outlining ability of another application as I try to figure out how best to structure the document.

Some cards are high-level and mostly about structure—a grouping item (e.g., as a top-level heading) pointing to other grouping items (second-level headings). In line with Chapter 7's discussion of situated searches, these grouping item cards have a centroid reflecting the contents in cards that the grouping item card points to.

Other cards at the lowest level are mostly about content. A "leaf-level" card may contain only a single thought or idea, expressed through text, a picture, a graphic or some combination of these and where possibly some elements of the card are excerpted (as an image or quote) from the Web (e.g., from an article, blog post, discussion board comment, etc.). For any such excerpt, the card keeps a link back to the element's source as well as additional COinS citation information. If the link is clicked, the web page is displayed, with the excerpt highlighted.

I can then imagine that the book as a document might have emerged—better, faster, more easily—through a kind of dialog between the cards of the document and the Web. If I'm on the Web already and come across a web page that relates to the book, I simply highlight a portion of the page (e.g., an image or text to quote). As an option, I then add my own thoughts concerning the page and how its information relates to the book. A card is created. Also, I can choose to link from other grouping item cards to this card, aided as I do so, by a search that matches card contents to the centroids of existing grouping item cards.

In the other direction, as I'm working on the document—whether as a listing of cards, an outline, or a "page layout" view, I might select text or an image and then request to see a streamlined

---

[367] See http://en.wikipedia.org/wiki/HyperCard. Hypercard was preceded by NoteCards (Halasz, Moran, & Trigg, 1987; Halasz, 2001).

pop-up version of my preferred web browser with search results listed. Again, I can make a selection that is then excerpted for inclusion in the document (on a new or existing card).

Things might be further streamlined if I'm able to select using gestures or eye movements and can then add my own comments via voice. Also, portions of the document might be shared in the form of a blog post on the Web as invitation for the comments of others. The dialog then expands to connect author through document excerpts as blog posts to readers through the comments on these posts. And then, we might ask, who still needs the published book?

9.5 WHERE DO WE "PIM" IN 2057?

In the highly acclaimed science fiction animation film WALL-E[368] the people depicted are couch potatoes in the extreme, nearly incapable of movement and almost completely detached from their physical surroundings as they view "reality" through video screens and are serviced by robots.

But an alternate future has us much more mobile with many more options to do PIM—at home, at work, and at play even as we move through and exercise in physical (not virtual) space.

There is already an increasing use of a "third place"[369]—neither home nor work but often a coffee shop—as a place to work and, more generally, to interact with our information ("do PIM"). Larson identifies the third place phenomenon as a key success factor for Starbucks.[370] He attributes Starbucks use as a third place in part to "the increasing use of the Internet and mobile computing devices capable of accessing it." Laptop use is so prevalent that Starbucks apparently now needs to contend with people who sit for many hours and only drink one or two cups of coffee.[371]

In fact I may be one of those people…

I also go to the library—especially the public library of the town in which I live. I know a fellow professor at University of Washington who completed much of the writing of his dissertation while sitting at a picnic area near the "It's a small world" ride in Disneyland in Anaheim, CA. (He lived locally and had an annual pass).

Why? Why leave a perfectly good work office and possibly another perfectly good home office to work in a public place? I do so for what I term "communitude":

Communitude—A desired state of being and working alone but around other people or in a public place.

I like to work without disruption but can start to feel lonely and "deprived" if I work for long periods of time in my office at the university or at home. As an alternative, I may work in the living room of my home where I'm nearer to other members of my family. Or I may go to the library or

---

[368] http://en.wikipedia.org/wiki/WALL-E; http://www.imdb.com/title/tt0910970/.

[369] See for example, http://usatoday30.usatoday.com/life/2006-10-04-third-space_x.htm.

[370] Larson, 2008, pp. 32–33

[371] (http://news.cnet.com/8301-17852_3-20087817-71/has-starbucks-had-enough-of-laptop-loungers/, http://gawker.com/5843279/the-great-starbucks-laptop-hobo-war-has-begun), http://www.sfchronicle.com/restaurants/article/Coffee-shops-limit-perks-to-move-Wi-Fi-squatters-4722190.php?t=586106004d8cb1714c.

to the coffee shop where I can work mostly without interruption while still having the stimulation of other people nearby. Sometimes I work even better. On those occasions when someone I know happens into the same space, it's always a welcome and, usually, short interruption ("Great to see you! Sorry… can't talk long now…"). If I look around, I see that I am not "alone." I see many other people at my favorite coffee shop or in the library working on their laptops, too. Communitude.

Using the natural interfaces as reviewed in Chapter 5 we may have even more opportunities to break away from the "desktop." Sitting for long periods of time is bad for us so maybe we stand as we work.[372] Or maybe we workout as we work, listening and responding to emails, for example, as we walk, run or bike.

Gaming devices, such as "omni-directional" or "360 degree" treadmills[373] will give us a chance to walk or run in a virtual space. But virtual environments needn't be purely fictional. Why not, instead, run or walk through the streets of Paris (as simulated via Google Earth, for example)— pursued or pursuing as we do, other players in our game? We get exercise, have fun, and learn more about Paris (or London or New York) all at the same time.

And then, sometime soon (long before 2057) imagine traveling through a virtual space representing a place in history—colonial America, for example or Athens in its golden age or a Jurassic period swamp? Or we might travel through a virtual space of our own information.

Real walking/running through a virtual learning space to compete in a multi-person game is an example of *multi-goaling* as we discussed before. We contrast multi-goaling with multi-tasking. In multi-tasking, we do an uneasy time-slice switching between several tasks (doing none especially well). With multi-goaling, one activity accomplishes several goals (the proverbial two birds killed with one stone). With synergy between goals we often do even better in the completion of one goal for the presence of the others. We run faster because it's fun and we're *just* about to catch the person in front of us. We keep walking just to see what's around the next Parisian corner.

The larger point was made already in Chapter 3 (Part 1). PIM is everywhere. Let's make it work for us in our lives.

9.6 CONCLUDING THOUGHTS ON TRANSFORMING TECHNOLOGIES

Will technology eliminate (the need for) PIM?

No.

Will it transform the way we do PIM?

Yes, with certainty.

---

[372] http://www.economist.com/news/science-and-technology/21583239-real-science-lies-behind-fad-standing-up-work-standing-orders.

[373] See http://www.theverge.com/2013/4/22/4253698/virtuix-omni-treadmill-oculus-rift-integration-kickstart-er-pricing; and, http://www.youtube.com/watch?v=BQw1tsgrJOs.

For starters, we considered input/output technologies such as voice recognition, gesture recognition, zooming and animation, eye-tracking, eye glasses with small screens (or even working whole-lens as filters and overlays to our visual experience). Combine these and related technologies in support of a more natural interface. Add a ubiquity of computing and constant, high bandwidth connectivity to the Web.

The result is that our ways of interacting with our information will change dramatically. But the result isn't an elimination of PIM.

To the contrary, we're faced with the potential for constant interaction with and a constant need to manage our information. To the bad, we have little hope for privacy in such a world—not in public places to be sure, possibly not even in private places. Digital information is everywhere. To the good, our ways of doing PIM may be much more integral to our ways of living. No need to lug a laptop or a camera. No need to pull out a credit card or even a palmtop device. No need to use a keyboard or even a touch screen. Our interactions with our information will be accomplished "naturally" through our eyes and hands and voices as aided through accessories we can wear rather than "lug."

Beyond the interface, we have the information itself. What if information for everything that matters to us could be saved, searched, and structured?

We started with the technical feasibility of **saving** "everything." Suppose, for starters, we could make a life log of everything we've experienced? A reasonably detailed life log might already be constructed for most of us based upon our interactions with our various devices (laptops, smartphones, tablets, etc.) and various applications (especially web-based services such as Gmail). We anticipate life logs that are increasingly integrated (one log rather than many logs scattered across different applications) recording events with increasing fidelity (e.g., pictures, sound and video as well as text).

Life logs may help us to recollect the events of our lives, *reminisce* (e.g., as we relive a special event), *retrieve* (e.g., "the picture we took at the soccer game"), *reflect* (what might have gone better in that exchange?) and "*remember our intentions*" ("Did I do what I said I would do?").

Assuming technical feasibility, many other issues remain. How to protect the privacy and security of a life log? How to guard against sudden loss (e.g., a virus attack) and also the gradual, inevitable degradation in the media used for storage? Technologies of storage may greatly extend a store's lifetime. Even so, our own internal memories will fade with the passage of time and, as these memories fade, the evocative power of digital life logs also appears to decline. More relevant for many of us may be the reality of a busy schedule that leaves us little time to reap the benefits of the "5 Rs" listed above. We're too busy living for today and tomorrow to spend much time on "yesterday."

And then, as we store more and more information, how to retrieve the "needle" of a particular event or information item from the haystack of "everything" informational?

The question takes us on to **search**—a second major technology with a potential to greatly transform PIM. Search, especially as situated in a larger context, has enormous potential to help us in the management of information that is "ours" in each of the senses in which information can be personal.

Search can help us to find information that is "owned by" us (**P1**)—the right version of a document, for example, and representing weeks of work. Search can help us to locate information about us (**P2**) on the Web especially as search technologies make more sophisticated use of the context surrounding references to names such as "William Jones." There is a natural segue from information about us (**P2**) to the information we send or share (**P4**). Search can help us to determine the impact that this information is having (good and bad). Search can help us to track the uses others are making of this information (with and without attribution).

Search can help us to filter and categorize the information directed toward us (**P3**) and, more generally, search can help us to sift and sort the information experienced by us (**P5**) and that flows by us constantly in each waking moment.

Search as a method of return to information is often placed in opposition to more stepwise navigational returns to information (a.k.a. "browsing"). However, the technology of search can work in ways unseen "behind the scenes" to make information navigation faster, easier, and less error-prone.

Situated searches can persist as a permanent part of our information landscape to help us locate information of relevance to us (**P6**) and our current information need. These searches—situated in connection with folders and other structuring items—may even help to improve our chances of serendipitously coming across useful information "by chance."

But then from search to **structure**. Any search that we do is structured by its scope. Structure provides a basis for query constraints (e.g., not just "Harry" but "Harry as author"). Structure provides a basis for navigating to information—either as a complement to search or as a primary method of information access. And structure helps people to recognize a desired item in the returned list of results.

But then back again to technologies to **save**. Fast searching depends not only on the fast access/seek times of storage but also on larger capacities needed to store indexes that may be a significant percentage (perhaps 100% or more) in storage size of the collections of information being indexed. The series of inserts on "Taking back our information" considered ways to take back our structures to be "first class" with existence separate from any single application but also able to be viewed and worked on through many applications. But the practical "mirroring" approach toward making structures first class also generates a need for more storage.

Technologies to save. Technologies to search. Technologies to structure. Each needs the other.

Yes, there's a "whole" in this bucket of transforming technologies.[374] The good kind. Technologies complement one another. Dependencies don't produce a flat, futile circularity. Rather, technologies interrelate to produce benefits that are much greater than what we could realize from a singular focus on just one (or another) of these technologies.

Technologies transform but don't eliminate PIM. Instead, technologies help us to be better at PIM. Technologies can increasingly take over the clerical burdens of PIM freeing us to focus more on the creative aspects of PIM. What is our information telling us? And how can we use it to best effect? PIM doesn't go away. Instead, PIM becomes a more integral part of and enabler of the lives we wish to live.

But, as we manage our information to manage our lives, we are not alone. We, ourselves and our information, are part of a social fabric linking us to others at home, at work, at play, and "at large." How can we manage our information in group situations? And how can we be assisted and energized through our interactions with others? These are questions for Chapter 10, "GIM and the social fabric of PIM." Chapter 10 is the first chapter in the final Part 3 to "The Future of Personal Information Management." In Part 3 we have the challenge to piece together all that has been learned in our explorations of PIM so that we might—really, literally—build a better world with our information.

---

[374] The children's song "There's a hole in the bucket" tells a story of circular dependences: "Henry has got a leaky bucket, and Liza tells him to repair it. But to fix the leaky bucket, he needs straw. To cut the straw, he needs a knife. To sharpen the knife, he needs to wet the sharpening stone. To wet the stone, he needs water. However, when Henry asks how to get the water, Liza's answer is 'in a bucket,'" http://en.wikipedia.org/wiki/There's_a_Hole_in_My_Bucket.

References

Adar, E., Karger, D., & Stein, L. A. (1999). Haystack: per-user information environment. In *8th Conference on Information and Knowledge Management (CIKM 1999)* (pp. 413–422). Kansas City, MO: ACM. Retrieved from http://haystack.lcs.mit.edu/papers/cikm99.pdf. DOI: 10.1145/319950.323231. 73

Adar, Eytan, Teevan, J., & Dumais, S. T. (2009). Resonance on the web: web dynamics and revisitation patterns. In *Proceedings of the 27th international conference on Human factors in computing systems* (pp. 1381–1390). Boston, MA, USA: ACM. DOI: 10.1145/1518701.1518909. 34

Aït-Kaci,, H. (2009). Children's magic won't deliver the semantic web. *Commun. ACM*, 52(3), 8–9. DOI:10.1145/1467247.1467250. 74

Allen, D. (2001). *Getting things done: The art of stress-free productivity*. New York: Penguin. Retrieved from http://www.davidco.com/. DOI: 10.1016/j.lrp.2008.09.004. 37

Anderson, J. R. (1990). *The adaptive character of thought*. Hillsdale, NJ: Lawrence Erlbaum Associates. DOI: 10.1037/0003-066X.51.4.355. 24

Anderson, K. M. (2005). Toward lightweight structural computing techniques with the SmallSC framework. In *Proceedings of the 2005 symposia on Metainformatics* (p. 1). Esbjerg, Denmark: DOI: 10.1145/1234324.1234325. 76, 101

Anderson, K. M., Sherba, S. A., & Lepthien, W. V. (2002). Toward large-scale information integration. In *Proceedings of the 24th International Conference on Software Engineering* (pp. 524–534). Orlando, Florida: ACM. ACM. DOI: 10.1145/581339.581403. 100

Anderson, K. M., Sherba, S. A., & Lepthien, W. V. (2003). Structure and behavior awareness in themis. In *Proceedings of the fourteenth ACM conference on Hypertext and hypermedia* (pp. 138–147). Nottingham, UK: ACM. DOI: 10.1145/900051.900082. 101

Anderson, K. M., Taylor, R. N., & E. James Whitehead, J. (1994). Chimera: hypertext for heterogeneous software environments. In *Proceedings of the 1994 ACM European conference on Hypermedia technology* (pp. 94–107). Edinburgh, Scotland: ACM. DOI: 10.1145/352595.352596. 100

André, P., schraefel, m. c., Teevan, J., & Dumais, S. T. (2009). Discovery is never by chance: designing for (un)serendipity. In *Proceedings of the seventh ACM conference on Creativity and cognition* (pp. 305–314). New York, NY, USA: ACM. DOI:10.1145/1640233.1640279. 43

Arampatzis, A., & Kamps, J. (2008). A study of query length. In *Proceedings of the 31st annual international ACM SIGIR conference on Research and development in information retrieval* (pp. 811–812). New York, NY, USA: ACM. DOI: 10.1145/1390334.1390517. 30

Bälter, O. (1997). Strategies for organising email messages. In *Proceedings of the Twelfth Conference of the British Computer Society Human Computer Interaction Specialist Group - People and Computers XII* (pp. 21–38). Bristol, UK: Springer. xix

Bao, X., Herlocker, J. L., & Dietterich, T. G. (2006). *Fewer clicks and less frustration: reducing the cost of reaching the right folder.* DOI: 10.1145/1111449.1111490. 37

Barreau, D. (2008). The persistence of behavior and form in the organization of personal information. *J. Am. Soc. Inf. Sci. Technol.*, 59(2), 307–317. DOI: 10.1002/asi.20752. 27

Barreau, D., & Nardi, B. A. (1995). Finding and reminding: file organization from the desktop. *SIGCHI Bull.*, 27(3), 39–43. 24

Barsalou, L. W. (1983). Ad hoc categories. *Memory & Cognition*, 11(3), 211–227. DOI: 10.3758/BF03196968. 66

Barsalou, L. W. (1991). Deriving categories to achieve goals. In *The psychology of learning and motivation: Advances in research and theory*. New York: Academic Press.

Bates, M. J. (1989). The design of browsing and berrypicking techniques for the online search interface. *Online Review*, 13, 407–424. DOI: 10.1108/eb024320. 32

Bates, Marcia J. (2002). After the dot-bomb: Getting Web information retrieval right this time. *First Monday*, 7(7). Retrieved from http://www.firstmonday.dk/issues/issue7_7/bates/. DOI: 10.5210%2Ffm.v7i7.971. 99

Beale, R. (2007). Supporting serendipity: Using ambient intelligence to augment user exploration for data mining and web browsing. *Int. J. Hum.-Comput. Stud.*, 65(5), 421–433. DOI:10.1016/j.ijhcs.2006.11.012. 43

Belkin, N. J., & Croft, W. B. (1992). Information filtering and information retrieval: two sides of the same coin? *Commun. ACM*, 35(12), 29–38. DOI: 10.1145/138859.138861. 42

Belkin, N., Marchetti, P. G., & Cool, C. (1993). Braque: Design of an interface to support user interaction in information retrieval. *Information Processing and Management*, 29(3), 325–344. DOI: 10.1016/0306-4573(93)90059-M. 32

Bell, G. (2001). A personal digital store. *Communications of the ACM*, 44(1), 86–91. Retrieved from http://portal.acm.org/citation.cfm?doid=357489.357513. DOI: 10.1145/357489.357513. 8

Bell, M., Reeves, S., Brown, B., Sherwood, S., MacMillan, D., Ferguson, J., & Chalmers, M. (2009). EyeSpy: supporting navigation through play. In *Proceedings of the 27th international conference on Human factors in computing systems* (pp. 123–132). Boston, MA, USA: ACM. DOI: 10.1145/1518701.1518723. 4

Bellotti, V., Ducheneaut, N., Howard, M., Smith, I., & Grinter, R. (2005). Quality vs. quantity: Email-centric task-management and its relationship with overload. *Human-Computer Interaction*, 20(1-2), 89–138. DOI: 10.1207/s15327051hci2001&2_4. xix

Bellotti, V., & Smith, I. (2000). Informing the design of an information management system with iterative fieldwork. In *Conference on Designing interactive systems (DIS 2000)* (pp. 227—237). New York City, NY: ACM Press. DOI: 10.1145/347642.347728. xix

Bennett, P. N., Dumais, S. T., & Horvitz, E. (2005). The Combination of Text Classifiers Using Reliability Indicators. *Inf. Retr.*, 8(1), 67–100. DOI:10.1023/B:INRT.0000048491.59134.94. 39

Berghel, H. (1997). Email : the good, the bad and the ugly. *Communications of the ACM*, 40(4), 11–15. Retrieved from http://portal.acm.org/citation.cfm?doid=248448.248450. DOI: 10.1145/248448.248450. xix

Bergman, O., Beyth-Marom, R., & Nachmias, R. (2006). The project fragmentation problem in personal information management. In *Proceedings of the SIGCHI conference on Human Factors in computing systems* (pp. 271–274). Montreal, Quebec, Canada: ACM. DOI: 10.1145/1124772.1124813. 36, 60

Bergman, O., Beyth-Marom, R., Nachmias, R., Gradovitch, N., & Whittaker, S. (2008). Improved search engines and navigation preference in personal information management. *ACM Trans. Inf. Syst.*, 26(4), 1–24. DOI: 10.1145/1402256.1402259. 86, 27

Bergman, O., Gradovitch, N., Bar-Ilan, J., & Beyth-Marom, R. (2013). Folder versus tag preference in personal information management. *Journal of the American Society for Information Science and Technology*, n/a–n/a. DOI:10.1002/asi.22906. 29

Bergman, O., Tucker, S., Beyth-Marom, R., Cutrell, E., & Whittaker, S. (2009). It's not that important: demoting personal information of low subjective importance using GrayArea. In *Proceedings of the 27th international conference on Human factors in computing systems* (pp. 269–278). Boston, MA, USA: ACM. DOI: 10.1145/1518701.1518745. 13

Bergman, O., Whittaker, S., Sanderson, M., Nachmias, R., & Ramamoorthy, A. (2010). The effect of folder structure on personal file navigation. *J. Am. Soc. Inf. Sci. Technol.*, 61(12), 2426–2441. DOI: 10.1002/asi.21415. 27, 29, 65

Bergman, O., Whittaker, S., Sanderson, M., Nachmias, R., & Ramamoorthy, A. (2012). How do we find personal files?: the effect of OS, presentation & depth on file navigation. In *Proceedings of the 2012 ACM annual conference on Human Factors in Computing Systems* (pp. 2977–2980). New York, NY, USA: ACM. DOI:10.1145/2208636.2208707. 27, 29

Berners-Lee, T. (2005, 15 12-15, 1998). Semantic Web roadmap: An attempt to give a high-level plan of the architecture of the Semantic Web. Retrieved from http://www.w3.org/DesignIssues/Semantic.html. 70

Berners-Lee, T., Hendler, J.A, & Lassila, O. (n.d.). The semantic web. *Scientific American*, v284(i5), 34–43. 70, 71

Bernstein, M., Kleek, M. V., Karger, D., & Schraefel, M. C. (2008). Information scraps: How and why information eludes our personal information management tools. *ACM Trans. Inf. Syst.*, 26(4), 1–46. DOI: 10.1145/1402256.1402263. 38

Biegel, G., & Cahill, V. (2004). A Framework for Developing Mobile, Context-aware Applications. In *Proceedings of the Second IEEE International Conference on Pervasive Computing and Communications (PerCom'04)* (p. 361–). Washington, DC, USA: IEEE Computer Society. Retrieved from http://dl.acm.org/citation.cfm?id=977406.978672. DOI: 10.1109/PERCOM.2004.1276875. 32

Blair, D. C., & Maron, M. E. (1985). An evaluation of retrieval effectiveness for a full-text document-retrieval system. *Communications of the ACM*, 28(3), 289–299. DOI: 10.1145/3166.3197. 46

Blanc-Brude, T., & Scapin, D. L. (2007). What do people recall about their documents?: implications for desktop search tools. In *Proceedings of the 12th international conference on Intelligent user interfaces* (pp. 102–111). Honolulu, Hawaii, USA: ACM. DOI: 10.1145/1216295.1216319. 27

Boardman, R., & Sasse, M. A. (2004). "Stuff goes into the computer and doesn't come out" A cross-tool study of personal information management. In *ACM SIGCHI Conference on Human Factors in Computing Systems* (CHI 2004). Vienna, Austria. DOI: 10.1145/985692.985766. 28, 36, 60

Boisvert, R. F., & Irwin, M. J. (2006). Plagiarism on the rise. *Commun. ACM*, 49(6), 23–24. DOI:10.1145/1132469.1132487. 35

Bowman, D. A., McMahan, R. P., & Ragan, E. D. (2012). Questioning naturalism in 3D user interfaces. *Commun. ACM*, 55(9), 78–88. DOI:10.1145/2330667.2330687. 4

Brin, S., & Page, L. (1998). The anatomy of a large-scale hypertextual Web search engine. *Comput. Netw. ISDN Syst.*, 30(1-7), 107–117. DOI: 10.1016/S0169-7552(98)00110-X. 30

Broadbent, D. E. (1958). *Perception and communication*. London, U.K.: Pergamon Press. DOI: 10.1037/10037-000. 14

Bruce, H., Wenning, A., Jones, E., Vinson, J., & Jones, W. (2010). Seeking an ideal solution to the management of personal information collections. In *Information Seeking in Context Conference -(ISIC)* 2010. Murcia, Spain. 59, 60

Brutlag, J. D., & Meek, C. (2000). Challenges of the Email Domain for Text Classification. In *Proceedings of the Seventeenth International Conference on Machine Learning* (pp. 103–110). San Francisco, CA, USA: Morgan Kaufmann Publishers Inc. Retrieved from http://dl.acm.org/citation.cfm?id=645529.657817. 38

Bryan, K., & Leise, T. (2006). The $25,000,000,000 Eigenvector: The Linear Algebra behind Google. *SIAM Review*, 48(3), 569–581. DOI:10.1137/050623280. 55

Buchanan, G., Blandford, A., Thimbleby, H., & Jones, M. (2004). Integrating information seeking and structuring: exploring the role of spatial hypertext in a digital library. In *Proceedings of the fifteenth ACM conference on Hypertext and hypermedia* (pp. 225–234). Santa Cruz, CA, USA: ACM. DOI: 10.1145/1012807.1012864. 67

Budzik, J., Hammond, K., & Birnbaum, L. (2001). Information access in context. *Knowledge based systems*, 14(1-2), 37–53. DOI: 10.1016/S0950-7051(00)00105-2. 32

Burrow, A. L. (2004). Negotiating access within Wiki: a system to construct and maintain a taxonomy of access rules. DOI: 10.1145/1012807.1012831. 67

Bush, V. (1945). As We May Think. *The Atlantic Monthly*, 176(1), 641–649. Retrieved from http://www.theatlantic.com/doc/194507/bush. 8

Byrne, D., Doherty, A. R., Jones, G. J. F., Smeaton, A. F., Kumpulainen, S., & Järvelin, K. (2008). The SenseCam as a tool for task observation. In *Proceedings of the 22nd British HCI Group Annual Conference on People and Computers: Culture, Creativity, Interaction - Volume 2* (pp. 19–22). Swinton, UK, UK: British Computer Society. Retrieved from http://dl.acm.org/citation.cfm?id=1531826.1531832. 8

Cai, Y., Dong, X. L., Halevy, A., Liu, J. M., & Madhavan, J. (2005). Personal information management with SEMEX. In *ACM SIGMOD International Conference on Management of Data*,. Baltimore, MD. DOI:10.1145/1066157.1066289. 35

Capra, R. G. (2006, March 23). An Investigation of Finding and Refinding Information on the Web. Retrieved July 21, 2013, from http://scholar.lib.vt.edu/theses/available/etd-03022006-154809/. 34

Capra, R., & Pérez-Quiñones, M. A. (2005). Using Web Search Engines to Find and Refind Information. *IEEE Computer*, 38(10), 36–42. DOI: 10.1109/MC.2005.355. 22, 34

Capra,III, R. G., & Pérez-Quiñones, M. A. (2005). Mobile refinding of web information using a voice interface: an exploratory study. In *Proceedings of the 2005 Latin American conference on Human-computer interaction* (pp. 88–99). New York, NY, USA: ACM. DOI:10.1145/1111360.1111369. 22

Carlson, N. (2012, November 22). The End Of The Smartphone Era Is Coming. Business Insider. Retrieved March 21, 2013, from http://www.businessinsider.com/the-end-of-the-smartphone-era-is-coming-2012-11. 2

Carpineto, C., & Romano, G. (2012). A Survey of Automatic Query Expansion in Information Retrieval. *ACM Comput. Surv.*, 44(1), 1:1–1:50. DOI:10.1145/2071389.2071390. 39

Carr, N. (2008, August). Is Google Making Us Stupid? *The Atlantic*. Retrieved from http://www.theatlantic.com/magazine/archive/2008/07/is-google-making-us-stupid/6868/. 46

Carr, N. G. (2011). *The shallows: what the Internet is doing to our brains.* New York: W.W. Norton. 46

Catarci, T., Dong, L., Halevy, A., & Poggi, A. (2007). Structure everything. In *Personal Information Management* (William Jones and Jaime Teevan.). University of Washington Press. 72

Chaffee, J., & Gauch, S. (2000). Personal ontologies for web navigation. In *CIKM 2000 : 9th International Conference on Information Knowledge Management* (pp. 227–234). MacLean, VA.: ACM. DOI: 10.1145/354756.354823. 72

Chaisson, E. J. (2002). *Cosmic Evolution: The Rise of Complexity in Nature.* Harvard University Press. 57

Chau, D. H., Myers, B., & Faulring, A. (2008). What to do when search fails: finding information by association. In *Proceeding of the twenty-sixth annual SIGCHI conference on Human factors in computing systems* (pp. 999–1008). Florence, Italy: ACM. DOI: 10.1145/1357054.1357208. 33

Chen, A. (2013, March 11). Google Glass will be the next Apple Newton. *Quartz*. Retrieved March 21, 2013, from http://qz.com/61145/google-glass-will-be-the-next-apple-newton/. 2

Chirita, P. A., Gavriloaie, R., Ghita, S., Nejdl, W., & Paiu, R. (2005). Activity based metadata for semantic desktop search. In *The Semantic Web: Research and Applications* (pp. 439–454). Springer. Retrieved from http://link.springer.com/chapter/10.1007/11431053_30. DOI: 10.1007/11431053_30. 72

Christian, B. (2012). *The most human human: what artificial intelligence teaches us about being alive.* New York: Anchor Books. 62

Chrysikou, E. G. (2006). When shoes become hammers: Goal-derived categorization training enhances problem-solving performance. *Journal of Experimental Psychology: Learning, Memory, and Cognition*, 32(4), 935–942. DOI:10.1037/0278-7393.32.4.935. 66

Civan, A., Jones, W., Klasnja, P., & Bruce, H. (2008). Better to Organize Personal Information by Folders Or by Tags?: The Devil Is in the Details. In *68th Annual Meeting of the American Society for Information Science and Technology* (ASIST 2008). Columbus, OH. 29

Cockburn, A., Greenberg, S., Jones, S., McKenzie, B., & Moyle, M. (2003). Improving web page revisitation : analysis, design and evaluation. *IT&Society*, 1(3), 159–183. Retrieved from http://www.stanford.edu/group/siqss/itandsociety/v01i03/abstract.html#9. 34

Cockburn, A., & McKenzie, B. (2001). What do web users do ? : an empirical analysis of web use. *International Journal of Human-Computer Studies*, 54(6), 903–922. Retrieved from http://dox.doi.org/10.1006/ijhc.2001.0459. DOI: 10.1006/ijhc.2001.0459. 34

Collins, A. M., & Quillian, M. R. (1969). Retrieval time from semantic memory. *Journal of Verbal Learning & Verbal Behavior*, 8(2), 240–247. DOI: 10.1016/S0022-5371(69)80069-1. 66

Craik, F. I. M., & Lockhart, R. S. (1972). Levels of processing: A framework for memory research. *Journal of Verbal Learning and Verbal Behavior*, 11(6), 671–684. DOI:10.1016/S0022-5371(72)80001-X. 12

Csikszentmihalyi, M. (1991). *Flow: The Psychology of Optimal Experience*. HarperCollins. 118

Cutrell, E., Dumais, S., & Teevan, J. (2006). Searching to eliminate personal information management. *Communications of the ACM*, 49(1), 58–64. DOI: 10.1145/1107458.1107492. 24

Cutrell, E., Robbins, D., Dumais, S., & Sarin, R. (2006). Fast, flexible filtering with phlat. DOI: 10.1145/1124772.1124812. 32

Czerwinski, M., Dumais, S. T., Robertson, G., Dziadosz, S., Tiernan, S., & van Dantzich, M. (1999). Visualizing implicit queries for information management and retrieval. In *ACM SIGCHI Conference on Human Factors in Computing Systems (CHI 99)* (pp. 560–567). Pittsburgh, PA.: ACM SIGCHI. Retrieved from http://doi.acm.org/10.1145/302979.303158. DOI: 10.1145/302979.303158. 32

Czerwinski, Mary, Horvitz, E., & Wilhite, S. (2004). A diary study of task switching and interruptions. In *Proceedings of the SIGCHI conference on Human factors in computing systems* (pp. 175–182). Vienna, Austria: ACM. DOI: 10.1145/985692.985715. 38

Dabbish, L. A., & Kraut, R. E. (2006). Email overload at work: an analysis of factors associated with email strain. In *Proceedings of the 2006 20th anniversary conference on Computer supported cooperative work* (pp. 431–440). Banff, Alberta, Canada: ACM. DOI: 10.1145/1180875.1180941. xix

Davies, S., Allen, S., Raphaelson, J., Meng, E., Engleman, J., King, R., & Lewis, C. (2006). Popcorn: the personal knowledge base. In *Proceedings of the 6th conference on Designing Interactive sys-*

tems (pp. 150–159). University Park, PA, USA: ACM. DOI: 10.1145/1142405.1142431. 72

Davis, H., Hall, W., Heath, I., Hill, G., & Wilkins, R. (1992). Toward an integrated information environment with open hypermedia systems. In *Proceedings of the ACM conference on Hypertext* (pp. 181–190). Milan, Italy: ACM. DOI: 10.1145/168466.168522. 100

Davis, J. P., Eisenhardt, K. M., & Bingham, C. B. (2009). Optimal structure, market dynamism, and the strategy of simple rules. *Administrative Science Quarterly*, 54(3), 413–452. Retrieved from http://asq.sagepub.com/content/54/3/413.short. DOI: 10.2189/asqu.2009.54.3.413. 57

De Bruijn, O., & Spence, R. (2008). A New Framework for Theory-Based Interaction Design Applied to Serendipitous Information Retrieval. *ACM Trans. Comput.-Hum. Interact.*, 15(1), 5:1–5:38. DOI:10.1145/1352782.1352787. 43

Decker, S., & Frank, M. (2004). The social semantic desktop. In *WWW2004 Workshop Application Design, Development and Implementation Issues in the Semantic Web* (Vol. 9, p. 10). Retrieved from http://sws.deri.ie/fileadmin/documents/DERI-TR-2004-05-02.pdf. 72

Deerwester, S., Dumais, S., Landauer, T. K., Furnas, G. W., & Harshman, R. A. (1990). Indexing by latent semantic analysis. *Journal of the Society for Information Science*, 41(6), 391–407. Retrieved from http://superbook.telcordia.com/~remde/isi/papers/JASIS90.ps. DOI: 10.1002/(SICI)1097-4571(199009)41:6<391::AID-ASI1>3.0.CO;2-9. 38

Dieng, R., & Hug, S. (1998). Comparison of Personal Ontologies Represented through Conceptual Graphs. In *ECAI* (Vol. 98, pp. 341–345). Retrieved from http://citeseerx.ist.psu.edu/viewdoc/download?doi=10.1.1.82.140&rep=rep1&type=pdf. 72

Dividino, R., Sizov, S., Staab, S., & Schueler, B. (2009). Querying for provenance, trust, uncertainty and other meta knowledge in RDF. *Web Semantics: Science, Services and Agents on the World Wide Web*, 7(3), 204–219. Retrieved from http://www.sciencedirect.com/science/article/pii/S1570826809000237. DOI: 10.1016/j.websem.2009.07.004. 94

Domingos, P. (2012). A few useful things to know about machine learning. *Commun. ACM*, 55(10), 78–87. DOI: 10.1145/2347736.2347755. 39

Dong, X., Halevy, A., & Madhavan, J. (2005). Reference reconciliation in complex information spaces. DOI: 10.1145/1066157.1066168. 35

Douglas Engelbart. (2013, March 19). In *Wikipedia, the free encyclopedia*. Retrieved from http://en.wikipedia.org/w/index.php?title=Douglas_Engelbart&oldid=542012197.

Dourish, P., Edwards, W. K., LaMarca, A., Lamping, J., Petersen, K., Salisbury, M., … Thornton, J. (2000). Extending document management systems with user-specific active properties.

ACM Transactions on Information Systems, 18(2), 140–170. Retrieved from http://portal. acm.org/citation.cfm?id=348758&coll=portal&dl=ACM&CFID=5562955&CFTO-KEN=52182225. DOI: 10.1145/348751.348758. 40

Dourish, P., Edwards, W. K., LaMarca, A., & Salisbury, M. (1999). Using properties for uniform interaction in the Presto Document System. In *The 12th Annual ACM Symposium on User Interface Software and Technology (UIST'99)*. Asheville, NC. DOI: 10.1145/320719.322583. 29, 40

Dredze, M., Lau, T., & Kushmerick, N. (2006). Automatically classifying emails into activities. In *Proceedings of the 11th international conference on Intelligent user interfaces* (pp. 70–77). New York, NY, USA: ACM. DOI: 10.1145/1111449.1111471. 38

Drucker, P. (2009). *Landmarks of Tomorrow: A Report on the New Post-Modern World*. Transaction Publishers. 110

Ducheneaut, N., & Bellotti, V. (2001). E-mail as habitat. *Interactions*, 8(5), 30–38. Retrieved from http://delivery.acm.org/10.1145/390000/383305/p30-ducheneaut.pdf?key1=383305& key2=7070797201&coll=portal&dl=ACM&CFID=3551004&CFTOKEN=19024722. DOI: 10.1145/382899.383305. xix

Dumais, S., Cutrell, E., Cadiz, J., Jancke, G., Sarin, R., & Robbins, D. (2003). Stuff I've seen: a system for personal information retrieval and re-use. In *SIGIR* 2003: 26th Annual International ACM SIGIR Conference on Research and Development in Information Retrieval (pp. 72—79). Toronto, Canada. DOI: 10.1145/860435.860451. 29

Dumais, S. T. (2004). Latent semantic analysis. *Annual Review of Information Science and Technology*, 38(1), 188–230. DOI: 10.1002/aris.1440380105. 38

Dumais, S. T., & Landauer, T. K. (1984). Describing categories of objects for menu retrieval systems. *Behavior Research Methods, Instruments, & Computers*, 16(2), 242–248. Retrieved from http://link.springer.com/article/10.3758/BF03202396. DOI: 10.3758/BF03202396. 45

Elsweiler, D., Baillie, M., & Ruthven, I. (2008). Exploring memory in email refinding. *ACM Trans. Inf. Syst.*, 26(4), 1–36. DOI: 10.1145/1402256.1402260. 28

Erdelez, S. (2004). Investigation of information encountering in the controlled research environment. *Inf. Process. Manage.*, 40(6), 1013–1025. DOI:10.1016/j.ipm.2004.02.002. 36

Erickson, T. (1996). The design and long-term use of a personal electronic notebook: a reflective analysis. In *Proceedings of the SIGCHI conference on Human factors in computing systems: common ground* (pp. 11–18). Vancouver, British Columbia, Canada: ACM. DOI: 10.1145/238386.238392. 59

Fails, J. A., & Olsen,Jr., D. R. (2003). Interactive machine learning. In *Proceedings of the 8th international conference on Intelligent user interfaces* (pp. 39–45). New York, NY, USA: ACM. DOI:10.1145/604045.604056. 39

Fertig, S., Freeman, E., & Gelernter, D. (1996a). Lifestreams: an alternative to the desktop metaphor. In *Conference on Human Factors in Computing Systems (CHI 1996)* (pp. 410–411). Vancouver, B.C.: ACM. DOI: 10.1145/257089.257404. 8, 117

Fertig, S., Freeman, E., & Gelernter, D. (1996b). Finding and reminding reconsidered. *SIGCHI Bulletin*, 28(1), 7 pp. Retrieved from http://www.acm.org/sigchi/bulletin/1996.1/fertig. html. 29, 46

Franz, T., Ansgar, S., & Staab, S. (2009). Are semantic desktops better?: summative evaluation comparing a semantic against a conventional desktop. In *Proceedings of the fifth international conference on Knowledge capture* (pp. 1–8). New York, NY, USA: ACM. DOI: 10.1145/1597735.1597737. 73

Freeman, E., & Gelernter, D. (1996). Lifestreams: A storage model for personal data. *ACM SIGMOD Record (ACM Special Interest Group on Management of Data)*, 25(1), 80–86. DOI: 10.1145/381854.381893. 8, 117

Gamberini, L., & Bussolon, S. (2001). Human navigation in electronic environments. *CyberPsychol. Behav.*, 4(1), 57–65. DOI: 10.1089/10949310151088398. 67

GeekWire. (2011, November 23). "Hello, computer!" UW prof and students search outside the box - GeekWire. *GeekWire*. Retrieved March 27, 2013, from http://www.geekwire. com/2011/computer-uw-prof-students-search-box/. 31

Gemmell, J., Bell, G., & Lueder, R. (2006). MyLifeBits: a personal database for everything. *Commun. ACM*, 49(1), 88–95. DOI: 10.1145/1107458.1107460. 8

Gemmell, J., Bell, G., Lueder, R., Drucker, S., & Wong, C. (2002). Mylifebits: fulfilling the memex vision. In *2002 ACM workshops on Multimedia* (pp. 235–238). Juan-les-Pins, France: ACM Press. DOI: 10.1145/641007.641053. 8

Gemmell, J., Lueder, R., & Bell, G. (2003). The MyLifeBits lifetime store. In *ACM SIGMM 2003 Workshop on Experiential Telepresence (ETP 2003)* (pp. 80–83). Berkeley, CA. DOI: 10.1145/982484.982500. 8

Gemmell, J., Williams, L., Wood, K., Bell, G., & Lueder, R. (2004). Passive capture and ensuing issues for a personal lifetime store. In *The First ACM Workshop on Continuous Archival and Retrieval of Personal Experiences (CARPE '04)* (pp. 48–55). New York). DOI: 10.1145/1026653.1026660. xvi

Goldman, N., Bertone, P., Chen, S., Dessimoz, C., LeProust, E. M., Sipos, B., & Birney, E. (2013). Toward practical, high-capacity, low-maintenance information storage in synthesized DNA. *Nature*. DOI: 10.1038/nature11875. 19

Goncalves, D., & Jorge, J. A. (2003). Analyzing personal document spaces. In *Human-Computer Interaction International 2003*. Lawrence Erlbaum Associates. 33

Gray, W. D., & Fu, W.-T. (2001). Ignoring perfect knowledge in-the-world for imperfect knowledge in-the-head. In *Proceedings of the SIGCHI conference on Human factors in computing systems* (pp. 112–119). Seattle, Washington, United States: ACM. DOI: 10.1145/365024.365061. 12

Greenberg, S., & Cockburn, A. (1999). Getting back to back : alternate behaviors for a web browser`s Back button. In *5th Conference on Human Factors and the Web : the Future of Web Applications* (p. 7 pp.). Gaithersburg, MD. Retrieved from http://www.itl.nist.gov/iaui/vvrg/hfweb/proceedings/greenberg/. 34

Groza, T., Handschuh, S., & Moeller, K. (2007). The nepomuk project-on the way to the social semantic desktop. Retrieved from http://ir.library.nuigalway.ie/xmlui/handle/10379/437. 72

Gruber, T. (2009). *Ontology*. Retrieved from http://queksiewkhoon.tripod.com/ontology_01.pdf. 97

Grudin, J. (1988). Why CSCW applications fail: problems in the design and evaluation of organization of organizational interfaces. DOI: 10.1145/62266.62273. 121

Grudin, Jonathan. (2011). Kai: how media affects learning. *interactions*, 18(5), 70–73. DOI: 10.1145/2008176.2008192. 46

Grudin, Jonathan, & Poole, E. S. (2010). Wikis at work: success factors and challenges for sustainability of enterprise Wikis. In *Proceedings of the 6th International Symposium on Wikis and Open Collaboration* (pp. 5:1–5:8). New York, NY, USA: ACM. DOI: 10.1145/1832772.1832780. 67

Guarino, N., Oberle, D., & Staab, S. (2009). What is an Ontology? In *Handbook on ontologies* (pp. 1–17). Springer. Retrieved from http://link.springer.com/chapter/10.1007/978-3-540-92673-3_0. DOI: 10.1007/978-3-540-92673-3_0. 96

Gwizdka, J. (2002). Reinventing the inbox : supporting the management of pending tasks in email. In *ACM SIGCHI Conference on Human Factors in Computing Systems, Doctoral Consortium (CHI 2002)* (pp. 550–551). Minneapolis, MN: ACM SIGCHI. DOI: 10.1145/506443.506476. xix

Haase, P., Hotho, A., Schmidt-Thieme, L., & Sure, Y. (2005). Collaborative and usage-driven evolution of personal ontologies. In *The semantic web: research and applications* (pp. 486–499).

Springer. Retrieved from http://link.springer.com/chapter/10.1007/11431053_33. DOI: 10.1007/11431053_33. 72

Halasz, F. G. (2001). Reflections on "Seven Issues": hypertext in the era of the web. *ACM J. Comput. Doc.*, 25(3), 109–114. DOI: 10.1145/507317.507328. 122

Halasz, F. G., Moran, T. P., & Trigg, R. H. (1987). Notecards in a nutshell. In *Proceedings of the SIG-CHI/GI conference on Human factors in computing systems and graphics interface* (pp. 45–52). Toronto, Ontario, Canada: ACM Press. DOI: 10.1145/1165387.30859. 122

Haller, D. H. (2010). Knitting the kNet - Toward a Global Net of Knowledge. Retrieved from http://www.community-of-knowledge.de/beitrag/knitting-the-knet-toward-a-global-net-of-knowledge/. 71

Harper, R., Randall, D., Smythe, N., Evans, C., Heledd, L., & Moore, R. (2007). Thanks for the memory. In *Proceedings of the 21st British HCI Group Annual Conference on HCI 2008: People and Computers XXI: HCI...but not as we know it - Volume 2* (pp. 39–42). University of Lancaster, United Kingdom: British Computer Society. 10

Hartig, O. (2009). Provenance Information in the Web of Data. In *LDOW*. Retrieved from http://www.dbis.informatik.hu-berlin.de/fileadmin/research/papers/conferences/2009-ldow-hartig.pdf. 94

Heath, T., & Bizer, C. (2011). Linked Data: Evolving the Web into a Global Data Space. *Synthesis Lectures on the Semantic Web: Theory and Technology*, 1(1), 1–136. DOI: 10.2200/S00334ED1V01Y201102WBE001. 75

Henzinger, M., Chang, B.-W., Milch, B., & Brin, S. (2003). Query-free news search. In *2th International World Wide Web Conference*. DOI: 10.1007/s11280-004-4870-6. 32

Hilbert, M., & López, P. (2011). The World's Technological Capacity to Store, Communicate, and Compute Information. *Science*, 332(6025), 60–65. DOI: 10.1126/science.1200970. 9

Hodges, S., Williams, L., Berry, E., Izadi, S., Srinivasan, J., Butler, A., ... Wood, K. (2006). Sense-Cam: a retrospective memory aid. In *Proceedings of the 8th international conference on Ubiquitous Computing* (pp. 177–193). Berlin, Heidelberg: Springer-Verlag. DOI: 10.1007/11853565_11. 10, 11

Hollindale, C. (2013). You've Started Self-Tracking. Now What? *Lifehacker*. Retrieved July 5, 2013, from http://lifehacker.com/youve-started-self-tracking-now-what-493562901. 17

Holt, J. (2011, March 3). Smarter, Happier, More Productive. *London Review of Books*, pp. 9–12. Retrieved from http://www.lrb.co.uk/v33/n05/jim-holt/smarter-happier-more-productive. 46

Hong, L., Chi, E. H., Budiu, R., Pirolli, P., & Nelson, L. (2008). SparTag.us: a low cost tagging system for foraging of web content. In *Proceedings of the working conference on Advanced visual interfaces* (pp. 65–72). Napoli, Italy: ACM. DOI: 10.1145/1385569.1385582. 32

Horrocks, I. (2008). Ontologies and the semantic web. *Commun. ACM*, 51(12), 58–67. DOI: 10.1145/1409360.1409377. 70, 72, 74

Horvitz, E., & Apacible, J. (2003). Learning and reasoning about interruption. DOI: 10.1145/958432.958440. 51

Hsu, J. (2008, September 18). The Secrets of Storytelling: Why We Love a Good Yarn: Scientific American. *Scientific American Mind*. Retrieved January 22, 2012, from http://www.scientificamerican.com/article.cfm?id=the-secrets-of-storytelling#comments. 33

Huhns, M. N., & Stephens, L. M. (1999). Personal ontologies. *IEEE Internet Computing*, 3(5), 85–87. DOI: 10.1109/4236.793466. 72

Isaacs, E., Konrad, A., Walendowski, A., Lennig, T., Hollis, V., & Whittaker, S. (2013). Echoes from the past: how technology mediated reflection improves well-being. In *Proceedings of the SIGCHI Conference on Human Factors in Computing Systems* (pp. 1071–1080). New York, NY, USA: ACM. DOI: 10.1145/2470654.246613. 11

Jain, A. K., Murty, M. N., & Flynn, P. J. (1999). Data clustering: a review. *ACM Comput. Surv.*, 31(3), 264–323. DOI: 10.1145/331499.331504. 50

Jensen, C., Lonsdale, H., Wynn, E., Cao, J., Slater, M., & Dietterich, T. G. (2010). The life and times of files and information: a study of desktop provenance. In *Proceedings of the 28th international conference on Human factors in computing systems* (pp. 767–776). Atlanta, Georgia, USA: ACM. DOI: 10.1145/1753326.1753439. 94

Jin, C., Pan, M., & Zhang, D. (2010). A Novel Web Page Watermark Scheme for HTML Security. In *2010 International Conference of Information Science and Management Engineering (ISME)* (Vol. 1, pp. 35–38). Presented at the 2010 International Conference of Information Science and Management Engineering (ISME). DOI: 10.1109/ISME.2010.60. 35

Johnson, S. (2007). A framework for mobile context-aware applications. *BT Technology Journal*, 25(2), 106–111. DOI: 10.1007/s10550-007-0033-5. 32

Jones, W. (1986a). On the applied use of human memory models: The Memory Extender personal filing system. *International Journal of Man Machine Studies*, 25, 191–228. DOI: 10.1016/S0020-7373(86)80076-1. 39

Jones, W. (1986b). The memory extender personal filing system. DOI: 10.1145/22339.22387. 39

Jones, W. (2007). *Keeping Found Things Found: The Study and Practice of Personal Information Management*. San Francisco, CA: Morgan Kaufmann Publishers. xix, 2, 9, 13, 21, 26, 30, 101

Jones, W., & Anderson, J. R. (1987). Short vs. long term memory retrieval: A comparison of the effects of information load and relatedness. *Journal of Experimental Psychology: General*, 116, 137–153. DOI: 10.1037/0096-3445.116.2.137. 118

Jones, W., Bruce, H., & Dumais, S. (2003). How do people get back to information on the web? How can they do it better? In *9th IFIP TC13 International Conference on Human-Computer Interaction (INTERACT 2003)*. Zurich, Switzerland. 36

Jones, W., Bruce, H., & Foxley, A. (2006). Project Contexts to Situate Personal Information. In *SIGIR 2006*. Seattle, WA: ACM Press. DOI: 10.1145/1148170.1148342. 36

Jones, W., Bruce, H., Foxley, A., & Munat, C. (2006). Planning personal projects and organizing personal information. In *69th Annual Meeting of the American Society for Information Science and Technology (ASIST 2006)* (Vol. 43). Austin, TX: American Society for Information Science & Technology. 36

Jones, W., Dumais, S., & Bruce, H. (2002). Once found, what then? : A study of "keeping" behaviors in the personal use of web information. Presented at the 65th Annual Meeting of the American Society for Information Science and Technology (ASIST 2002), Philadelphia, PA. 38

Jones, W., Klasnja, P., Civan, A., & Adcock, M. (2008). The Personal Project Planner: Planning to Organize Personal Information. In *ACM SIGCHI Conference on Human Factors in Computing Systems (CHI 2008)* (pp. 681–684). Florence, Italy: ACM, New York, NY. DOI: 10.1145/1357054.1357162. 36

Jones, W., & Maier, D. (2003). *Report from the session on personal information management. Workshop of the information and data management program.* Seattle, WA: National Science Foundation Information. Retrieved from http://dada.cs.washington.edu/nsf2003/final-reports/Summary%20of%20IDM03%20session%20on%20Personal%20Information%20Management.pdf. 21

Jones, W., Munat, C., & Bruce, H. (2005). The Universal Labeler: Plan the project and let your information follow. In *68th Annual Meeting of the American Society for Information Science and Technology (ASIST 2005)* (p. TBD.). Charlotte, NC: American Society for Information Science & Technology. Retrieved from http://kftf.ischool.washington.edu/UL_ASIST05.pdf. 36, 67

Jones, W., Phuwanartnurak, A. J., Gill, R., & Bruce, H. (2005). Don't take my folders away! Organizing personal information to get things done. In *ACM SIGCHI Conference on Human Factors in Computing Systems (CHI 2005)* (Vol. 2005, pp. 1505–1508). Portland, OR: ACM Press. DOI: 10.1145/1056808.1056952. 25, 29, 60, 65

Jones, W., & Teevan, J. (2007). *Personal Information Management*. Seattle, WA: University of Washington Press. 11

Jones, William. (2010). No knowledge but through information. *First Monday*, 15(9). Retrieved from http://firstmonday.org/htbin/cgiwrap/bin/ojs/index.php/fm/article/viewArticle/3062/2600. 72, 96

Jones, William. (2011). XooML: XML in support of many tools working on a single organization of personal information. In *Proceedings of the 2011 iConference* (pp. 478–488). Seattle, Washington: ACM. Retrieved from http://delivery.acm.org/10.1145/1950000/1940827/p478-jones.pdf?key1=1940827&key2=5397719921&coll=DL&dl=ACM&ip=205.175.115.100&CFID=11076833&CFTOKEN=71585935.

Jones, William. (2012). *The Future of Personal Information Management, Part I*. San Rafael: Morgan & Claypool Publishers. Retrieved from http://www.morganclaypool.com/doi/abs/10.2200/S00411ED1V01Y201203ICR021. DOI: 10.2200/S00411ED1V01Y-201203ICR021. xvii, 4, 9, 61, 69, 72

Jones, William, & Anderson, K. M. (2011). Many Views, Many Modes, Many Tools... One Structure: Toward a Non-disruptive Integration of Personal Information. In *Proceedings of the 22nd ACM conference on Hypertext and hypermedia* (pp. 113–122). Eindhoven, The Netherlands: ACM. DOI: 10.1145/1995966.1995984. 87

Jones, William, Anderson, K. M., & Whittaker, S. (2012). Representing our information structures for research and for everyday use. In *CHI '12 Extended Abstracts on Human Factors in Computing Systems* (pp. 151–160). New York, NY, USA: ACM. DOI: 10.1145/2212776.2212793. 87

Jones, W., Bruce, H., Jones, E., & Vinson, J. (2009). Providing for Paper, Place and People in Personal Projects. Presented at the PIM 2009, Vancouver, B.C. Retrieved from http://pimworkshop.org/2009/index.php?page=acceptedpapers. 26

Jones, William, Hou, D., Sethanandha, B. D., & Bi, E. S. (2009). Planz: Writing New Stories for the Same Old File System. Presented at the PIM 2009, Vancouver, B.C. Retrieved from http://pimworkshop.org/2009/papers/jones-demo-pim2009.pdf. 37

Jones, William, Hou, D., Sethanandha, B. D., Bi, S., & Gemmell, J. (2010). Planz to put our digital information in its place. In *Proceedings of the 28th of the international conference extended abstracts on Human factors in computing systems* (pp. 2803–2812). Atlanta, Georgia, USA: ACM. DOI: 10.1145/1753846.1753866. 37

Kalnikait\.e, V., & Whittaker, S. (2008). Cueing digital memory: how and why do digital notes help us remember? In *Proceedings of the 22nd British HCI Group Annual Conference on People and Computers: Culture, Creativity, Interaction - Volume 1* (pp. 153–161). Swinton, UK, UK: British Computer Society. Retrieved from http://dl.acm.org/citation. cfm?id=1531514.1531536. 13

Kalnikaite, V., & Whittaker, S. (2012). Synergetic Recollection: How to Design Lifelogging Tools That Help Locate the Right Information. In *Human-Computer Interaction: The Agency Perspective* (pp. 329–348). Springer. Retrieved from http://link.springer.com/chapter/10.1007/978-3-642-25691-2_14. DOI: 10.1007/978-3-642-25691-2_14. 10, 37

Kalnikaité, V., & Whittaker, S. (2007). Software or wetware?: discovering when and why people use digital prosthetic memory. In *Proceedings of the SIGCHI Conference on Human Factors in Computing Systems* (pp. 71–80). New York, NY, USA: ACM. DOI: 10.1145/1240624.1240635. 12

Kaptelinin, V. (2003). Integrating tools and tasks: UMEA: translating interaction histories into project contexts. In *ACM SIGCHI Conference on Human Factors in Computing Systems (CHI 2003)* (pp. 353—360). Ft. Lauderdale, FL. DOI: 10.1145/642611.642673. 36

Karger, D. R. (2007). Unify Everything: It's All the Same to Me. In *Personal Information Management*. (William Jones & Jaime Teevan.). Seattle, WA: University of Washington Press. 59, 73, 101

Karger, D. R., Bakshi, K., Huynh, D., Quan, D., & Sinha, V. (2005a). Haystack: A general purpose information management tool for end users of semistructured data. In *Second Biennial Conference on Innovative Data Systems Research (CIDR 2005)*. Asilomar, CA. Retrieved from http://www-db.cs.wisc.edu/cidr/cidr2005/papers/P02.pdf. 73

Karger, D. R., Bakshi, K., Huynh, D., Quan, D., & Sinha, V. (2005b). Haystack: A customizable general-purpose information management tool for end users of semistructured data. In *Proc. of the CIDR Conf.* Retrieved from http://cs.brown.edu/courses/cs295-11/2006/haystack.pdf. 73

Karousos, N., Pandis, I., Reich, S., & Tzagarakis, M. (2003). Offering open hypermedia services to the WWW: a step-by-step approach for developers. In *Proceedings of the 12th international conference on World Wide Web* (pp. 482–489). Budapest, Hungary: ACM. DOI: 10.1145/775152.775221. 100

Katifori, A., Vassilakis, C., Daradimos, I., Lepouras, G., Ioannidis, Y., Dix, A., … Catarci, T. (2008). Personal ontology creation and visualization for a personal interaction management system. In *Proceedings of PIM Workshop, CHI* (p. 15). Retrieved from http://www.alandix.com/academic/papers/PIM2008-personal-ontology/pim2008-katifori-etal.pdf. 72, 74

Kim, N., Lee, H. S., Oh, K. J., & Choi, J. Y. (2009). Context-aware mobile service for routing the fastest subway path. *Expert Syst. Appl.*, 36(2), 3319–3326. DOI: 10.1016/j.eswa.2008.01.054. 32

Knight, W. (2012, October 11). What Comes After the Touch Screen? | MIT Technology Review. *MIT Technology Review*. Retrieved March 21, 2013, from http://www.technologyreview. com/news/429546/what-comes-after-the-touch-screen/. 4

Kraft, R., Maghoul, F., & Chang, C. C. (2005). Y!Q: contextual search at the point of inspiration. DOI: 10.1145/1099554.1099746. 32

Krevelen, D. W. F. V., & Poelman, R. (2010). A Survey of Augmented Reality Technologies , Applications and Limitations. *International Journal*, 9(2), 1–20. DOI: 10.1155/2011/721827. 2

Lansdale, M. (1988). The psychology of personal information management. *Appl. Ergon.*, 19(1), 55–66. DOI: 10.1016/0003-6870(88)90199-8. 12, 21

Larson, R. C. (2008). Starbucks a Strategic Analysis. Past Decisions and Future Options. Retrieved from http://coe.brown.edu/documents/StarbucksaStrategicAnalysis_R.Larson_honors_2008.pdf. 123

Lee, E. S., & Raymond, D. R. (1993). Menu-driven systems. *Encyclopedia of Microcomputers,* 11, 101–127. Retrieved from http://www.darrellraymond.com/menus.pdf. 45

Licklider, J. C. R. (1960). Man-computer symbiosis. *IRE Transactions on Human Factors in Electronics*, HFE-1, 4–11. DOI: 10.1109/THFE2.1960.4503259. 109

Licklider, J. C. R. (1965). *Libraries of the future*. Cambridge, MA: The MIT Press. 109

Lindley, Siân E., Harper, R., Randall, D., Glancy, M., & Smyth, N. (2009). Fixed in time and "time in motion": mobility of vision through a SenseCam lens. In *Proceedings of the 11th International Conference on Human-Computer Interaction with Mobile Devices and Services* (pp. 2:1–2:10). New York, NY, USA: ACM. DOI: 10.1145/1613858.1613861. 8, 10

Lindley, Siín E., Glancy, M., Harper, R., Randall, D., & Smyth, N. (2011). "Oh and how things just don't change, the more things stay the same": Reflections on SenseCam images 18 months after capture. *Int. J. Hum.-Comput. Stud.*, 69(5), 311–323. DOI: 10.1016/j. ijhcs.2010.12.010. 11

Loftus, E. (1993). The reality of repressed memories. *American Psychologist*, 48(5), 518–537. DOI: 10.1037/0003-066X.48.5.518. 12

Lovejoy, T., & Grudin, J. (2003). Messaging and Formality: Will IM follow in the Footsteps of Email. In *Proc. Interact 2003* (pp. 817–820). Retrieved from http://courses.ischool.utexas. edu/Turnbull_Don/2008/fall/INF_385Q/readings/grudin.pdf. xix

Ma, Z., Pant, G., & Sheng, O. R. L. (2007). Interest-based personalized search. *ACM Trans. Inf. Syst.*, 25(1), 5. DOI: 10.1145/1198296.1198301. 33

Mackay, W. E. (1988). Diversity in the use of electronic mail : a preliminary inquiry. *ACM Transactions on Office Information Systems*, 6(4), 380–397. DOI: 10.1145/58566.58567. xix

Malone, T. W. (1983). How do people organize their desks: implications for the design of office information-systems. *ACM Transactions on Office Information Systems*, 1(1), 99–112. DOI: 10.1145/357423.357430. 13

Mann, S. (2004). "Sousveillance": inverse surveillance in multimedia imaging. In *Proceedings of the 12th annual ACM international conference on Multimedia* (pp. 620–627). New York, NY, USA: ACM. DOI: 10.1145/1027527.1027673. 61

Mann, S., Sehgal, A., & Fung, J. (2004). Continuous lifelong capture of personal experience using eyetap. In *First ACM Workshop on Continuous Archival and Retrieval of Personal Experiences (CARPE '04)* (pp. 1–21.). New York, NY, USA. DOI: 10.1145/1026653.1026654. 8

Marchionini, G. (1995). *Information seeking in electronic environments*. Cambridge, UK: Cambridge University Press. DOI: 10.1017/CBO9780511626388. 25, 32

Marchionini, Gary. (2006). Exploratory search: from finding to understanding. *Communications of the ACM*, 49(4), 41–46. DOI: 10.1145/1121949.1121979. 46

Marchionini, Gary. (2008). Human–information interaction research and development. *Library & Information Science Research*, 30(3), 165–174. DOI: 10.1016/j.lisr.2008.07.001. 16

Marsden, G., & Cairns, D. E. (2003). Improving the usability of the hierarchical file system. 27

Marshall, C. C. (2009). No bull, no spin: a comparison of tags with other forms of user metadata. In *Proceedings of the 9th ACM/IEEE-CS joint conference on Digital libraries* (pp. 241–250). Austin, TX, USA: ACM. DOI: 10.1145/1555400.1555438. 33

Marshall, C. C., & Frank M. Shipman, I. I. I. (1995). Spatial hypertext: designing for change. *Commun. ACM*, 38(8), 88–97. DOI: 10.1145/208344.208350. 67, 70, 76

Maslow, A. H. (1972). *The farther reaches of human nature*. Maurice Bassett. Retrieved from http://books.google.com/books?hl=en&lr=&id=QbPVIsjlQ-EC&oi=fnd&pg=PR11&d-q=Maslow,+A.+(1971).+The+farther+reaches+of+human+nature.+&ots=KMy388jcGX-&sig=dSsrSJEYJq4cqkyZZmuwFICuyo4. 118

McCool, R. (2005). Rethinking the semantic web. Part I. *Internet Computing, IEEE*, 9(6), 88–86. Retrieved from http://ieeexplore.ieee.org/xpls/abs_all.jsp?arnumber=1541954. DOI: 10.1109/MIC.2005.133. 74

McCool, R. (2006). Rethinking the Semantic Web, Part 2. *IEEE Internet Computing*, 10(1), 96–95. DOI: 10.1109/MIC.2006.18. 75

McKenzie, B., & Cockburn, A. (2001). An empirical analysis of Web page revisitation. In *34th Hawaiian International Conference on Systems Sciences, HICSS34* (p. 9 pp.). Maui, Hi.: IEEE Computer Society Press. Retrieved from http://ieeexplore.ieee. org/iel5/7255/20032/00926533.pdf?isNumber=20032 http://www.cosc.canterbury. ac.nz/~andy/papers/hiccsWeb.pdf. DOI: 10.1109/HICSS.2001.926533. 34

Millard, D. E., Moreau, L., Davis, H. C., & Reich, S. (2000). FOHM: a fundamental open hypertext model for investigating interoperability between hypertext domains. In *Proceedings of the eleventh ACM on Hypertext and hypermedia* (pp. 93–102). San Antonio, Texas, United States: ACM. DOI: 10.1145/336296.336334. 70, 76

Naisbitt, J. (1984). *Megatrends: Ten new directions transforming our lives*. New York: Warner. 110

Nardi, B., & Barreau, D. K. (1997). "Finding and reminding" revisited : appropriate metaphors for file organization at the desktop. *SIGCHI Bulletin*, 29(1). Retrieved from http://www.acm. org/sigchi/bulletin/1997.1/nardi.html. DOI: 10.1145/251761.248508. 27

Neisser, U. (1967). *Cognitive psychology*. New York: Appleton-Century Crofts. 26, 27

Nelson, T. H. (1982). *Literary machines*. Sausalito, CA: Mindful Press. 102

Nelson, Theodor H. (1999). Xanalogical structure, needed now more than ever: parallel documents, deep links to content, deep versioning, and deep re-use. *ACM Computing Surveys (CSUR)*, 31(4es), 33. DOI: 10.1145/345966.346033. 70, 76

Nürnberg, P. J., Leggett, J. J., & Schneider, E. R. (1997). As we should have thought. In *Proceedings of the eighth ACM conference on Hypertext* (pp. 96–101). Southampton, United Kingdom: ACM. DOI: 10.1145/267437.267448. 70, 76

Nürnberg, P. J., Wiil, U. K., & Hicks, D. L. (2004). Rethinking structural computing infrastructures. In *Proceedings of the fifteenth ACM conference on Hypertext and hypermedia* (pp. 239–246). Santa Cruz, CA, USA: ACM. DOI: 10.1145/1012807.1012868. 101

Ogollah, K., & Bolo, A. Z. (2009). Strategy Structure Environment Linkage and corporate performance: A conceptual overview. Retrieved from http://erepository.uonbi.ac.ke/handle/123456789/31576. 57

Olston, C., & Chi, E. H. (2003). ScentTrails: Integrating browsing and searching on the Web. ACM Trans. *Comput.-Hum. Interact.*, 10(3), 177–197. DOI: 10.1145/937549.937550. 25

Østerbye, K., & Wiil, U. K. (1996). The flag taxonomy of open hypermedia systems. In *Proceedings of the the seventh ACM conference on Hypertext* (pp. 129–139). Bethesda, Maryland, United States: ACM. DOI: 10.1145/234828.234841. 70, 76

Patalano, A. L., & Seifert, C. M. (1997). Opportunistic planning: Being reminded of pending goals. *Cognitive Psychology*, 34, 1–36. Retrieved from http://works.bepress.com/andrea_patalano/15. DOI: 10.1006/cogp.1997.0655. 43

Petrelli, D., & Whittaker, S. (2010). Family memories in the home: contrasting physical and digital mementos. *Personal Ubiquitous Comput.*, 14(2), 153–169. DOI: 10.1007/s00779-009-0279-7. 12

Phuwanartnurak, A. J. (2009). Did you put it on the wiki?: information sharing through wikis in interdisciplinary design collaboration. In *Proceedings of the 27th ACM international conference on Design of communication* (pp. 273–280). Bloomington, Indiana, USA: ACM. DOI: 10.1145/1621995.1622049. 67

Pitkow, J., Schutze, H., Cass, T., Cooley, R., Turnbull, D., Edmonds, A., … Breuel, T. (2002). Personalized search : a contextual computing approach may prove a breakthrough in personalized search efficiency. *Communications of the ACM*, 45(9), 50–55. Retrieved from http://portal.acm.org/citation.cfm?doid=567498.567526. DOI: 10.1145/567498.567526. 33

Potthast, M., Stein, B., Barrón-Cedeño, A., & Rosso, P. (2010). An evaluation framework for plagiarism detection. In *Proceedings of the 23rd International Conference on Computational Linguistics: Posters* (pp. 997–1005). Stroudsburg, PA, USA: Association for Computational Linguistics. Retrieved from http://dl.acm.org/citation.cfm?id=1944566.1944681. 35

Pullan, W., & Bhadeshia, H. (2000). Structure: In *Science and Art*. Cambridge University Press. 57

Qu, Y., & Furnas, G. W. (2005). Sources of structure in sensemaking. 83

Qu, Y., & Furnas, G. W. (2008). Model-driven formative evaluation of exploratory search: A study under a sensemaking framework. *Inf. Process. Manage.*, 44(2), 534–555. DOI: 10.1016/j.ipm.2007.09.006. 83

Quan, D., Huynh, D., & Karger, D. R. (2003). Haystack: A platform for authoring end user Semantic Web applications. In *2nd International Semantic Web Conference* (ISWC 2003). Sanibel Island, FL. DOI: 10.1007/978-3-540-39718-2_47. 73

Raskin, J. (2000). *The Humane Interface: New Directions for Designing Interactive Systems*. Reading, Massachusetts: Addison Wesley. Retrieved from http://rchi.raskincenter.orghttp://jefthemovie.com/jef_project_notes.htm. 36

Ravasio, P., Schär, S. G., & Krueger, H. (2004). In pursuit of desktop evolution: User problems and practices with modern desktop systems. *ACM Trans. Comput.-Hum. Interact.*, 11(2), 156–180. DOI: 10.1145/1005361.1005363. 27

Rhodes, B., & Maes, P. (2000). Just-in-time information retrieval. *IBM Systems Journal*, 39, 3–4. DOI: 10.1147/sj.393.0685. 32

Ringel, M., Cutrell, E., Dumais, S. T., & Horvitz, E. (2003). Milestones in time: The value of landmarks in retrieving information from personal stores. In *INTERACT'03*. 34

Ronallo, J. (2012). HTML5 Microdata and Schema.org. *The Code4Lib Journal*, (16). Retrieved from http://journal.code4lib.org/articles/6400. 79

Rosch, E. (1978). Principles of categorization. In *Cognition and categorization* (pp. 27–48). Hillsdale, NJ: Lawrence Erlbaum Associates. 45

Rosch, E., Mervis, C. B., Gray, W., Johnson, D., & Boyes-Braem., P. (1976). Basic objects in natural categories. *Cognitive Psychology*, 8, 382—349. DOI: 10.1016/0010-0285(76)90013-X. 45, 66

Ross Hudgens. (2013, March 22). *How to Get a Job in SEO*. Retrieved from http://www.slideshare.net/RossHudgens/how-to-get-hired-in-seo?from_search=6.

Salton, G., & McGill, M. J. (1986). *Introduction to Modern Information Retrieval*. New York, NY, USA: McGraw-Hill, Inc. 38

Sauermann, L. (2005a). The semantic desktop - A basis for personal knowledge management. In *I-Know '05, 5th International Conference on Knowledge Management*. Graz, Austria. Retrieved from http://i-know.know-center.tugraz.at/content/download/405/1592/file/Sauermann_paper.pdf. 72

Sauermann, L. (2005b). The Gnowsis Semantic Desktop for Information Integration. In *Wissensmanagement* (pp. 39–42). Retrieved from http://citeseerx.ist.psu.edu/viewdoc/download?doi=10.1.1.169.2519&rep=rep1&type=pdf. 72

Sauermann, L., Bernardi, A., & Dengel, A. (2005). Overview and Outlook on the Semantic Desktop. In *Semantic Desktop Workshop*. Retrieved from https://courses.ischool.utexas.edu/donturn/2008/fall/INF_385T-SW/readings/Sauermann-2005-Semantic_Desktop.pdf. 72

Sauermann, L., Grimnes, G. A., Kiesel, M., Fluit, C., Maus, H., Heim, D., … Dengel, A. (2006). Semantic desktop 2.0: The gnowsis experience. In *The Semantic Web-ISWC 2006* (pp. 887–900). Springer. Retrieved from http://link.springer.com/chapter/10.1007/11926078_64. DOI: 10.1007/11926078_64. 72

Sauermann, L., & Heim, D. (2008). Evaluating Long-Term Use of the Gnowsis Semantic Desktop for PIM. In *Proceedings of the 7th International Conference on The Semantic Web* (pp. 467–482). Berlin, Heidelberg: Springer-Verlag. DOI: 10.1007/978-3-540-88564-1_30. 72, 73

Schon, D. A. (1984). *The Reflective Practitioner: How Professionals Think In Action*. Basic Books. 67

Schwartz, D. L., & Bransford, J. (1998). A Time for Telling. *COGNITION AND INSTRUCTION*, 16(4), 475–522. DOI: 10.1207/s1532690xci1604_4. 45

Segal, R. B., & Kephart, J. O. (1999). MailCat: An intelligent assistant for organizing e-mail. In *Third Annual Conference on Autonomous Agents* (pp. 276–282). Seattle, WA: ACM. DOI: 10.1145/301136.301209. 38

Sellen, A. J., Fogg, A., Aitken, M., Hodges, S., Rother, C., & Wood, K. (2007). Do life-logging technologies support memory for the past?: an experimental study using sensecam. In *Proceedings of the SIGCHI conference on Human factors in computing systems* (pp. 81–90). San Jose, California, USA: ACM. DOI: 10.1145/1240624.1240636. 8, 11

Sellen, A. J., & Whittaker, S. (2010). Beyond total capture: a constructive critique of lifelogging. *Commun. ACM*, 53(5), 70–77. DOI: 10.1145/1735223.1735243. 10

Shah, S. (2010). Caution: Reported Trends In Search Query Length May Be Misleading. *Search Engine Land*. Retrieved July 9, 2013, from http://searchengineland.com/caution-reported-trends-in-search-query-length-may-be-misleading-41641. 30

Shamos, M. (2007). Privacy and Public Records. In *Personal Information Management*. Seattle: University of Washington Press. 113

Shen, J., Li, L., Dietterich, T. G., & Herlocker, J. L. (2006). A hybrid learning system for recognizing user tasks from desktop activities and email messages. DOI: 10.1145/1111449.1111473. 38, 51

Shen, X., Tan, B., & Zhai, C. (2007). Privacy protection in personalized search. *SIGIR Forum*, 41(1), 4–17. DOI: 10.1145/1273221.1273222. 33

Shipman, F. M., Hsieh, H., Moore, J. M., & Zacchi, A. (2004). Supporting personal collections across digital libraries in spatial hypertext. DOI: 10.1145/996350.996433. 67

Simon, H. A. (1971). Designing organizations for an information-rich world. In *Computers, communications and the public interest* (pp. 40–41). Baltimore, MD: The Johns Hopkins Press. 57

Simon, Herbert A. (1962). The architecture of complexity. *Proceedings of the American philosophical society*, 106(6), 467–482. Retrieved from http://www.jstor.org/stable/10.2307/985254. 57

Singer, E. (2011, June 9). Is "Self-tracking" the Secret to Living Better? | MIT Technology Review. *MIT Technology Review*. Retrieved July 5, 2013, from http://www.technologyreview.com/view/424252/is-self-tracking-the-secret-to-living-better/. 17

Singh, M. P. (2002). The pragmatic web: Preliminary thoughts. In *Proc. of the NSF-OntoWeb Workshop on Database and Information Systems Research for Semantic Web and Enterprises* (pp. 82–90). Retrieved from http://www.csc.ncsu.edu/faculty/mpsingh/papers/positions/nsf-02.pdf. 74, 76

Slamecka, N. J., & Graf, P. (1978). The generation effect: Delineation of a phenomenon. *Journal of Experimental Psychology: Human Learning and Memory*, 4, 592–604. DOI: 10.1037/0278-7393.4.6.592. 12

Sparrow, B., Liu, J., & Wegner, D. M. (2011). Google Effects on Memory: Cognitive Consequences of Having Information at Our Fingertips. *Science*, 333(6043), 776 –778. DOI: 10.1126/science.1207745. 24

Stumpf, S., Rajaram, V., Li, L., Burnett, M., Dietterich, T., Sullivan, E., ... Herlocker, J. (2007). Toward harnessing user feedback for machine learning. In *Proceedings of the 12th international conference on Intelligent user interfaces* (pp. 82–91). New York, NY, USA: ACM. DOI: 10.1145/1216295.1216316. 39

Stumpf, S., Rajaram, V., Li, L., Wong, W.-K., Burnett, M., Dietterich, T., ... Herlocker, J. (2009). Interacting meaningfully with machine learning systems: Three experiments. *Int. J. Hum.-Comput. Stud.*, 67(8), 639–662. DOI: 10.1016/j.ijhcs.2009.03.004. 39

Taghavi, M., Patel, A., Schmidt, N., Wills, C., & Tew, Y. (2012). An analysis of web proxy logs with query distribution pattern approach for search engines. *Computer Standards & Interfaces*, 34(1), 162–170. DOI: 10.1016/j.csi.2011.07.001. 30

Tauscher, L. M., & Greenberg, S. (1997a). How people revisit web pages : empirical findings and implications for the design of history systems. *Int. J. Hum.-Comput. Stud.*, 47(1), 97–137. DOI: 10.1006/ijhc.1997.0125. 34, 36

Tauscher, L. M., & Greenberg, S. (1997b). Revisitation patterns in World Wide Web navigation. In *ACM SIGCHI Conference on Human Factors in Computing Systems (CHI 1997)* (pp. 399–406). Atlanta, GA: ACM Press. DOI: 10.1145/258549.258816. 34

Teevan, J. (2006a). *Supporting finding and re-finding through personalization*. Massachusetts Institute of Technology. 33

Teevan, J. (2006b). The Re:Search Engine: Helping People Return to Information on the Web. In *ACM Symposium on User Interface Software and Technology (UIST '05)*. Seattle, WA. 55

Teevan, J., Alvarado, C., Ackerman, M. S., & Karger, D. R. (2004). The perfect search engine Is not enough: A study of orienteering behavior in directed search. In *ACM SIGCHI Conference on Human Factors in Computing Systems (CHI 2004)* (pp. 415–422). Vienna, Austria. DOI: 10.1145/985692.985745. 24, 65

Teevan, J., Dumais, S. T., & Horvitz, E. (2005). Personalizing search via automated analysis of interests and activities. In *SIGIR 2005* (pp. 449–456). Salvador, Brazil. DOI: 10.1145/1076034.1076111. 33

Teevan, Jaime. (2008). How people recall, recognize, and reuse search results. *ACM Trans. Inf. Syst.*, 26(4), 1–27. DOI: 10.1145/1402256.1402258. 52

Teevan, Jaime, Liebling, D. J., & Ravichandran Geetha, G. (2011). Understanding and predicting personal navigation. In *Proceedings of the fourth ACM international conference on Web search and data mining* (pp. 85–94). New York, NY, USA: ACM. DOI: 10.1145/1935826.1935848. 33

The Economist. (From the print edition: Technology Quarterly). Phase-change memory: Altered states. *The Economist.* Retrieved from http://www.economist.com/node/21560981.

The Economist. (2012a, Technology Quarterly: Q4). The eyes have it. The ability to determine the location of a person's gaze is opening up an enormous range of new applications. *The Economist.* Retrieved March 2, 2013, from http://www.economist.com/news/technology-quarterly/21567195-computer-interfaces-ability-determine-location-persons-gaze. 4

The Economist. (2012b, June 2). Prophets of zoom. *The Economist,* (Technology Quarterly: Q2 2012). Retrieved from http://www.economist.com/node/21556097. 2

Thudt, A., Hinrichs, U., & Carpendale, S. (2012). The bohemian bookshelf: supporting serendipitous book discoveries through information visualization. In *Proceedings of the SIGCHI Conference on Human Factors in Computing Systems* (pp. 1461–1470). New York, NY, USA: ACM. DOI: 10.1145/2207676.2208607. 43

Tulving, E. (1983). *Elements of episodic memory.* Oxford: Oxford University Press. 66

Van Kleek, M. G., Bernstein, M., Panovich, K., Vargas, G. G., Karger, D. R., & Schraefel, M. C. (2009). Note to self: examining personal information keeping in a lightweight note-taking tool. In Proceedings of the 27th international conference on Human factors in computing systems (pp. 1477–1480). Boston, MA, USA: ACM. 38

Voit, K., Andrews, K., & Slany, W. (2012). Tagging might not be slower than filing in folders. In *Proceedings of the 2012 ACM annual conference extended abstracts on Human Factors in Computing Systems Extended Abstracts* (pp. 2063–2068). New York, NY, USA: ACM. DOI: 10.1145/2223656.2223753. 28

Völkel, M., & Haller, H. (2009). Conceptual data structures for personal knowledge management. *Online Information Review*, 33(2), 298–315. DOI: 10.1108/14684520910951221. 72

Ware, M., Frank, E., Holmes, G., Hall, M., & Witten, I. H. (2002). Interactive machine learning: letting users build classifiers. *Int. J. Hum.-Comput. Stud.*, 56(3), 281–292. Retrieved from http://dl.acm.org/citation.cfm?id=514412.514417. 39

Whittaker, S., Bellotti, V. M. E., & Gwizdka, J. (2007). Email as PIM. In *Personal Information Management.* Seattle, WA: University of Washington Press. xix

Whittaker, S., & Sidner, C. (1996). Email overload: exploring personal information management of email. Retrieved from http://www.acm.org/sigchi/chi96/proceedings/papers/Whittaker/sw_txt.htm. DOI: 10.1145/238386.238530. xix

Whittaker, Steve, Bergman, O., & Clough, P. (2010). Easy on that trigger dad: a study of long term family photo retrieval. *Personal Ubiquitous Comput.*, 14(1), 31–43. DOI: 10.1007/s00779-009-0218-7. xvii, 12

Whittaker, Steve, Matthews, T., Cerruti, J., Badenes, H., & Tang, J. (2011). Am I wasting my time organizing email?: a study of email refinding. In *PART 5 -------- Proceedings of the 2011 annual conference on Human factors in computing systems* (pp. 3449–3458). Vancouver, BC, Canada: ACM. DOI: 10.1145/1978942.1979457. xix

Williams, R. L., & Eggert, A. C. (2002). Notetaking in College Classes: Student Patterns and Instructional Strategies. *The Journal of General Education*, 51(3), 173–199. DOI: 10.1353/jge.2003.0006. 12

Williams, R. L., & Worth, S. L. (2002). Thinking Skills and Work Habits: Contributors to Course Performance. *The Journal of General Education*, 51(3), 200–227. DOI: 10.1353/jge.2003.0007. 13

Wong, H.-S. P., Kim, S., Lee, B., Caldwell, M. A., Liang, J., Wu, Y., … Yu, S. (2011). Recent Progress of Phase Change Memory (PCM) and Resistive Switching Random Access Memory (RRAM). In *Memory Workshop (IMW), 2011 3rd IEEE International* (pp. 1–5). Presented at the Memory Workshop (IMW), 2011 3rd IEEE International. DOI: 10.1109/IMW.2011.5873188. 9

Zhao, Q., & Lu, H. (2005). A PCA-based watermarking scheme for tamper-proof of web pages. *Pattern Recognition*, 38(8), 1321–1323. DOI: 10.1016/j.patcog.2004.12.012. 35

Zhou, C., Frankowski, D., Ludford, P., Shekhar, S., & Terveen, L. (2007). Discovering personally meaningful places: An interactive clustering approach. *ACM Trans. Inf. Syst.*, 25(3). DOI: 10.1145/1247715.1247718. 50

Author Biography

William Jones is a Research Associate Professor in the Information School at the University of Washington where he works on the challenges of "Keeping Found Things Found" (kftf.ischool.washington.edu). He has published in the areas of personal information management (PIM), human-computer interaction, information retrieval, and human cognition. Prof. Jones wrote the book *Keeping Found Things Found: The Study and Practice of Personal Information Management* and, more recently, *The Future of Personal Information, Part 1: Our Information, Always & Forever"* (for which this lecture is Part 2, with Part 3 to follow).

He holds several patents relating to search and PIM from his work as a program manager at Microsoft in Office and then in MSN Search. Prof. Jones received his doctorate from Carnegie-Mellon University for research into human memory.

Printed in the United States
by Baker & Taylor Publisher Services